HOT Springs
& Hot Pools
of the Southwest

HOT Springs & Hot Pools of the Southwest

Jayson Loam's Original Guide

Marjorie Gersh-Young

AQUA THERMAL ACCESS

Hot Springs and Hot Pools of the Southwest: Jayson Loam's Original Guide

Copyright 1998 by Marjorie Gersh-Young

Design, layout and production
by Marjorie Gersh-Young

Front Cover - Valley View Hot Springs, Colorado
Barbara Hanson

ISBN 1-890880-01-9

Manufactured in the United States

Published by: **Aqua Thermal Access**
55 Azalea Lane
Santa Cruz, CA 95060
831 426-2956
e-mail: hsprings@ix.netcom.com
web page: www.hotpools.com

Reprint: 1999

Grateful acknowledgements

All of the regional contributors who always went above and beyond their assignment to make this book interesting and accurate. All of you who have written in with updates and information. Staff members at state parks, national forests, national parks, and hot springs resorts for their cooperation and encouragement.

A special thank you to Eileen Bonomo who ran interference to make sure the book was printed the best way possible, Susanne Viverito for her editing, Karen Barnett for the cover design, and Henry Young (my husband) for acting as my sounding board and making the computer run right.

To

Jayson Loam

August 29, 1918 - February 22, 1994

"King of the Hot Springs"

who pursued with passion what he truly

loved to do most and, therefore, benefited

us all.

May you soak in peace.

HOT Springs & Hot Pools
of the Southwest

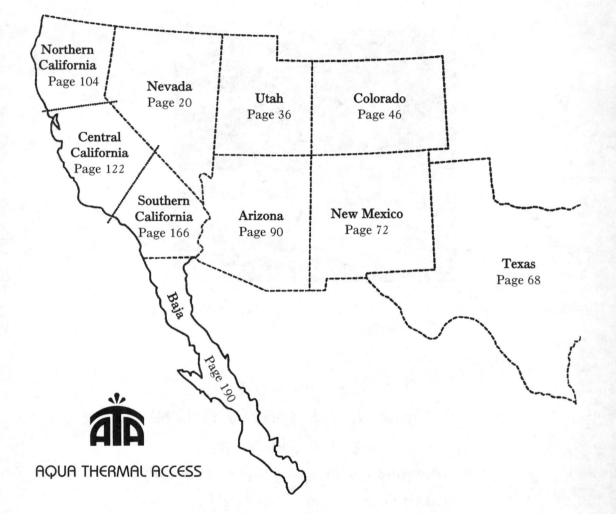

Northern California
Page 104

Nevada
Page 20

Utah
Page 36

Colorado
Page 46

Central California
Page 122

Southern California
Page 166

Arizona
Page 90

New Mexico
Page 72

Texas
Page 68

Baja
Page 190

AQUA THERMAL ACCESS

Companion volume to
Hot Springs and Hot Pools of the Northwest

TABLE OF CONTENTS

INTRODUCTION

By Marjorie Gersh-Young

This book was written with the premise that there is nothing more enjoyable than to soak in a hot spring in ideal conditions. To me this means a beautiful pool with water at 104° cascading in over the rocks out in the middle of the forest at the end of a moderate hike. While definitions of the perfect pool may differ, there does seem to be some standard information that everyone wants to know in order to make an informed choice.

Our hot springs research program started with an analysis of the 1,600 springs listed in the NOAA springs list published by the National Oceanic and Atmospheric Administration. Only seven percent of the listed springs were on public land, accessible without charge, and another fifteen percent were private, commercial enterprises open to the public. Nearly one-third of the locations had temperatures below 90°, so we eliminated them as simply not hot enough. The remaining two-thirds required individual investigation, usually involving personal inspection, which reduced the NOAA list to a usable twenty-two percent. The unusable seventy-eight percent were often old resorts that had burned down, seeps too small to get into, functioning as cattle troughs, or on posted, private land, making them not usable by the public (NUBP).

As many of you may know, Jayson Loam was the original creator of these hot spring books almost twenty years ago. At that time he did the initial field work and made many decisions as to what information should be included or excluded. Over the years we have refined the format, but without going into an analysis of the chemicals in the water, have maintained the basic premise that soaking in geothermal water does feel good. We have continued to designate hot water as anything above 90° and to include hot wells, treating them the same as hot springs. (Occasionally I will include a spring at a lower temperature due to its natural beauty or location.) Rental tub locations, which have now become an integral part of many people's lives, are also included. And, as a special service and option for many of our readers, there is now a listing of nudist/naturist resorts and parks in those states where there are springs listed that welcome visitors with advance reservations. One thing we do not do is send people onto private property where they can get arrested or shot.

This edition retains these basic criteria while expanding the descriptions, providing more detailed directions with GPS sightings, and adding a bit of history whenever possible. I feel sure that the blending of our styles and interests will ensure you, the user, continued enjoyment from the book.

Barbara Hanson, who was my traveling companion in Colorado and New Mexico, took this picture of me at Spence, one of the jewels in New Mexico's crown of wonderful hot springs. She also took the picture on the front cover.

REGIONAL CONTRIBUTORS

JUSTINE HILL is a travel writer, photographer, and visual anthropologist who has traveled extensively and has written about and photographed other cultures, travel locations, sacred sites and the great outdoors. She currently lives surrounded by nature in Topanga, California, where she has a stock of over 50,000 photos that appear frequently in calendars, posters, magazines, postcards, travel literature, and coffee-table books. For information about her photo collection and related services, contact Justine Hill at PO Box 608, Topanga, CA 90290. 310 455-3409.

ROB WILLIAMS has devoted his life to locating, soaking, and now developing hot springs in remote areas of Baja California. Four-wheel drive vehicles are used to reach hidden canyons filled with palm forests and natural hot springs. The best time of year to explore these remote, dry wilderness areas is during the winter and spring. To reserve a place on one of Rob's tours, or to acquire maps and up-to-date information, contact Rob's Baja Tours, PO Box 4003, Balboa, CA 92261. 714 673-2670.

CHRIS ANDREWS, who lives and works in Idaho seems to like nothing better than to hop in his truck, often with his lovely wife and daughter, and travel to hot springs all over the west. He takes won-derful photographs and doesn't mind how far he has to hike to find a spring he hasn't visited.

PHIL WILCOX, also known as "the Solar Man," is semi-retired and lives on a remote piece of land in Northern California. He loves to travel often in search of hot springs and has recently been seen in Alaska, Canada, Oregon, Washington, New Mexico, Nevada, and points west. When not traveling, he designs, sells, and installs remote home solar power systems. Send $4.00 for a complete catalog to THE SOLAR MAN, 20560 Morgan Valley Rd., Lower Lake, CA 95457. GPS: N 38.5354 W 122.3136.

CAMILLA VAN SICKLE AND BILL PENNINGTON have fulfilled their dream. After many years of traveling to track down hundreds of remote locations, with an emphasis on hot springs where hiking and camping are permitted in the buff, they now own El Dorado Hot springs near Phoenix, Arizona with natural, hot mineral water which they are developing for your pleasure. They have provided details on springs across the United States. All of this information is published in hard copy or on a series of disks that can be ordered from PO Box 10, Tonopah, AZ 85354. 623 393-0750. HotSpring@El-Dorado.com.

STEVE HEEREMA AND SHARA BRIGGS are hot springs enthusiasts who are spending part of their two-year break from the work world visiting hot springs, many that are in the back country, taking photos and updating information.

HUNTING FOR HOT WATER:
Where it Comes From

The cataclysmic folding and faulting of the earth's crust over millions of years, combined with just the right amount of underground water and earth core magma, has produced a hot surface geothermal flow that often goes on for centuries.

Volcanic activity dies down. Igneous rocks which have solidified from hot liquids such as magma are formed in pockets deep in the earth below the remains of the volcano. The magma produces heat which is conducted through a layer of solid rock into the porous level where new water, or water which has never before been on the surface, is believed to be formed from available molecules. Fissures are formed in the solid rock layer above the porous layer and steam and hot water escape producing hot springs, geysers, and fumaroles. A hot spring is considered to be a natural flow of water from the ground at a single point. It is called a seep if it does not have enough flow to create a current. Springs may come up on dry land or in the beds of streams, ponds, and lakes.

ARTESIAN SPRING

Artesian spring water comes from a source that is located at a higher elevation than the springhead. The water travels from this source deep into the ground where it absorbs heat from the surrounding earth. As gravity forces water down from the source, heated water is forced up to the surface through cracks in the earth. The water here has an average temperature of 95° F.

Photos by Justine Hill

Natural geothermal areas lie in the earthquake and volcano belts along the earth's crustal plates. In many areas due to the earth shifting and moving the hot magma has worked its way closer to the earth's surface. Surface water (water from rain, for instance) soaks into the earth through cracks and crevices down to the area where the hot magma again provides the heat source for the water. If there are no fissures or cracks for the water to use to come to the surface, water can be drilled for, for example. Each of the resorts in Desert Hot Springs California has its own well.

Water temperatures vary greatly. When the water is at least fourteen degrees hotter than the average temperature of the air it is considered to be thermal water (or a hot springs). This definition means that there is a very wide range of what is considered thermal water as the air temperature in Iceland is certainly different from that of a California desert. The overall temperature of the water can range up to the boiling point. Geothermal resources in Italy, New Zealand, California and Iceland have been used for a number of years to heat municipal and private buildings, and even whole towns. In Iceland the early Norse carried hot water to their homes through wooden pipes.

As the water travels up through varying layers of the earth it accumulates different properties. These are classified as alkaline, saline, chalybeate or iron, sulfurous, acidulous, and arsenical. At least as far back as the time of the Greeks and the Romans medicinal cures were attributed to the different chemicals and certain springs were alleged to cure certain diseases from venereal diseases to stomach and urinary tract weaknesses. The waters were administered in a combination of drinking it and soaking in it.

Of the thousands of hot springs found in the United States, most are found in the Western mountains.

THIS IS THE ORIGINAL
HOT SPRINGS WATER

INDUSTRIAL ANALYSIS

Acidity None	
Acid Carbonate	31.16
Aluminum	.61
Calcium	5.18
Chlorine	35.18

HYDROGEN SULPHATE TRACES

Iron	.61
Magnesium	.44
Potassium	2.76
Silicate	3.89
Sodium	18.08
Sulphate	2.40

GASES

Carbon Dioxide
Hydrogen
Menthane
Nitrogen
Oxygen

FORMATION
AT OVERFLOW CONTAINS

Arsenic	
Lithium	TEMPERATURE
Sulphur	154° 186°
Phosphate	
Borates	

The sign above is posted at the Jemez Springs Bathhouse in New Mexico which offers a wide range of health services. Ojo Caliente, also in New Mexico, has several different soaking areas, each one with its own mineral specialty. This Lithia spring has a pump handle on it to encourage you to drink the water and to take it home with you.

A Bit of History

Long before the "white man" arrived to "discover" hot springs, the Native American believed that the Great Spirit resided in the center of the earth and that "Big Medicine" fountains were a special gift from The Creator. Even during tribal battles over territory or stolen horses, it was customary for the sacred "smoking waters" to be a neutral zone where all could freely be healed. Back then, hot springs belonged to everyone, and understandably, we would like to believe that nothing has changed.

The Native American tradition of free access to hot springs was initially imitated by the pioneers. However, as soon as mineral water was perceived to have some commercial value, the new settlers' private property laws were invoked at most of the hot spring locations. Histories often include bloody battles with "white men" over hot spring ownership, and there are colorful legends about Indian curses that had dire effects for decades on a whole series of ill-fated owners. After many fierce legal battles, and a few gun battles, some ambitious settlers were able to establish clear legal titles to the properties. Then it was up to the new owners to figure out how to turn their geothermal flow into cash flow.

Pioneering settlers dismissed as superstition the Native American's spiritual explanation of the healing power of a hot spring. However, those settlers did know from experience that it was beneficial to soak their bodies in mineral water, even if they didn't know why or how it worked. Commercial exploitation began when the owner of a private hot spring started charging admission, ending centuries of free access.

Photos by Marjorie Young

The shift from outdoor soaks to indoor soaks began when proper Victorian customers demanded privacy, which required the erection of canvas enclosures around the bathers in the outdoor springs. Then affluent city dwellers, as they became accustomed to indoor plumbing and modern sanitation, were no longer willing to risk immersion in a muddy-edged, squishy-bottom mineral spring, even if they believed that such bathing would be good for their health. Furthermore, they learned to like their urban comforts too much to trek to an outdoor spring in all kinds of weather. Instead, they wanted a civilized method of "taking the waters," and the great spas of Europe provided just the right model for American railroad tycoons and land barons to follow, and to surpass.

Around the turn of the century, American hot spring resorts fully satisfied the combined demands of Victorian prudery, modern sanitation, and indoor comfort by offering separate men's and women's bathhouses with private individual porcelain tubs, marble shower rooms, and central heating. Scientific mineral analysis of the geothermal water was part of every resort merchandising program, which included flamboyant claims of miraculous cures and glowing testimonials from medical doctors. Their promotion material also featured additional social amenities, such as luxurious suites, sumptuous restaurants, and grand ballrooms.

In recent decades, patronage of these resorts has declined, and many have closed down because the traditional medical claims were outlawed and modern medical plans refuse to reimburse anyone for a mineral water "treatment." A few of the larger resorts have managed to survive by adding new facilities such as golf courses, conference and exhibition spaces, fitness centers, and beauty salons. The smaller hot spring establishments have responded to modern demand by installing larger (six persons or more) communal soaking tubs and family-size soaking pools in private spaces for rent by the hour. Most locations continue to offer men's and women's bathhouse facilities in addition to the new communal pools, but most have discontinued the use of cast iron, one-person bath tubs.

In addition to the privately owned hot spring facilities, there are several dozen locations that are owned and operated by federal, state, county, or city agencies. States, counties, and cities usually staff and operate their own geothermal installations. Locations in US National Forests and National Parks are usually operated under contract by privately owned companies. The nature and quality of the mineral water facilities offered at these publicly owned, privately operated hot spring locations varies widely.

In 1862, David and Harriet Walley built an elegant spa and luxury hotel in Genoa, Nevada with gourmet dining on the same spot that *Walley's* is located today. It was adjacent to the Pony Express route and the Emigrant Trail. Once a gathering place for the Ute Indians, *Waunita Hot Springs Ranch* in Gunnison, Colorado was a thriving health spa by the early 1900s.

Although natural mineral water (from a spring or well) is required for a truly authentic traditional "therapeutic soak," there is a new generation of dedicated soakers who will not patronize a motel unless it has a hot pool. They know full well that the pool is filled with gas-heated tap water and treated with chlorine, but it is almost as good as the real thing and a lot more convenient. We chose to include in our hunt for hot water those locations that offer private-space hot tubs for rent by the hour.

According to California legend, the historic redwood tub was invented by a Santa Barbara group who often visited Big Caliente Hot Springs. One evening a member of the group wished out loud that they could have their delicious outdoor communal soaks without having to endure the long dusty trips to and from the springs. Another member of the group suggested that a large redwood wine cask might be used as an alternate soaking pool in the city. It was worth a try, and it was a success. Over time, other refugees from the long Big Caliente drive began to build their own group soaking pools from wine casks, and the communal hot tub era was born.

Photos by Marjorie Young

The buggy pictured above was part of *Gilroy Hot Springs*' interesting history. First opened in 1868 Gilroy Hot Springs was a destination resort attracting enough people to have its own post office and a shuttle to the resort supplied by the Southern Pacific Railway. It was purchased by H.K. Sakata, a successful Japanese American Farmer from Watsonville, in 1938 and renamed Yamato Onsen (Japan Hot Spring). It was the only Japanese American owned commercial hot spring in California. It became a hide-out for Japanese Americans who were ostracized before the start of World War II. Mr. Sakata himself was interned. Upon his release he returned to the springs where he set up a hostel for other refugees from the camps who had nowhere else to go.

The main facilities were destroyed by a fire twenty years ago. The present owner is in the process of redeveloping the property under the name of Gilroy Yamato Hot Springs. The pools and much of the grounds are open. The hot springs is officially California State Historical Landmark #1017.

Sweetwater Gardens in Mendocino, California has a wooden communal hot tub which is very popular with both the locals and visitors alike.

USING THIS GUIDE

The primary tool in this guide is the KEY MAP, which is provided for each state or geographical subdivision. The KEY MAP INDEX on the outside back cover tells the page number where each of the KEY MAPS can be found. Each KEY MAP includes significant cities and highways, but please note that it is designed to be used with a standard highway map.

Within every KEY MAP, each location has been assigned a number that is printed next to the identifying circle or square. On the pages following the KEY MAP you will find descriptions of each location listed in numerical order.

The Master Alphabetical Index of Mineral Water Locations is printed at the end of the book and gives the page number on which each location description will be found. If you know the specific hot spring name, this alphabetical index is the place to start.

The following section describes the quick-read symbols that are used on the KEY MAPS and in the location descriptions.

●Non-Commercial Mineral Water Locations

On the key maps and in each hot spring listing, a solid round dot is used to indicate a non-commercial hot spring, or hot well, where no fee is required and pools are generally created by the rearranging of rocks or by using easily available material. At a few remote locations, you may be asked for a donation to help the work of a nonprofit organization that has a contract with the Forest Service to protect and maintain the spring.

The first paragraph of each listing is intended to convey the general appearance, atmosphere, and surroundings of the location, including the altitude, which can greatly affect the weather conditions. The phrase "open all year" does not mean that all roads and trails are kept open regardless of snowfalls or fire seasons. Rather, it means that there are no seasonally closed gates or doors, as at some commercial resorts. Where there is a particular problem we try to note it.

The second paragraph describes the source and temperature of the mineral water and then conveys the manner in which that water is transported or guided to a usable soaking pool. "Volunteer-built pool" usually implies some crude combination of at-hand material such as logs, rocks, and sand. If the situation requires that the pool water temperature be controlled, the method for such control is described. River-edge and creek-edge pools are vulnerable to complete washouts during high runoff months, so often volunteers have to start from scratch

every year. Whether bathing suits are optional or not is indicated. There is also a mention of handicap accessibility.

The third paragraph identifies the facilities and services available on the premises or nearby and states the approximate distance to other facilities and services.

If needed, there is a final paragraph of directions, which should be used in connection with a standard highway map, a National Forest map if applicable, or any local area map.

The trek up to *Big Caliente* outside Santa Barbara is rumored to have been the impetus for the building of home hot tubs. Also, long before there were government mandates about making areas handicap accessible, that pool was equipped with railings for this purpose.

■Commercial Mineral Water Locations

On the key maps in this book and in the hot springs listings, a solid square is used to indicate a mineral water commercial location. A phone number and address are provided for the purpose of obtaining rates, additional information, and reservations.

The first paragraph of each listing is intended to convey the size, general appearance, atmosphere, and surroundings of the location. "Open all year" does not imply that the facility is open twenty-four hours of every day, only that it does not have a "closed" season.

The second paragraph of each listing focuses on the water facilities available at the location. It describes the origin and temperature of the mineral water, the means of transporting that water, the quantity, type, and location of tubs and pools, the control of soaking water temperatures, and the chemical treatment used, if any.

In all states, health department standards require a minimum treatment of public pool water with chlorine, bromine, or the equivalent. A few fortunate locations are able to meet these standards by operating their smaller mineral water pools on a continuous flow-through basis, thereby eliminating the need for chemical treatment. Many other locations meet these standards by draining and refilling tubs and pools after each use or after the end of each business day.

Natural mineral water as it percolates up through the earth picks up a variety of minerals. As the minerals accumulate around the water source they often form a cone or tufa mound as they do here at the *Spring Inn* in Colorado.

There actually are a few commercial locations where rare geothermal conditions (and health department rules) make it possible to soak in a natural sand-bottom hot spring open to the sky.

At those hot springs resorts that are being run as a business, bathing suits are normally required in public spaces. A few locations have a policy of clothing optional in the pools and sometimes everywhere on the grounds. Handicap accessibility is mentioned for those locations that provide it.

The third paragraph of a commercial hot spring listing briefly mentions the principal facilities and services offered, plus approximate distances to other nearby services and if credit cards are accepted. This information is intended to advise you if overnight accommodations, RV hookups, restaurants, health clubs, beauty salons, etc., are available on the premises, but it does not attempt to assign any form of quality rating to those amenities. There is no such thing as a typical hot spring resort and no such thing as typical accommodations at such a resort. Phone and ask questions.

❑Tubs Using Gas-heated Tap Water or Well Water

Listings of rent-a-tub locations, indicated by a white square, begin with an overall impression of the premises and with the general location, usually within a city area. This is followed by a description of the private spaces, tubs, and pools, water treatment methods, and water temperature policies. Generally, unless stated otherwise, clothing is optional in private spaces and required elsewhere. Facilities and services available on the premises are described. Credit cards accepted, if any, are noted. Nearly all locations require reservations, especially during the busy evening and weekend hours.

In a separate section titled "For the Naturist" we have included a special listing of landed clubs in those states where there are hot springs to give skinny-dippers alternatives to conventional motels/hotels/resorts. Most of the nudist/naturist resorts specifically prohibit bathing suits in their pools and have a policy of clothing optional elsewhere on the grounds. Most nudist/naturist resorts are not open to the public for drop-in visits but the resorts listed in this book are often willing to offer a visitor's pass if you phone ahead and make arrangements.

Definitely open to the public are those resorts listed in the Palm Springs section. Just call for reservations.

A Word about Nudity

You had best start with the hard fact that any private property owner, county administration, park superintendent, or forest supervisor has the authority to prohibit "public nudity" in a specific area or in a whole park or forest. Whenever the authorities have to deal with repeated complaints about nude bathers at a specific hot spring, it is likely that the area will be posted with NO NUDITY ALLOWED signs, and you could get a citation without further warning.

The vast majority of natural hot springs on public property are not individually posted, but most jurisdictions have some form of general regulation prohibiting public nudity. However, there have been some recent court cases establishing that a person could not be found guilty of indecent exposure if he removed his clothes only after traveling to a remote area where there was no one to be offended.

In light of these court cases, one of the largest national forests has retained its general "nude bathing prohibited" regulation but modified its enforcement procedure to give a nude person an opportunity to put on a bathing suit before a complaint can be filed or a violation notice issued.

In practical terms, this means that a group at an unposted hot spring can mutually agree to be nude. As soon as anyone else arrives and requests that all present put on bathing suits, those who refuse that request risk a citation. If you are in the nude group, all you need from the newcomers is some tolerance. You may be pleasantly surprised at the number of people who are willing to agree to a policy of clothing-optional if, in a friendly manner, you offer them an opportunity to say "Yes."

Chris Andrews

The farther out in the wilderness you travel, the more likely it is you will find a place to soak nude without offending anyone. *Soldier's Meadow* in Nevada would certainly qualify.

Sign photos by Justine Hill
and Bill Pennington

CARING FOR THE OUTDOORS

This is an enthusiastic testimonial and an invitation to join in supporting the work of the US Forest Service, the National Park Service, and the several State Park Services. At all of their offices and ranger stations we have always received prompt, courteous service, even when the staff was busy handling many other daily tasks.

Nearly all usable primitive hot springs are in national forests, and many commercial hot spring resorts are surrounded by a national forest. Even if you will not be camping in one of their excellent campgrounds, we recommend that you obtain official Forest Service maps for all of the areas through which you will be traveling. Maps may be purchased from the Forest Service Regional Offices listed below. To order by mail, phone or write for an order form:

Rocky Mountain Region   303 275-5349
Eastern Wyoming, Colorado
740 Simms St., Lakewood, CO 80401

Intermountain Region   801 625-5352
Southern Idaho, Utah,
Nevada, and Western Wyoming
324 25th St., Ogden, UT 84401

Southwestern Region   800 280-2267
Arizona, New Mexico
Federal Bldg. 517 Gold Ave., SW
Albuquerque, NM 87102

Pacific Southwest Region   415 705-2874
California, Hawaii
630 Sansome St., San Francisco, CA 94111

When you arrive at a national forest, head for the nearest ranger station and let them know what you would like to do in addition to putting your body in hot mineral water. If you plan to stay in a wilderness area overnight, request information about wilderness permits and camping permits. Discuss your understanding of the dangers of water pollution, including giardia (back country dysentery) with the Forest Service staff. They are good friends as well as competent public servants.

The following material is adapted from a brochure issued by the Forest Service, Southwestern Region, Department of Agriculture and supplemented with up-to-date information by Nancy Pfeiffer.

In order to get to *Conundrum Hot Springs* in Colorado you must hike through the designated Wilderness Area of the White River National Forest.

CAUTION

NATURAL HOT SPRINGS

- Water temperatures vary by site, ranging from warm to very hot . . . 180°F.

- Prolonged immersion may be hazardous to your health and result in hyperthermia (high body temperature).

- Footing around hot springs is often poor. Watch out for broken glass. Don't go barefoot and don't go alone. Please don't litter.

- Elderly persons and those with a history of heart disease, diabetes, high or low blood pressure, or who are pregnant should consult their physician prior to use.

- Never enter hot springs while under the influence of: alcohol, anti-coagulants, antihistamines, vasodilators, hypnotics, narcotics, stimulants, tranquilizers, vasoconstrictors, anti-ulcer or anti-Parkinsonian medicines. Undesirable side effects such as extreme drowsiness may occur.

- Hot springs are naturally occurring phenomena and as such are neither improved nor maintained by the Forest Service.

Steve Heerema

17

DO NOT WASH IN STREAMS OR SPRINGS

Wash yourself, your dishes and your clothes in a container, away from water sources.

Food scraps, tooth paste, even biodegradable soap will pollute streams and springs. Remember, it's your drinking water, too!

Pour wash water on the ground away from streams and springs.

If you are near a hot springs, fill a garbage bag with hot water from the springs and wash your clothes in it.

Try to pack out trash left by others. Your good example may catch on!

PACK IT IN — PACK IT OUT

Bring trash bags to carry out all trash that cannot be completely burned.

DON'T SHORT CUT TRAILS.

Trails are designed and maintained to prevent erosion.

Cutting across switchbacks and trampling meadows can create a confusing maze of unsightly trails.

If you see an idyllic green grassy spot to camp right next to the springs, don't use it. Remember, that spot is idyllic to everyone else as well. Also wild animals, bears included, enjoy hot springs areas. Give them the right of way. How far away you should camp is up to your good judgement.

CAMPFIRES Use gas stoves when possible to conserve dwindlling supplies of firewood.

Use only fallen timber for firewood. Even standing dead trees are part of the beauty of wilderness, and are important to wildlife.

If you need to build a fire, use an existing campfire site if available.

Clear a circle of all burnable materials.

Dig a shallow pit for the fire.

Keep the sod intact.

If you need to clear a new fire site, select a safe spot away from rock ledges that would be blackened by smoke; away from meadows where it would destroy grass and leave a scar; away from dense brush, trees and duff where it would be a fire hazard. Keep fires small.

Never leave a fire unattended.

Put your fire COLD OUT before leaving, by mixing the coals with dirt & water. Feel it with your hand. If it's cold out, cover the ashes in the pit with dirt, replace the sod, and naturalize the disturbed area. Rockfire rings, if needed or used, should be scattered before leaving.

DON'T BURY TRASH!
Animals dig it up.

BURY HUMAN WASTE

When nature calls, select a suitable spot at least 200 feet from open water, campsites and trails. Dig a hole 4 to 6 inches deep. Try to keep the sod intact.

Don't pick flowers, dig up plants or cut branches from live trees. Leave them for others to see and enjoy.

After use, fill in the hole completely burying waste **and taking the toilet tissue with you as animals will dig it up. It can be burned or disposed of later.**

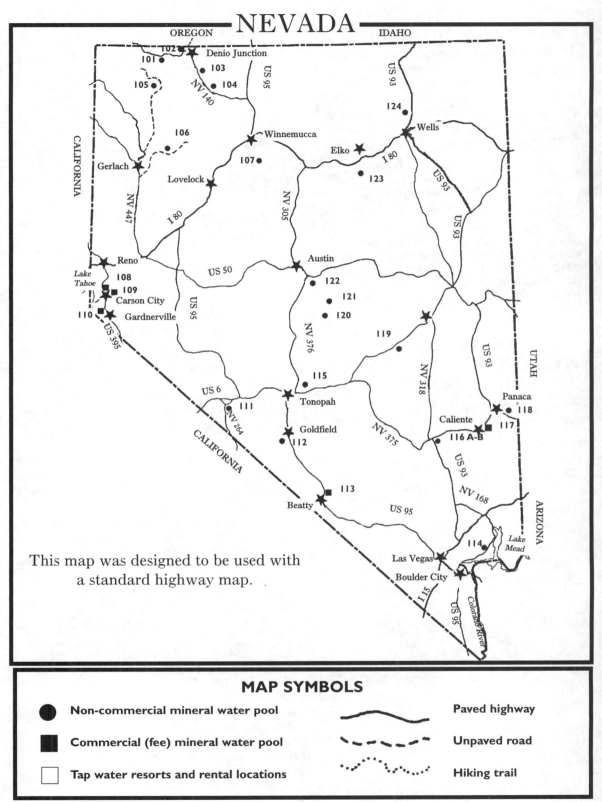

NEVADA

OREGON   IDAHO

CALIFORNIA

102 Denio Junction
101
103
105   104
NV 140

US 95

US 93

124

Wells

106   Winnemucca   Elko
Gerlach   I 80
107   123
Lovelock
NV 447
NV 305
US 93
NV 376
I 80
US 93

Reno   Austin
US 50
Lake
Tahoe   108   122
109   121
Carson City   120
110   119
Gardnerville
US 95
US 93
NV 318

US 395
UTAH

US 6   115
111   Tonopah
NV 264   Panaca
CALIFORNIA   Goldfield   Caliente   118
112   NV 375   116 A-B   117
ARIZONA
NV 168
113
Beatty   US 95
US 93

114   Lake
Mead

This map was designed to be used with   Las Vegas
a standard highway map.   Boulder City

Colorado River
I 15
US 95

MAP SYMBOLS

Symbol	Description	Symbol	Description
●	Non-commercial mineral water pool	〰️	Paved highway
■	Commercial (fee) mineral water pool	- - -	Unpaved road
□	Tap water resorts and rental locations	····	Hiking trail

Chris Andrews

The old adobe bathhouse and the area around the
pond have been renovated by Friends of the Refuge.

101   VIRGIN VALLEY WARM SPRING

● **In the Sheldon Wildlife Refuge**

A charming, gravel-bottom, warm pond adjacent to a
small campground in the high desert foothills near the
Nevada-Oregon border. Elevation 5,100 feet. Open all
year, subject to snow blocking the road.

Natural mineral water emerges from the pond
bottom (and is piped from other nearby springs) at 89°.
The rate of flow maintains pond temperature at
approximately 85°, depending on air temperature and
wind speed. A new cement pad and ladder into the pond
have been installed and the bank between the pond and
the bathhouse has been reinforced. No chemical
treatment of the water is necessary. Bathing suits are
required. The pool and facilities are handicap accessible
with assistance.

Natural hot water continually flows through two
indoor showers and to an outside pump for washing. The
campground is equipped with chemical toilets. Free
camping is available. Services are 27.5 miles away in Denio.

Directions: On NV 140, 27.5 miles west of Denio
Junction and 10 miles east of the Cedarville Road
Junction, watch for a road sign to Virgin Valley, Royal
Peacock Mine. Go south on the gravel road 2.5 miles to
campground.

GPS: N 41.85318 W 119.00230

102   BOG HOT SPRINGS

● **Near the town of Denio**

A large, sand-bottom ditch carrying hot mineral water
to an irrigation pond. Located on brush-covered, flat land
just below the Nevada-Oregon border. Elevation 4,300
feet. Open all year.

Natural mineral water flows out of several springs at
122°, is gathered into a single man-made channel, and
gradually cools as it travels toward the reservoir. A dam
with spillway pipe has been built at the point where the
temperature is approximately 105°, depending on air
temperature and wind speed. Water flows profusely
through the pipe as it fills the two-foot deep soaking
pond. Around the dam, brush has been cleared away for
easy access and nearby parking, but it is possible to soak
in the ditch farther upstream if a warmer water
temperature is desired. Clothing optional is probably the
custom at this remote location.

There are no services available, but there is an
abundance of level space on which overnight parking is
not prohibited. It is almost fourteen miles to a restaurant,
store, service station, motel, and RV hookups in Denio
Junction.

Directions: From Denio Junction, go west on NV 140
9.2 miles, turn right and drive north 4 miles on gravel road
to a pond on the left. At .4 of a mile past the pond turn
left and drive 100 yards to ditch and turn around area.

GPS: N 41.92168 W 118.80131

Justine Hill

There may be no facilities and no shade, but there is a 360-degree view of the surrounding mountains.

Photos by Chris Andrews

This part of the world seems to have found the perfect way to recycle old bathtubs.

103   HOWARD HOT SPRING

● **South of Denio Junction**

Small soaking tub one mile off Highway 140 on a barren plateau between Denio Junction and Winnemucca with a view of rolling hills on both sides. Elevation 4,200 feet. Open all year; wet weather could make road impassable.

Natural mineral water exits the ground at 135° and flows across the ground. At a spot where the water has cooled to 108° there is an old porcelain bathtub with pipes carrying the hot water to a log-and-rock pool which tends to be filled with algae. Bring a shovel and wire brush. Clothing is optional.

There are no restrictions against camping at the spring. All services are eighteen miles away in Denio Junction.

Directions: From Denio Junction, head south (toward Winnemucca) on Hwy 140 for 17 miles. Just past mile post 49, turn left on dirt road. Continue 1 mile; take the left fork and then a right fork through a gate, staying on the main road for .25 miles. Spring is visible on the right.

Coming from Winnemucca, turn right just past the sign reading "Denio Junction 20 miles."

GPS: N 41.72134 W 118.50554

104   DYKE HOT SPRING

● **South of Denio Junction**

Old porcelain bathtub set in a ravine against the hills on the western side of the Quinn River valley with hills to the west and broad vistas across the valley to the east. Elevation 4,000 feet. Open all year.

A small natural mineral water stream with a slight sulfur smell flows out of the hills at 150° and is carried by plastic pipe into the old bathtub. To control the temperature in the tub, remove the hot water pipe and allow the water to cool down. If tub water is dirty, empty tub and refill. Clothing is optional even though the tub is near the road. Traffic is seldom a problem.

Overnight camping is not restricted. All services are thirty-nine miles away in Denio Junction.

Directions: From Denio Junction, drive south about 26 miles (9 miles south of road to Howard Hot Spring). Just past mile post 41, turn onto Big Creek Road. (Sign says "Dyfurrena Ranch and Photo Gallery.") Go 7 miles to "T" and turn left onto Woodward Road. Pass ranch on left (2 miles) and take first left (another 2 miles). Park at obvious pullout and walk a few yards back toward the road and tub, which is hidden in the ravine.

GPS: N 41.56699 W 118.56652

Chris Andrews

105   SOLDIER MEADOWS

● North of the town of Gerlach

Delightful, deep pond located in the middle of a large meadow with a beautiful view of the surrounding desert and nearby Calico Mountains. Near High Rock Lake in the Black Rock Desert of northwest Nevada. Elevation 4,500 feet. Open all year; may be difficult to reach during winter storms. Spring and fall are best times.

Mineral water seeps up through the bottom of this natural, two-foot deep, sand and stone pond. A wooden ladder leads into the pond from a small wooden deck. Water temperatures range from 90-102°, depending on air and wind conditions. A second, small squishy-bottom pond at about 100° is about half a mile away, surrounded by alkali desert. The apparent local custom is clothing optional.

The hot springs are located on the private property of Soldier Meadows Guest Ranch and Lodge, a private working ranch and bed and breakfast. (For reservations: PO Box 67, Likely, CA 96116, 916 233-4881.) There are no services available, but the owners do not mind anyone using the springs. Please close all gates and camp outside the ranch fence and posted areas. It is 62 miles to a service station and mini-mart in Gerlach.

You can choose to stay over and be part of the crew on the nearby working ranch or you can dig for opals and explore the wonders of the desert and the great outdoors.

Directions: From Gerlach, take Hwy 34 north and east for 12.2 miles. Turn right on Soldier Meadows Road (mostly good gravel surface) for 50 miles. Bear left toward Summit Lake and first Soldier Meadow sign (Humboldt County Road 217). Turn left. At .5 miles from the sign follow the dirt road that veers off to the left for .2 miles to the white alkali meadow and small pond. Or, continue straight from the sign for 1 mile to the big pond on the right.

Note: There are numerous other hot springs on the road to High Rock Lake, but a four-wheel-drive vehicle is recommended since the road is rough.

GPS: N 41.37989 W 119.18140

106   TREGO HOT DITCH

● **Northeast of the town of Gerlach**

A hot ditch next to Western Pacific railroad tracks. Located in the Black Rock Desert with a backdrop of the Pahsupp Mountains. Elevation 4,000 feet. Open all year.

Natural mineral water bubbles up out of the ground by the railroad tracks at 120° and cools gradually as it flows toward a small man-made dam. Wooden stairs lead into the water where the water temperature varies greatly depending on air and wind conditions and may be as cool as 80°. Clothing is optional, but pools can be seen from the tracks and trains pass frequently.

No services are available, but overnight parking is not prohibited. It is 20 miles to a service station and mini-mart in Gerlach.

Directions: From Gerlach, go 3.5 miles south on Route 447. Turn left on gravel county road 48 (sign to Winnemucca, 96 miles). Continue 17 miles and turn left toward railroad radio antenna. Continue 1 mile and turn right at the first fork, left at the second, and right at the third (antenna on left). Take the next left toward the railroad track (pool not visible) and continue on a one-lane, sandy, dirt road for .3 miles up a gradual slope. Bear left across clearing with campfire rings, toward railroad tracks. Pool and ditch are on the right.

Note: There are rumors to the effect that on the way back to Gerlach, about three miles on your right, there is another pool. Check it out.

GPS: N 40.77173 W 119.11640

107   KYLE HOT SPRINGS

● **Near the town of Mill City**

Two stock tanks with crystal-clear water located on a barren mountainside in the East Humboldt Range overlooking a scrub-covered valley with a magnificent 360-degree view. Elevation 4,500 feet. Open all year.

High-sulphur-content mineral water flows out of the ground at over 110°. Hot sulphur dioxide steam comes out of a nearby vent. A plastic pipe carries water from the source to the first six-foot round galvanized stock tank where it measures 104°. A hose carries the overflow to the adjacent six-foot stock tank where water temperature measures around 80°. Clothing is optional. The tubs are handicap accessible with assistance.

There are no services available and no shade, but overnight parking is not prohibited. There is a truck stop/restaurant/mini-mart along I80 in Mill City (26 miles) for gas, provisions, RV park, and laundromat. All other services are 53 miles away in Winnemucca.

Directions: From Mill City exit 149 on Hwy 80, proceed south on Hwy 400 approximately 15.6 miles. Turn left at Kyle Hot Springs sign and drive 9.7 miles on a gravel road. Bear left at the fork at 9 miles and proceed toward the white hill with a corral at the bottom. The spring is on top of the knoll; you can drive right to it.

GPS: N 40.40708 W 117.88485

Note: Since this was originally written reports have come in that a drilling operation has drastically reduced the water flow to the tubs and the water is murky and too cool to soak.

108 BOWERS MANSION
4005 US 395 North   702 849-1825
■   **Carson City, NV 89704**

A Washoe County Park with extensive picnic, playground, and parking facilities, in addition to a large modern swimming pool. Elevation 5,100 feet. Park open all year; pools open Memorial Day to Labor Day. There is a charge for using the facilities.

Natural mineral water, pumped from wells at 116°, is combined with cold well water as needed. The swimming pool and children's wading pool are maintained at 80°. Both pools are treated with bromine. Bathing suits are required. Pool and picnic facilities are A.D.A. handicap accessible.

There are no services available on the premises. Tours of the mansion are conducted from Mother's Day to the end of October. It is four miles to restaurants, motels, service stations, and RV hookups in Carson City.

Directions: Go 10 miles north of Carson City on US 395. Watch for signs and turn west on side road 1.5 miles to location.

Phil Wilcox

109 CARSON HOT SPRINGS
1500 Hot Springs Rd.
702 882-9863
■   **Carson City, NV 89701**

Older hot springs plunge with swimming pool and nine large private rooms, each containing a sunken tub large enough for eight persons. Located in the northeast outskirts of Carson City. Elevation 4,300 feet. Open all year.

Natural mineral water flows out of the ground at 126°. Air spray and evaporative cooling are used to lower the water temperature when pools are drained and refilled each day. No chemical or city water is added. The outdoor swimming pool temperature is maintained at 98° in the summer and 102° in the winter. Individual room pool temperatures can be controlled as desired, from 95-110°. Bathing suits are required in the swimming pool, optional in the private rooms.

Massage, restaurant, bar, and RV parking (no-hookups) are available on the premises. No credit cards are accepted. It is one mile to a store and service station.

Directions: From US 395 at the north end of Carson City, go east on Hot Springs Road 1 mile to plunge.

110 WALLEY'S HOT SPRINGS RESORT

PO Box 26   702 782-8155
2001 Foothill Rd.   800 628-7831

■ Genoa, NV 89411

Tastefully restored 1862 spa and luxury hotel located twelve miles east of Lake Tahoe at the foot of the Sierra Nevada Mountains. Elevation 4,700 feet. Open all year.

Natural mineral water flows from several wells at temperatures up to 160° and is then piped to the bathhouse and to six outdoor cement pools (two with jets) where the temperatures are maintained from 96-104°. The cement swimming pool uses bromine-treated creek water and averages 80°. Bathing suits required in the outdoor pools. Handicap accessible.

Overnight accommodations are available. The main building is a two-story health club with separate men's and women's sections, each containing a sauna, steambath and weight training equipment. Massage is also available in each section. Facilities include dining rooms and bars. Visa, MasterCard, and American Express are accepted. It is seven miles to a store, service station, and RV hookups. Phone for rates and reservations.

Photos by Jayson Loam

In refurbishing *Walley's* the new owners carried on the tradition of relaxed elegance that was the signature of the original resort built in 1862.

111   FISH LAKE HOT WELL

● **Near the town of Dyer**

A cement-lined soaking pool on the edge of a barren desert wash in Fish Lake Valley, approximately half-way between Reno and Las Vegas. Winter is most beautiful, with snow-capped peaks encircling the valley. Elevation 4,800 feet. Open all year.

Natural mineral water emerges from a well casing at 105° and at a rate of more than fifty gallons per minute. The well was discovered in the 1880s when ranchers were drilling for oil. The well casing is surrounded by a six-foot by six-foot cement sump that maintains a water depth of four feet above a gravel bottom. From there it flows into a large, 102° cement soaking pool that can easily hold ten to twelve people. A three-foot wide cement walk surrounds the pool, with cinderblock and wooden benches on three sides. Overflow goes into a large man-made swimming hole stocked with a variety of large goldfish where water temperature measures 95°. Then the water flows into a second pond at 85° and into a third cooler pool. Posted signs say no nude bathing, but the custom seems to be clothing optional at your own discretion, depending on the people present. The pool is handicap accessible with assistance.

There is an abundance of level space for overnight parking. Facilities include a fenced-off area around the tub and pools, metal barbeque stands, campfire rings, and trash receptacles. Signs about not trashing or vandalizing the area reflect the feeling that this is now a heavily used party and camping site. Please help keep it clean.

Directions: From the junction of NV 264 and NV 773, go 5.7 miles south on NV 264 to a gravel road on the east side of the highway. Follow this for 7 miles to a fork, then bear left for .1 mile to the springs. The gravel road is subject to flash-flood damage and should not be attempted at night.

Source maps: USGS *Davis Mountain* and *Rhyolite Ridge* (well not shown on map).

The county is doing its best to keep *Fish Lake* open—please do your best to help.

Justine Hill

112   ALKALI (SILVER PEAK)
HOT SPRING

● **Near the town of Goldfield**

Two remote, brick-lined soaking pools at the edge of a salt flat in the remains of an abandoned turn-of-the-century hot springs resort with stunning views of the high Sierra to the west. Elevation 5,000 feet, Open all year.

Natural mineral water flows out of the ground through a flow pipe at 115°. On one edge of the source spring, volunteers have used bricks to build two large (four-six person) soaking pools in which the temperature is controlled by diverting or admitting hot water as desired. Wooden steps lead to the pools, and pieces of old carpet are around for sitting or sunning. Trash cans are available to collect the party trash. The apparent local custom is clothing optional.

There are no services on the premises, but there is plenty of level ground on which overnight parking is not prohibited. It is eleven miles to a store, service station, and motel in Goldfield.

Directions: From the town of Goldfield (27 miles south of Tonopah) drive north on US 95 for 4 miles and look for a sign to "Alkali/Silver Peak" on the west side of the highway. Turn west and drive 6.8 miles on a rough paved road to a power substation. A large abandoned swimming pool is near the road, just past the power station. Follow the channel 50 feet up the hill toward the station to the soaking pools. This area can be very muddy after rain or snow.

113   BAILEY'S HOT SPRINGS
Box 387   702 553-2395
■   **Beatty, NV 89003**

An older hot spring, rich in railroad history, now primarily an RV park with three large indoor, hot mineral water soaking pools. Located in the high desert country just east of Death Valley National Monument. Elevation 3,500 feet. Open all year.

Natural, crystal clear, odorless mineral water emerges from the ground at 110° and bubbles up through the gravel bottoms of three indoor soaking pools that used to be railroad water reservoirs. Flow rates are controlled to maintain different temperatures in the three pools, approximately 98°, 103°, and 105°. The rate of flow-through is sufficient to eliminate the need for chemical treatment of the water. Bathing suits are optional in the private-space pools. Pool use is included in the overnight RV fee, and pools are available on a day-use basis to tent campers and the general public for a small fee.

Facilities include tree-shaded full hookup RV spaces with picnic area and barbeque pits, showers, restroom, and a lawn for tent camping. No credit cards are accepted. It is five miles to a store, cafe, and service station.

Directions: From the only traffic signal in Beatty, go 5.5 miles north on US 95. Watch for the large sign on the east side of the road.

Phil Wilcox

Photos by Justine Hill

114   ROGERS WARM SPRING

● **Near the town of Overton**

A refreshing warm pond and shady picnic oasis on the barren north shore of Lake Mead in the Lake Mead National Recreation Area. Elevation 1,600 feet. Open all year.

Natural mineral water at approximately 90° flows directly up through a gravel bottom into a 100-foot-diameter pool at a sufficient rate to maintain the entire three-foot-deep pool at approximately 80°. Hundreds of gallons per minute flow over a cement and rock spillway in a series of small waterfalls. Bathing suits would be advisable at this location in the daytime.

There are no services available, and overnight parking (after 10 PM) is prohibited. It is eight and one-half miles to a store, restaurant, and service station in Overton, and five miles to a campground.

Directions: From the intersection of US 93 and NV 147 in the city of Henderson, go northeast on Lake Mead Drive. At the intersection with Northshore Road (NV 169), follow Northshore Road northeast toward Overton. Rogers Warm Spring is 4 miles beyond the Echo Bay Marina turnoff.

Alternate Directions: When approaching from the north, take the I-15 exit Logandale/Overton. Turn east on NV 169 to "Lake Mead National Recreation Area" and continue south for 27 miles to the Rogers Spring sign.

GPS: N 36.378 W 114.443

115   WARM SPRINGS

● **East of Tonopah**

A hot, sandy-bottom ditch pool formed in a channel that originally fed a large outdoor swimming pool surrounded by barren, nearly treeless high desert. Elevation 1,800 feet. Open all year.

Natural mineral water at more than 120° emerges from the ground with a cloud of steamy vapors and flows down a well-maintained trench with white calcium deposits on both sides (volunteers keep it clean). Just before the water flows through a wide pipe under the road, the channel has been dammed and widened to form a two-foot pool where water temperature measures 110°. When the water emerges on the south side of US 6, the foot-deep channel measures 106-108° and gradually cools as it follows NV 375 for nearly a mile before disappearing into the terrain. Bathing suits are suggested since the pools are right along the road, even though traffic is sparse.

No services are available. There is still a phone for outgoing credit card and collect calls only, at the now closed Warm Springs Bar.

Directions: Warm Springs is on US 6, 50 miles east of Tonopah, 160 miles from Bishop, CA, and 190 miles northwest of Las Vegas NV.

Construction is scheduled to begin in 1998 to rebuild the adjacent resort property. How that will affect *Ash Springs* is uncertain. Check at "R Place" across from the springs for status of construction.

116A   ASH SPRINGS

● **North of the Town of Alamo**

Natural warm-water swimming holes formed in deep channels under ash and cottonwood trees, surrounded by barren desert foothills. Elevation 4,000 feet. Open all year.

Hundreds of gallons per minute of natural mineral water flows out of several springs on Bureau of Land Management (BLM) property and gradually cools as it runs off though clear, large, wide sandy-bottom ditches which are currently on private property and fenced off. The water is approximately 92°. A heavy knotted rope hanging from a shade tree gives this pool the feeling of "Ye Olde Swimming Hole." A separate spring feeds a nearby rock, brick, and cement pool where water temperature measures 98°. Bathing suits are a good idea.

Facilities include a picnic area, firepits, trash collection, and level BLM land for parking with a two hour limit. No overnight camping. "R Place," a service station, restaurant, store, campground, and RV park is open across the highway 24 hours a day. Do not enter any marked, private land.

Directions to BLM land pools: From Las Vegas, drive 90 miles north on US 93 to Alamo. Continue four miles on US 93 to Ash Springs Resort on the right (east) side of the highway. Continue north beyond the end of the resort property fence and turn right on a narrow dirt road for 100 yards to the camping/campfire area and adjoining soaking pools.

116B   CRYSTAL SPRINGS

● **Near Ash Springs**

Warm water pours through a wide irrigation spout into an overgrown pool just off "Extraterrestrial Highway" near Nellis Air Force Base. Elevation 4,000 feet. Open all year.

Spray rises from the profuse flow of 75° water as it is funnelled through the irrigation spout into a broad pool where it seeps into the shrubbery along the banks. The spring and pool are located behind a barbed wire fence with paths leading to the running water. Although it is near the highway, the water is not visible to the few motorists who pass by, so bathing suits are optional.

There are no services or facilities. There are level areas along the highway for overnight parking. Most services can be found approximately seven miles away at "R Place," across from Ash Springs.

Directions: Drive approximately 100 miles north from Las Vegas to the intersections of US 93 and NV 375. Go west .5 miles to an area of shade trees and greenery. Walk 20 yards south to the spring

Photos by Justine Hill

Even though the water is only warm, *Crystal Springs* was included as a nice place to cool off while driving in summer in the middle of the hot Nevada desert.

117   CALIENTE HOT SPRINGS MOTEL
Box 216   702 726-3777
■   Caliente, NV 89008

Primarily a motel, with some hot-water facilities. Located on the edge of Caliente in beautiful Rainbow Canyon, one hundred and fifty miles north of Las Vegas. Elevation 4,400 feet. Open all year.

Natural mineral water flows from a spring at 115° and is piped to three indoor, family-size, newly retiled soaking pools in which hot mineral water and cold tap water may be mixed as desired by the customer. No chemical treatment is necessary because soaking pools are drained, cleaned, and refilled after each use. Soaking pools may be rented by the public on an hourly basis; free to motel guests.

There are six rooms with kitchenettes and a hydrojet tub using hot mineral water and cold tap water. Major credit cards are accepted. A restaurant, store, and service station are within a few blocks.

118   PANACA WARM SPRINGS
●   North of Panaca, NV

A large, warm swimming hole maintained by the town of Panaca, located on BLM land surrounded by low mountains and ranch land in the high desert of eastern Nevada near the Utah border. Elevation 4,742 feet. Open all year.

Natural warm springs flow out of the mountain and through a marsh into a large dammed pond which is as deep as five and one-half feet near the dam, and varies in temperature from 78-80°. A five-step ladder leads into the pond. Once a year the pond is drained and cleaned by the town. The water is clean, but there is a lot of broken glass in the surrounding area. There are no clothing requirements, however the springs is right along a heavily traveled, unpaved road.

Overnight parking is not prohibited. Gas, store, and a mini-mart are available in Panaca and auto service and a restaurant are five miles away at the Highway 93 junction.

Directions: In Panaca turn north off Main Street to Fifth Street. Follow the straight dirt road for .3 miles to the spring.

GPS: N 37.807 W 114.380

A sign at *Panaca Springs* says: "The large and constant flow of sweet warm water from this spring makes possible the desert oasis of Meadow Valley. First noted by Manley's Death Valley party of 1849. Dependent on these spring waters, Mormons built the first permanent settlement in southern Nevada at Panaca in 1864. For 30 years this water was used for all domestic purposes."

Justine Hill

● **Southwest of Currant, NV**

Narrow, shallow irrigation ditch surrounded by rangeland near Humboldt National Forest in the high desert of Nevada near the Utah border. Elevation approximately 6,000 feet. Open all year.

A two-foot wide, shallow irrigation ditch with 80° water has been dug between the rangeland brush on both sides of US 6 near Blackrock Station. The ditch is filled with moss and surrounded by tall grass. As the ditch is right along the highway, bathing suits are recommended if you decide to soak.

There is nothing available on the premises, but services at Blackrock Station include gas, a store/mini-mart, and a telephone.

Directions: Located along US 6, 22 miles southwest of Currant, approximately half way between Ely and Tonopah.

If you happen to be driving along this road *Locke's Spring* is nice to know about, but it is not worth a special trip to see.

Justine Hill

● **Southeast of Austin, NV**

Volcanic crater filled with very hot water whose overflow forms a wide body of water for soaking. Elevation 6,700 feet. Open all year.

Natural mineral water at 183° runs down from Diana's Punch Bowl forming a hot creek about five miles wide allowing the water temperature to cool down to the low 100s at the further end of the creek. Several dams have been built along the waterway providing areas to soak, many at least waist high. Clothing optional. Very difficult handicap access.

There are no services on the premises but there is a lot of flat, unposted area to camp overnight. Toquima Campground is sixteen miles away. All other services are 46 miles away in Austin.

Directions: From the intersection of US 50 and NV 376 go 100 yards south on 376. Bear left on a gravel road. Consider this point 0 on your odometer. This is FS Road 001. At 14.4 miles pass the road to your left, and at 17.8 miles pass Toquima Campground. At 24.2 miles bear right at a major fork in the road. At 24.5 you'll pass through a ranch yard, bear left. Bear right at the fork at 28 miles. At 32.7 miles turn left on a small dirt road toward a large conical butte a couple of miles away. This butte is Diana's Punch Bowl. It is worth a hike up to the top to see the spring inside. A road goes around to the right to the springs (about .5 miles).

GPS: N 39.03097 W 116.66632

The view into the volcanic crater known as *Diana's Punch Bowl.*

Chris Andrews

Most of the time it is only you and the cows at *Pott's Ranch Hot Spring.*

Photos by Chris Andrews

This hot water ditch was formed from the overflow from *Diana's Punch Bowl.*

121   POTT'S RANCH HOT SPRING

● **Southeast of Austin, NV**

A watering tank large enough for four set into the hillside with views of the high desert of the Monitor Valley, surrounded on both sides by the Toiyabe National Forest. Elevation 6,700 feet. Open all year.

Natural mineral water comes out of the source spring at 113° and is piped to an eight-foot round cattle tank and bathtub. Water temperature is adjusted by diverting the hot water pipes. Local volunteers have built a small wood deck and bench and help keep the area quite clean. Clothing optional. Handicap accessible with assistance.

There are no facilities out here so be prepared with everything you need as the nearest supplies are 43 miles away in Austin or 90 miles away in Tonopah. The Toquima Campground is 13.5 miles away.

Directions: See directions to Diana's Punch Bowl. The directions are the same until you come to the fork at the 28 mile odometer reading. To get to Pott's bear left at the cattle guard. At 30.4 pass an old ranch house on the left. At 30.8 bear right and the spring is at 31.3.

GPS: N 39.07971 W 116.63989

122　SPENCER HOT SPRINGS

● **Southeast of the town of Austin, NV**

A group of volunteer-built soaking pools on a knoll with a view of barren hills and snow-capped mountains. Elevation 5,700 feet. Open all year.

Natural mineral water flows out of several springs at 122°, then through a shallow channel down the slope of the knoll. Volunteers have dug a small, three-foot deep, sand-bottom soaking pool next to this channel. The temperature is 104°. A wooden slat deck has been built near the soaking pool. Volunteers have also installed a large metal stock tank downhill for soaking in 107° water. A second stock tank has been installed about one-quarter of a mile to the north where the water is about 112°. Water temperature is controlled by inserting or removing the pipe or hoses carrying the hot water. Clothing optional is the apparent local custom.

There are no services available, but there is a limited amount of level space on which overnight parking is not prohibited. A steel fire pit has been built near the metal soaking tank, and there are several large bins for trash collection. Please do your part to keep this location clean.

Directions: From the intersection of US 50 (12 miles east of Austin) and NV 376, go 100 yards south on NV 376 and turn left onto road 001 with a sign saying Monitor Valley. Continue 5.5 miles southeast on a gravel road bearing left on a dirt road that leads up to the hot-spring knoll.

GPS: N 39.32746 W 116.85569

Why not spend several days in the area around Austin visiting *Spencer, Diana's Punch Bowl,* and *Pott's* hot springs, all of which are within a few miles of each other?

Top photo by Chris Andres
Bottom photo by Justine Hill

Justine Hill

Chris Andrews

123   RUBY VALLEY HOT SPRINGS

● Near Elko, NV

Series of natural hot spring pools located in the spectacular high desert near Ruby Lake National Wildlife Refuge on the east side of the Ruby Mountains with views of Humboldt National Forest. Elevation approximately 7,000 feet. Open all year; may be impassable during heavy rains.

Hot, 122° water emerges up through the ground at various spots on a grassy knoll just outside the border fence of the Wildlife Refuge into several pools where water temperatures range from 106-122°. The area around the springs is a marshy bog and even with several wooden planks which have been set down as walkways you still sink into the marsh.

There are no facilities and no shade, but plenty of flat areas away from the marshy hot springs where you can park overnight. The nearest town is Jiggs (36 miles away) where you can purchase gas, food, and a drink.

Directions: Ruby Valley can be reached from US 93 (drive west), from I 80 east of Elko (drive south) or from I 50 (drive north). Follow signs along these highways to Ruby Valley National Wildlife refuge. from Elko, drive south on excellent paved NV 228 for 36 miles to Jiggs. Continue until the pavement ends and the road becomes unpaved Harrison Pass Road which crosses Humboldt National Forest at Harrison Pass (elevation 7,248 feet). The road is not maintained in winter. On the east side of the mountain, Harrison Pass Road ends at a wide gravel road. Turn left for .3 miles, then right onto a one lane dirt road. At 3.5 miles bear right at the fork and follow the fence around the wildlife refuge. At .3 miles go right when the road forks. The hot springs are on a knoll surrounded by dark green bullrushes which are visible from the refuge.

124   TWELVE MILE HOT SPRINGS

● North of Wells, NV

Very large soaking pool formed by a rock-and-concrete wall at the base of a large hill. Located in a small canyon near Bishop Creek. Elevation 5,000 feet. Open all year; roads may not be passable and fording Bishop Creek may be dangerous in wet weather or times of high water.

Natural mineral water flows out of the rocks directly into a large, clean, gravel-bottom pool about twelve feet wide, ninety feet long and approximately three feet deep, making it one of the biggest hot soaking pools at 104° that we've ever found. While the apparent local custom is clothing optional, keep a suit handy on the weekends.

All services, except level ground for overnight camping, are back in Wells.

Directions: Consider the intersection of 6th St. and Lake Ave. in downtown Wells as point 0. Turn northeast on Lake Ave. Cross the railroad tracks and turn left on 8th St. Continue across Wells Ave on what is now a dirt road. One mile further the road is again paved. Continue north. At 9.7 miles and just past 2 farmhouses the road curves sharply west. Turn onto the dirt road that comes off to the right and continue straight on this road to the main pool at 11.7 miles. (There is a large steel and wood bridge approximately .1 of a mile before the spring.) The road in is very rough and a very high clearance vehicle is suggested.

Grandma's Farmhouse B&B was recommended as a good place to stay Phone: 775 752-3065.

Note: There are hot water seeps along the banks lining Bishop Creek where other pools could be built.

GPS: N 41.24283 W 114.94816

UTAH

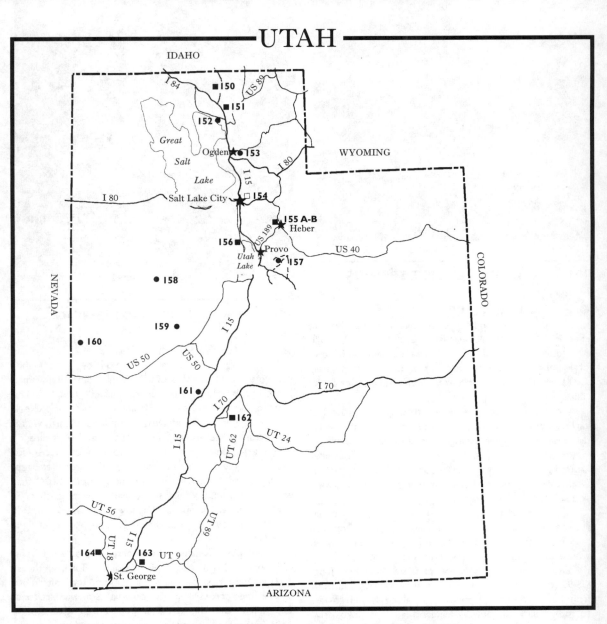

This map was designed to be used with a standard highway map.

MAP SYMBOLS

● Non-commercial mineral water pool

■ Commercial (fee) mineral water pool

□ Tap water resorts and rental locations

〜 Paved highway

- - - Unpaved road

··· Hiking trail

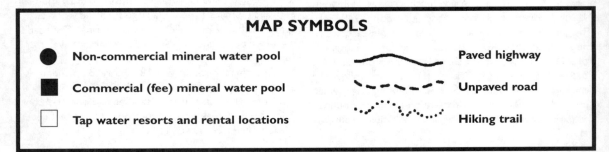

Phil Wilcox

150 BELMONT SPRINGS
Box 36   **801 458-3200**
■ **Fielding, UT 84311**

Modern, commercial plunge with RV park and golf course in a large northern Utah valley. Elevation 4,300 feet. Open April through October; scuba park open during winter.

Natural mineral water flows out of artesian wells at 125° and is piped to four outdoor pools, all of which are treated at night with minimal chlorine that burns off by daytime. The large swimming pool is maintained at 93°, a hot-tub soaking pool at 106°, and two hot-tub hydrojet pools at 106°. Bathing suits are required. Limited handicap accessibility.

Locker rooms, two picnic areas, golf course, overnight parking, tent camping, RV hookups, a scuba diving park, and a tropical fish farm which also raises red-claw lobsters are on the premises. A cafe, store, service station, and motel are available within ten miles. Scuba instructors and classes are welcome. No credit cards are accepted.

Directions: From the town of Plymouth (exit 394) on I-15, go one mile south and watch for resort sign.

Jayson Loam

In addition to the swimming and soaking pools, there is a 35-foot deep scuba pond open all year.

Crystal Hot Springs has been a commercial venture since 1901. The Native Americans, Chinese and Japanese who helped build the nearby railroad certainly didn't have the opportunity to choose among the five different pools with varying temperatures.

151 CRYSTAL HOT SPRINGS
8215 North Hwy 38   **801 547-0777**
■ **Honeyville, UT 84314**   **801 279-8104**

Small, historical resort featuring one of the world's largest side-by-side hot and cold springs. The property includes spacious, tree-shaded lawns for picnics and camping. Elevation 4,700 feet. Open all year.

Natural hot mineral water flowing out of a spring at 140° and a cold spring at 52°, is piped to an Olympic-size swimming pool, a "soaker pool" large enough to swim in, and three outdoor hydrojet pools on a flow-through basis requiring no chemical treatment. A lap pool and the catch pool for the two waterslides used city water and require a minimum of chlorine treatment. Various pools on the premises range from temperatures of 85-105°. Bathing suits are required. Facility is handicap accessible.

Locker rooms, snack bar (seasonal), large overnight camping area and RV hookups are available on the premises. It is four blocks to a store and fifteen miles to a motel. Visa and MasterCard are accepted.

Directions: From I-15, take the Honeyville exit. Go one mile east on UT 240 to UT 38, then 2.5 miles north to the resort on the west side of the highway.

155A   THE HOMESTEAD
700 N. Homestead Rd.   801 654-1102
800 327-7220
■   Midway, UT 84049

The only warm-water scuba sight in the continental US has been added to this upscale, historic, destination resort specializing in leisure vacations and group meetings, with extensive access to summer and winter sports and recreation. Elevation 5,600 feet. Open all year.

A 110-foot tunnel has been hollowed out of the tufa crater's north side providing access to scuba divers, snorkelers, swimmers and mineral bathers to enjoy the 96° water.

Natural mineral water flows from a tufa-cone spring at 96°. The water temperature is boosted, and the water is piped to one small outdoor mineral bath that averages 100° and is not treated with chemicals. All other pools use chlorine-treated tap water. The large outdoor swimming pool is maintained at 85°, the indoor hydrojet pool at 102°, and the indoor lap pool at 90°. There is also a dry sauna available. Pool use is available to registered guests and pool members. Bathing suits are required.

Locker rooms, dining rooms, a pub, an eighteen-hole championship golf course, hotel rooms, suites, condominiums, and bed and breakfast are available on the premises. During the winter there are snowmobiling, skiing, sleigh rides and guided trail rides; during the summer there are golf, tennis, trail rides and mountain biking. It is two miles to a store, service station, and RV hookups. Major credit cards are accepted.

Directions: From Heber City on US 189, go west on UT 113 to the town of Midway and follow signs to the resort.

155B   MOUNTAIN SPAA RESORT
800 North Mtn. Spaa Lane
801 654-0807
801 654-0721
■   Midway, UT 84049

Historic, rustic resort located in beautiful Heber Valley, one mile from Wasatch Mountain State Park. Elevation 5,700 feet. Open daily from Memorial Day to Labor Day and during April, May, September, and October, weather permitting.

Natural mineral water flows from cone-shaped tufa craters at 120° and is piped to two pools. The outdoor swimming pool, with kiddie slide and large deck area, is maintained at 86-98°. The indoor swimming pool, built inside a large crater, maintains a temperature of 87-103°. Both pools are drained twice weekly, disinfected, and refilled.

Guest house, cabins, soda fountain, snack bar, game room, locker rooms, lawn and picnic area, overnight camping, and RV hookups are available on the premises. Banquet room and pavilion facilities available for large groups. Visa and MasterCard are accepted.

Directions: From Heber City on US 189, go west on UT 113 to the town of Midway. Turn north on River Road, go .7 mile to 600 North in Midway, and follow signs to the resort.

The building in the background houses the swimming pool, which is built in a large natural crater.

152 STINKY SPRINGS

● **West of the town of Brigham City**

After the bathhouse was removed volunteers erected tents to cover the two remaining pools alongside a highway in the flat country north of the Great Salt Lake. Elevation 4,000 feet. Open all year.

Natural mineral water flows out of a spring at 118°, through a culvert under the highway, and into two cement soaking pits. Temperature within each pool is controlled by diverting the hot-water flow as desired. In recent years volunteers have kept the surrounding party trash to a minimum, but the water does have a sulfur-dioxide smell. The apparent local custom is clothing optional in the tents.

There are no services available on the premises.

Directions: From I-15, take the Golden Spike exit, then go 9 miles west through Corinne on UT 83 for 4 miles (mile marker 4). The springs are on the south side of the road shortly before you reach Little Mountain, a rocky hill on the north side of the road.

GPS: N 41.57655 W 112.23415

Makeshift tents cover the springs. Access to the two pools are to the right and left of the dividing post as pictured below.

Photos on this page by Chris Andrews

153 OGDEN HOT SPRINGS

● **East of the city of Ogden**

Small, primitive hot springs at the river's edge, located in a beautiful river gorge in Ogden Canyon. Elevation 4,800 feet. Open all year, subject to annual flooding.

Natural mineral water flows out of a spring at 130° and through a pipe and hoses to a volunteer-built, rock-and-mud pool at 107°. The water continues flowing into a rock-and-cement-bottomed pool at 101°. The sides have been built up to prevent the entrance of river water. The temperature is controlled by diverting the hoses when desired. The apparent local custom is clothing optional, even though the highway is visible.

There are no services available on the premises.

Directions: Exit I-15 in Ogden at SR 39 (12th St.) and go east 4.9 miles to the mouth of Ogden Canyon. Park on either side of the road just after passing under suspended water pipe. Short trail downstream to spring starts at mile 9 green marker. (If pulling a trailer, go 1 mile farther upstream to a turnaround and come back to park.)

GPS: N 41.23564 W 111.92378

154 WASATCH SPAS
3955 S. State St.   801 264-TUBS
❏   Salt Lake City, UT 84107

Private hot tub rentals, plus spa sales and service, on a main street in Salt Lake City.

Four indoor rooms and one out-of-doors area enclosed by a beautiful redwood gazebo are for rent to the public by the hour. Temperatures are set at 102° and tubs are treated with bromine. Major credit cards are accepted. Phone or e-mail (hottubs@aros.net) for rates, reservations, and directions.

Diamond Fork Hot Springs is indeed the jewel in Utah's crown. The best hot spring in the state offers three hot soaking pools and a spectacular waterfall.

156 SARATOGA RESORT
Saratoga Rd. at Utah Lake
801 768-8206
■ Lehi, UT 84043

Lakeside recreation resort with picnic ~'s, rides, and boat-launching facilities. Elevatior ~ Open May to September.

Natural mineral water is r ~ . at 120° and is piped to four o' ~ . which are treated with chlori ~ ⁄drojet pool is maintained at 10~ ~ ⁄ool, diving pool, and waterslide c~ ~ ~ained at 75-80°. Bathing suits are ~

~ ~ bar, overnight camping, and RV ~ ⁓ole on the premises. There are also ~ ⁓ement park rides. No credit cards are accepted.

Di~ections: From the town of Lehi on I-15, go west on UT 73 and follow signs to resort.

As of 1999 this resort was closed.

157 DIAMOND FORK HOT SPRINGS
(also known as Fifth Water Canyon)
● Spanish Fork, UT (South of Provo)

Three volunteer-built rock pools in a beautiful canyon at the end of an easy hike, with flowing creek and large waterfall. Elevation 5,800 feet. Open all year subject to snow.

Natural mineral water flows out of the ground at 125° and depending how rocks have been moved along the creek, combines with creek water to cool the higher pool to a comfortable temperature. The lower pool receives the overflow from the upper pool and is slightly cooler. The third pool is across the creek and is quite hot when the creek is low, but it cools some when creek water is high and flows over into the pool. The apparent local custom is clothing optional.

There are no services available on the premises, but overnight camping is not prohibited at the trailhead and at the many pull-out spots along the creek. It is fifteen minutes to a mini-mart in Spanish Fork.

Directions: From the junction of SR 89 and SR 6 (off I-15 south of Provo), proceed south on SR 6 for 6.2 miles. Turn left on paved road (Diamond Fork) and drive exactly 10 miles (passing many nice camping sites) to trailhead parking area. Cross bridge and start up trail. Stay straight and do not turn right over the second bridge. Cross the bridge over the creek. After 1 mile, proceed another 1.5

Chris Andrews

158   WILSON HEALTH SPRINGS

● **Northwest of Delta, UT**

Two bath tubs located on the salt flats near a very large hot source pool in the high Utah desert at the south edge of the Wendover Bombing and Gunnery Range. Elevation 4,500 feet. Open all year although roads are not maintained.

Natural mineral water at 120° flows through two channels dug out of the clay directly into the two bathtubs set further up along the channels. The temperature of the water is controlled by diverting the hot water with wooden gates in the channel. Clothing optional. Handicap accessible with assistance.

There are no facilites on the premises but lots of area for unofficial camping nearby. All services are located 95 miles away in Delta or 120 miles away in Wendover.

Directions: From Delta, travel northeast on US 5 to UT 174. Turn left and travel northwest approximately 80 miles following the signs to the Fish Springs National Wildlife Refuge. Continue past the ranger station another 4.9 miles and turn right near an old abandoned bus. The spring is on a small, 8-foot high butte, approximately .25 miles from the main gravel road. The roads can become a muddy quagmire during the rainy season.

Source map: USGS *Fish Springs NW* (spring not on map).

GPS: N 39.90650 W 113.43021

Photos by Chris Andrews

159   BAKER HOT SPRINGS

● **Northwest of Delta, UT**

Concrete soaking pools and a great place to soak are all that remain of an old resort located in the high desert in western Utah. Elevation 4,600 feet. Open all year although roads are not maintained.

Natural mineral water flows out of a spring at 122° into an earthen channel which directly feeds the three five-by eight-foot soaking pools. Each pool has a set of stairs leading down into the two-foot deep tubs. Cold spring water runs through a parallel channel and can be piped to each tub to cool the water to a comfortable temperature. Clothing optional. Handicap accessible with minimal assistance.

There are no facilites available on the premises but there is plenty of open land which can be used for camping. All services are 27 miles away in Delta.

Directions: From the junction of US 6 and UT 174 (10 miles northeast of Delta) drive west on 174 19 miles. Turn right on a good gravel road and drive 7 miles to the spring. The spring is about 150 yards on your right.

GPS: N 39.61050 W 112.73081

160   GANDY WARM SPRINGS

● **South of Gandy, UT**

Large, popular swimming hole at the base of a large volcano-shaped butte in the high Utah desert not far from the Utah-Nevada border. Elevation 5,300 feet. Open all year although roads are not maintained.

Natural mineral water flows from a spring at over 4,400 gallons per minute at a temperature of 82°. The warm water flows through a large creek to fill the swimming hole which is two- to four-feet deep. Temperatures range between 78-82° depending on winds and air temperature. While the local custom seems to be clothing optional it is a good idea to have a suit handy in case you need one. Handicap accessible with assistance.

There are no facilites available on the premises but there is plenty of open land which can be used for camping. Basic services are available in Baker, NV 42 miles away. All services can be found in Delta, UT 114 miles away.

Directions: From US 50 and US 6, 50 miles east of the Utah-Nevada border turn north on a gravel road towards Gandy, UT. Travel 28.2 miles and turn left (west) on another dirt road. (There's a small pump house on the east side of the road.) Reset your odometer to 0. At 1.3 miles bear right, at 1.9 miles bear left, at 2.4 miles bear left, and at 2.6 miles bear right. Spring is at 2.7 miles. Make sure you are heading towards the volcano-shaped butte.

GPS: N 39.45997 W 114.0291

Steve Heerema

161   MEADOW HOT SPRINGS

●   **South of Provo, near Meadow**

Delightful large pool, formed from travetine or mineral deposits, with ample sitting room on underwater stone ledges. Located in the pasture lands of Utah with unobstructed views of the Pahvant Mountain Range. Elevation 4,800 feet. Open all year.

Natural mineral water flows up through the bottom of a beautifully clear, room-sized pool at 100°. A heavy rope across the pool allows you to remain on the surface while viewing the clear, deeper portions of the pool. The apparent local custom is clothing optional.

There are no facilities on the premises, but overnight parking is not prohibited. It is six miles to a store in Meadow.

Directions: From I-15 (south of Provo) take exit 158 at Meadow. From Meadow on the east side of I 15, go south on Hwy 133 for 1.6 miles, turning right (west) on the gravel road half a mile south of mile marker 6. Head straight west for 5 miles to the end of the road. Spring is about 200 yards south.

GPS: N 38.864 W 112.506

Unfortunately there is no way in black and white to show the clarity of the water and the depth of the beautiful colors in this pool.

162 MYSTIC HOT SPRINGS OF MONROE

575 East First North   888 527-3286
Monroe, UT 84754

Older, funky RV park (under construction) with several hillside soaking pools, and a campground set about with razzleberry bushes, overlook a green agricultural valley with spectacular mountain views. Elevation 5,500 feet. Open all year.

Natural mineral water flows out of a spring at 168°, cooling as it flows across the mountains into a soaking pool where the temperature ranges from 100-105°. A huge tufa mound engulfs several bathtubs offering a soak for one or two persons. The water then flows on to the natural tropical fish ponds. If those present do not object, nude bathing is okay.

Biking and hiking trails, picnic area, camping, full RV hookups, and tepees are available on the premises. It is a short walk to the large and colorful Red Hill Spring, the natural warm water caves, and the adjoining tropical fish pond. A service station is within four blocks. Soaking is free with overnite stay. Major credit cards accepted.

Directions: From the town of Richfield on I-70, go 6 miles south on US 89, then 3 miles on UT 118 to the town of Monroe. Follow signs to the resort.

Phil Wilcox

163 PAH TEMPE MINERAL HOT SPRINGS RESORT

825 North 800 East   801 635-2879
**   Fax   801 635-2353**
Hurricane, UT 84737

Located in the spectacular Virgin River Canyon, eighteen miles from St. George and twenty miles southwest of Zion National Park. Elevation 3,000 feet. Open all year; reservations encouraged.

Natural mineral water flows up from the earth and into newly constructed soaking pools at approximately 106°. Much of the time there are also natural pools in the river. There is one shaded, outdoor swimming pool that averages 94° and does not require chemical treatment. Bathing suits are required; alcohol and tobacco are prohibited. Some areas are handicap accessible.

A bed and breakfast with nine charming rooms, some with private baths, and a central dining facility is available, as are two cabins with private baths. Camping and RV hookups are available. A retreat center is located on the premises for reunions, weddings, and special seminars. A vegetarian breakfast is served daily. Massage, facials, Yoga, and other therapy classes are offered. Visa, MasterCard and approved checks are accepted.

Directions: From St. George: Take I-15 to exit 16 (Zion National Park, the Grand Canyon). This ramp will merge into UT 9. Continue on UT 9 through the town of Hurricane and turn right onto Enchanted Way located just before a large bridge spanning the Virgin River. Follow the paved, winding road down to the gate.

From Zion National Park: Stay on UT 9 through the town of LaVerkin. Turn left onto Enchanted Way and follow the directions as above.

Note: Advanced reservations are encouraged. Please call for additional information.

Natural soaking areas located along the river, in addition to several constructed pools offer guests at *Pah Tempe* multiple choices of hot natural mineral water soaks. Be sure to stop there on the way to Zion National Park. Call ahead for reservations.

164　VEYO POOL
287 East Veyo Rd.

801 574-2300

■　Veyo, UT 84782

Located at the bottom of a deep canyon in the high Utah desert. Cottonwood trees, 100-feet high, form a canopy to protect the pools from the summer heat. The largest rock climbing park in the United States is located on the property. Elevation 4,600 feet. Open May 1 to Labor Day.

Natural mineral water flows out of an artesian well at a temperature of 85° and flows over a rock waterfall into the newly redone outdoor swimmin pool that is ozonated. The 85° water also fills a shallow, 140-foot long pond for the kids. Bathing suits are required. Management will provide any assistance neded for handicapped visitors.

Locker rooms, snack bar, restaurant, camping sites, a sand volleyball court, and a pcinic area are available on the premises. It is one mile to a store and service station, eight mile to overnight camping and RV hookups, and twelve miles to a motel. Credit cards are accepted. Call to reserve camp sites and picnic areas.

Directions: From the city of St. George on I-15, go 19 miles north on UT 18 to the town of Veyo and follow signs to the resort.

Courtesy of Veyo Hot Springs

Photos by Phil Wilcox

COLORADO

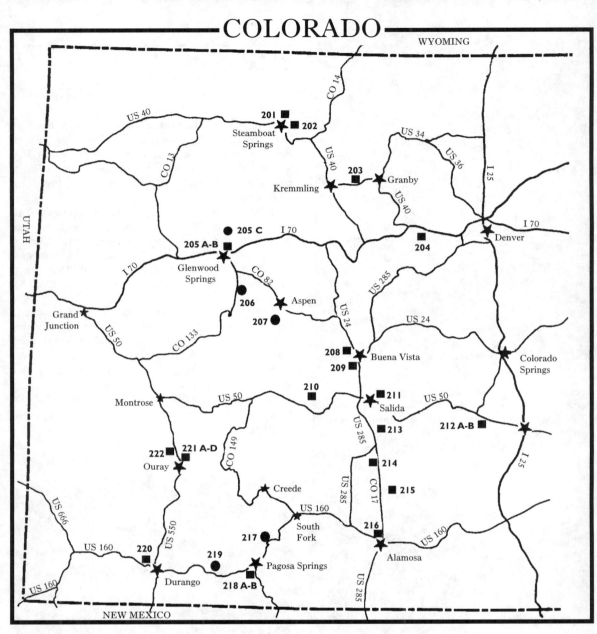

This map was designed to be used with a standard highway map.

MAP SYMBOLS

- ● Non-commercial mineral water pool
- ■ Commercial (fee) mineral water pool
- ☐ Tap water resorts and rental locations

- Paved highway
- Unpaved road
- Hiking trail

201 STRAWBERRY PARK HOT SPRINGS

PO Box 77332   970 879-0342
■ Steamboat Springs, CO 80477

A unique hot spring that manages to retain a maximum of primitive naturalness while providing improved services for a variety of hot-spring enthusiasts. Elevation 7,500 feet. Open all year.

Natural mineral water flows out of many hillside fissures at 146° and cools successively as it is channeled into a series of creek-bank, rock-and-masonry pools where it is combined with creek water to provide a range of soaking temperatures (from 100-105° in the upper pool down to 85° in the lower pool). Continuous flow-through in all pools eliminates the need for chemical treatment. A private pool with heated changing area is for rent by the hour. Bathing suits are required during the day (10 AM until dark); optional at night. Handicap access with assistance.

An 1890s railroad caboose with private bath and amenities, along with cabins, overnight camping, and catered private parties are available on the premises. Massage is also available. A bathhouse provides showers for overnight guests, and cold drinks can be purchased. It is seven miles to all other services. No credit cards are accepted.

Directions: From US 40 in the town of Steamboat Springs, go north on 7th St. and follow signs 7 miles to location at the end of County Road 36. The steep grades are not recommended for trailers. Four-wheel drive or tire chains are required on all vehicles during the winter season. Phone for hours, rates, reservations, and transportation from Steamboat Springs. Note: It is well worth the expense of the shuttle during the winter months, as the roads are narrow and very slippery, resulting in accidents and possible closure of the road during the winter.

Dramatic views, wonderful soaks, and lodging in a remodeled 1890s railroad caboose make a perfect stay.

Photos on this page by Phil Wilcox

Even before these springs were "discovered" by James Crawford they were known by the Ute Indians as Medicine Springs.

202 STEAMBOAT SPRINGS HEALTH AND RECREATION

PO Box 1211   970 879-1828
Steamboat Springs, CO 80477

Large community pool, diving board, hot pools, a 350 foot water slide, and sauna situated near the city center. Elevation 6,700 feet. Open all year.

Natural mineral water flows out of a spring at 103° and is piped to five pools that are treated with bromine and ozone. The soaking pools are maintained at a temperature of 101°, the water slide pick-up pool at 90°, and the large lap pool at 80°. Two large outdoor soaking pools, one with jets, are maintained at 102°. Bathing suits are required. Pools are handicap accessible.

Facilities include locker rooms, saunas, snack bar, weight room, cardiovascular equipment and tennis courts. Exercise classes, massage, and child care are available on the premises. It is three blocks to a cafe, store, service station, and motel and two miles to overnight camping and RV hookups. Visa and MasterCard are accepted.

Location: On the north side of US 40, at the east edge of the city of Steamboat Springs.

Courtesy of Steamboat Springs

203   HOT SULPHUR SPRINGS
■   PO Box 275   970 725-3306
Hot Sulphur Springs, CO 80451

Totally renovated resort on ninety scenic acres with a view of the Contintntal Divide, close to winter and summer sports. Elevation 7,600 feet. Open all year.

Natural mineral water flows out of a spring at 123° and is piped to a variety of pools. The outdoor swimming pool is open May to October and maintained around 80°. Fifteen outdoor soaking pools and one solarium pool are maintained at 100-108° on a flow-through basis that eliminates the need for chemical treatment. The outdoor Ute Cave Pool has a "do it yourself" massage waterfall. Two indoor pools in private spaces rent by the hour, and there are two indoor pools in separate men's and women's bathhouses. Temperatures in these pools are 108°. Bathing suits are required. Handicap accessible.

Dressing rooms, motel rooms, a conference area, snack bar, and picnic areas are available on the premises. Massage, facials and body wraps are available. A free campground on the river is located adjacent to the property. It is three blocks to a cafe, store, and service station, and seventeen miles to RV hookups. Credit cards are accepted.

Directions: From US 40 in the town of Hot Sulphur Springs, follow signs north across the bridge to the resort.

There's no extra charge for the spectacular views.

Courtesy of Hot Sulphur Springs

Marjorie Young

In addition to this tropical indoor setting under a dome, there are outdoor soaking pools and a special area for mudbaths.

204   INDIAN SPRINGS RESORT
■   302 Soda Creek Rd.   303 567-2191
Idaho Springs, CO 80452

Popular historic resort with geothermal caves just off I-70 in the Arapaho National Forest. Elevation 7,300 feet. Open all year.

Natural mineral water flows out of three underground springs at 124°. Within the men's cave are three walk-in soaking pools ranging in temperature from 104-112°. Within the women's cave are four similar pools. There are four private-space outdoor soaking pools and eleven private-space indoor tubs that are large enough for couples or families. Temperatures are approximately 106-108°. All of the above pools operate on a flow-through basis; a minimum of bromine is added. A minimum of bromine is also used in the large, landscaped indoor pool, which is maintained at 96° in winter and 90° in the summer. Bathing suits are required in the swimming pool and prohibited in the caves. Handicap access difficult.

Mud baths, locker rooms, massage, dining room, rooms in the hotel, inn and lodge, overnight camping, and RV hookups are available on the premises. It is five blocks to a store and service station. Visa and MasterCard are accepted.

Directions: From I-70, take the Idaho Springs exit to the business district, then follow signs south on Soda Springs Road to resort.

Courtesy of Glenwood Hot Springs

Snow on the mountains and a nip in the air doesn't discourage people from swimming in the world's largest outdoor hot springs pool (over two blocks long). Recreational activities abound in the area during all seasons.

205 A GLENWOOD HOT SPRINGS LODGE AND POOL

PO Box 308   **970 945-6571**
■   **Glenwood Springs, CO 81601**

A very large commercial resort, called by many "the grandaddy of them all," near the center of town on the north bank of the Colorado River. Elevation 5,700 feet. Open all year.

Natural mineral water flows out of the spring at 122°. The water is cooled by heat exchangers and supplies four pools. Three of these are treated with chlorine. The 104° therapy pool uses pure untreated spring water that turns over the entire pool contents every hour. The one-hundred-foot-long outdoor soaking pool has eight bubble jet therapy chairs. The two-block-long (405 foot) swimming pool is maintained at a temperature of 90° in summer and 93° in winter. It has a sand/charcoal filtration system that turns the entire pool over four times per day. Water is further purified by a high-tech ozonator system for water clarity. The water slide catch-pool is 85°, and the summer-only kiddie pool is kept at 92°. A private athletic club is available for walk-ins and includes a water jet indoor therapy pool maintained at 102° and treated with bromine. The club also has a steam room, sauna, weight room, and four racquetball courts. Bathing suits are required everywhere. The entire facility is handicap accessible.

Changing facilities, rental swimsuits and towels, a restaurant, sport shop, miniature golf course, massage, and a 107-room lodge are available on the premises. It is one block to a store and service stations and two miles to overnight camping and RV hookups. All major credit cards are accepted.

See their Web site: www.hotspringspool.com

Courtesy of Yampah Spa

205 B   YAMPAH SPA AND VAPOR CAVES
709 E. 6th   970 945-0667
■   Glenwood Springs, CO 81601

Natural underground geothermal steam baths located in historic, natural vapor caves whose use dates back to the time of the Ute Indians. Elevation 5,700. Open all year.

Natural mineral water creates vapor that emerges at 125° within three caves and maintains the caves at 112-115° year around. All caves are coed, and bathing suits are required. There are also two private-space hydrojet pools filled with tap water, treated with bromine, and maintained at 104°.

Changing facilities, massage, beauty salon, and a full range of health and beauty treatments including facials, herbal wraps, body scrubs, body mud, and massage are available on the premises. It is three blocks to a cafe, store, service station and motel and five miles to overnight camping and RV hookups. Visa and MasterCard are accepted.

Marjorie Young

A large, squishy pool with muddy banks and bottom adds the option of a mudbath facials and body treatment to a fun soak with friends.

205 C   SOUTH CANYON HOT SPRINGS

●   **West of Glenwood Springs**

A primitive, city-owned geothermal spring located in a narrow wooded canyon leading south off the Colorado River. Elevation 5,200 feet. Open all year.

Natural mineral water flows out of the ground at 118° cooling to approximately 107° as it flows into a large squishy-bottom pool up the hillside across from the creek. The area is not currently fenced or posted, and there is no recent pattern of harassment. The local custom is clothing optional.

There are no services on the premises but all major services can be found a couple of miles away in Glenwood Springs.

Directions: From Glenwood Springs take I-70 to the South Canyon exit 111, cross the Colorado River, cross the railroad tracks, and go up canyon .6 mile. Park along the west bank at a pull-out. Several easily visible trails head down hill towards the creek. Depending on which one you take you will either need to scramble up a pile of rocks or cross over the creek via a log and a short climb up the hill to the pool. The ground is very slippery due to seeps and rain can make the climb very treacherous.

GPS: N 39.552 W 107.412

It might be called *Penny Hot Springs* because the river water that overflows the pools often turns copper color after spring and summer rains.

206   PENNY HOT SPRINGS

● **North of the town of Redstone**

Primitive, riverbank hot spring pools, seasonally flooded by high water. Elevation 8,000 feet. Open all year (subject to flooding).

Natural mineral water flows out of a spring at 133° and drops directly into the Crystal River. Between annual high-water washouts, volunteers build rock-and-sand pools in which hot mineral water and cold river water can be mixed to a comfortable temperature. Because the location is close to the highway, bathing suits are strongly recommended. The view of the hills from the pools is quite pretty.

There are no services on the premises. All services are within three miles in the historic mining town of Redstone.

Directions: From Glenwood Springs, as you head toward Redstone, on the east side of CO 133 .8 mile south of mile marker 56, there is a small parking area on the east side of the highway next to the river. It is 12.8 miles on CO 133 after you make the turn off Hwy 82. A short, obvious trail goes down to the pools, visible from the embankment.

GPS: N 39.227 W107.224

207   CONUNDRUM HOT SPRINGS

● **South of the town of Aspen**

Three primitive pools surrounded by spectacular Rocky Mountain scenery in a designated Wilderness Area of the White River National Forest at the end of a difficult nine-mile, one-way trail. Elevation 11,200 feet. Open all year, subject to weather conditions.

Natural mineral water flows out of a spring at 120° and is piped into three volunteer-built rock-and-sand pools, three-to-four-feet deep with temperatures around 100° in the lower pools. The largest pool will accommodate at least a dozen hikers. This spring is off a popular trail. Clothing optional.

It is a nine mile, rugged, uphill hike from the trailhead, although you can camp along the trail. You should not, however, camp within 100-feet of the springs. Be sure to observe good wilderness camping practices and keep the area pristine. It is twenty miles to all other services.

The weather can change from minute-to-minute. Be sure to obtain information about current conditions at a White River National Forest ranger station before attempting the trip.

Directions: From Aspen take CO 82 northwest about .25 mile. Turn left at Maroon Creek Road (FS 102) and immediately split left on Castle Creek Drive. Continue 5 miles and turn right on Conundrum Road. Drive 1.1 miles to the Conundrum Creek trailhead parking lot. (Stay off private surrounding area.)

USGS: *Hayden Peak, Maroon Bells.*
GPS: N 39.012 W106.891

208 COTTONWOOD HOT SPRINGS INN
18999 County Rd. 306   719 395-6434
800 241-4119
■ **Buena Vista, CO 81211**

A small, relaxing rustic inn nestled in a high mountain valley, surrounded by the San Isabel National Forest in the highest mountain range in the continental US. Location in Colorado's "banana-belt" means 345 days of sunshine. Close to summer and winter recreation. Elevation 8,550 feet. Open all year.

Odorless natural mineral water flows out of a spring at 130° and is gravity fed into the entire facility, feeding three beautiful, natural, rock-lined soaking pools, each cabin's individual private tub, and three outdoor private hydropools (adult only, clothing optional) at 100-106°. All pools, including a cold plunge, operate on a flow-through basis that requires no chemical treatment. The mineral water is so pure that it is used as tap water throughout the resort. Bathing suits are optional within the fenced private spas. All pools are available to the public for a day-use fee. Registered guests need to pay extra only for the private tubs.

Twelve rooms with private baths are located on the second floor of the main lodge. There are three rustic, creekside cabins, each with an individual trough-type hot tub, and one three-bedroom cottage with a private tub on its deck. (Two-day minimum stay is required in cabins and cottage during high season.) Camping tepees are also available. There are no TVs or phones in any of the rooms. Available for your enjoyment are the community room, library, and kitchen. The community room is also available for group meetings, seminars, work shops, reunions, and special events. Meals can be arranged for groups, or the kitchen can be leased

Surrounded by the highest mountain range in the continental US, unlimited recreational activities are available in the area, such as hiking, fishing, mountain climbing, horseback riding, skiing, golfing, sightseeing, ghost towns, and some first-class water for white water rafting and kayaking.

for your use. All forms of massage are available. Major credit cards are accepted. It is five and one-half miles to all other services. Phone or write for rates and reservations.

Directions: From US 24 in Buena Vista, go west 5.5 miles on CO 306, the road to Cottonwood Pass. Watch for resort signs on the right side of the road.

Photos by Marjorie Young

Jayson Loam

Phil Wilcox

209 MOUNT PRINCETON HOT SPRINGS
County Road 162   719 395-2361
■ **Nathrop, CO 81236**

Large, modern resort between Leadville and Salida, surrounded by San Isabel National Forest. Elevation 8,500 feet. Open all year.

Natural mineral water flows out of a spring at 132°. Odorless and tasteless, this water is used in all pipes. Three outdoor swimming pools, one Olympic-size, are maintained at temperatures between 80-82° and are treated with chlorine. A regulation lap pool is kept at 86° and a soaking pool between 99-103° which is partially covered. All pools are available to the public for a fee and free to registered guests (extra fee for waterslide). The hot mineral pool and the slide are open only during the summer. There are several natural spots for soaking down in Chalk Creek, depending on the river level. Bathing suits are required. Some facilities are handicap accessible.

Locker rooms, restaurant, hotel rooms, picnic area, saddle horses, fishing, and hiking are available on the premises. Skiing and river rafting are close by. A conference center/party room is available for large groups. It is five miles to all other services. Major credit cards are accepted.

Directions: From US 285 in the town of Nathrop, go west 5 miles on CO 162 to resort.

210 WAUNITA HOT SPRINGS RANCH
8007 County Road 887
970 641-1266
■ **Gunnison, CO 81230**

American-plan guest ranch surrounded by Gunnison National Forest. Elevation 9,000 feet. Open all year.

Natural mineral water flows out of several springs at 175° and is piped to a swimming pool and to geo-thermal heating units in the buildings. The swimming pool is maintained at 95° and operates on a flow-through basis, so only a minimum of chlorine treatment is needed. Summer pool use is reserved for registered guests, with a minimum stay of six days by prior reservation only. Pool is available on a day-use basis from October to April. Call first. Bathing suits are required. Limited handicap accessibility.

Guest-ranch services, including rooms, meals, saddle horses, and fishing, are available on the premises. It is fifteen miles to a store, service station, and overnight camping and twenty-eight miles to RV hookups. No credit cards are accepted.

Directions: From the town of Gunnison, go 19 miles east on US 50. Turn left on CR 887 and follow signs 8 miles north to the ranch. Gunnison is served by several airlines and free pickup can be arranged.

Courtesy of Salida Hot Springs

Courtesy of Desert Reef

211   SALIDA HOT SPRINGS
410 West Rainbow Blvd.
719 539-6738
■   Salida, CO 81201

Modernized, indoor municipal pool, hot baths, park, picnic area and playground. Elevation 7,000 feet. Open all year.

Natural mineral water flows out of Poncha Springs at 150° and is piped six miles to Salida. The large indoor swimming pool is maintained at a temperature of 100-104°, the lap pool is maintained at 90-92°, and a shallow baby pool at 96°. All pools are treated with chlorine. There are six private indoor soaking pools that are drained and refilled after each use. The water temperature is controlled by the customer. An extensive warm-water program for people afflicted with arthritis is offered as well as boating instruction for moving-water safety in kayaks, canoes and rafts. Bathing suits are required everywhere except in private soaking pools. Handicap accessible with assistance.

Locker rooms are available on the premises. It is less than five blocks to all other services. No credit cards are accepted.

Directions: From the junction of US 50 and US 285, go 3.5 miles east on US 50. Look for signs on the north side of the street.

One of the six private, indoor soaking pools you can rent if the noise in the big pool gets to be too much.

Visible behind the hot waterfall at *Desert Reef* is the steam from the artesian well that keeps this beautiful tub filled at just the right temperature all year round. The sandy part of the beach consists of a regulation-size volleyball court to the left of the pool.

212 A   DESERT REEF BEACH CLUB
PO Box 503   719 784-6134
■   Penrose, CO 81240

A small, remote, recreation club located east of Florence, Colorado. The club has grown up around a geothermal well in the desert foothills south of Colorado Springs. Elevation 5,200 feet. Open all year Wednesday, Thursday, Saturday, and Sunday, 10 AM to 10 PM.

Natural mineral water flows out of an artesian well at 130° and is piped to a dramatic large pool where the water flows in over a waterfall on a flow-through basis so that no chemical treatment of the water is necessary. Flow rate is adjusted to maintain pool temperature within a comfortable range for soaking through all seasons. Bathing suits are optional. Not handicap accessible at this time.

There is a landscaped lawn area for sunning and picnicking, and cold drinks are available on the premises. A large greenhouse in which plants are raised is also used as a meeting room or shelter. Regulation size sand volleyball court and horseshoe pits are provided for your enjoyment.

Visa and MasterCard are accepted. It is two miles to all other services. As this is a membership facility, it is necessary to phone during business hours for information on guest passes, rates, and directions.

The rate of water flow is so great that no chemicals are ever needed in this large cement pool and whether or not you wear a bathing suit is entirely up to you.

212 B THE WELL
Hwy 50 at Penrose

719 372-9250
800 898-WELL

■   Penrose, CO 81240

Large, hot mineral water swimming/soaking pool located in the high desert country between two mountain ranges in a broad valley called the Banana Belt of Colorado, with sunshine 350 days a year. Just west of Pueblo and Colorado Springs. Elevation 5,200 feet. Open all year; closed Tuesdays.

Artesian well water at 108° emerges from a depth of 2,000 feet and flows through a pipe at 325 gallons per minute, showering into a large, oval-shaped, seventy-foot diameter cement pool. Pool temperature is maintained at approximately 98-100° in winter and 94° in summer and is controlled by the amount of aeration. No chemicals are added to the water, which remains clear due to CO_2 that bubbles into it. The pool is drained and cleaned once a week. Clothing or no clothing is entirely optional.

Facilities include overnight RV and tent sites (no hookups), modern bathhouse, cabana building with soft drink machine, volleyball, and horseshoes. Future plans include cabins, and a sauna. Massage is often available. No cameras, radios, or pets are allowed, and no glass of any kind in the pool area. Facilities are handicap accessible with assistance. Nonmembers are welcome to use the facilities as well as members, who receive discounted day-use and overnight fees. It is one and one-half miles to a motel, restaurant, gas station, and market in Penrose.

Directions: From the junction of US 50 and CO 115 (36 miles southwest of Colorado Springs, 27 miles west of Pueblo), drive west for 1 mile to the second highway crossover. The Well is at the only lamppost streetlight on the south side of the street.

Spectacular views, multiple pools, cabins, and places to camp are augmented by the wonderful hospitality of the hosts and the friendly attitude of the people who belong.

213   VALLEY VIEW HOT SPRINGS
PO Box 65   **719 256-4315**
■   **Villa Grove, CO 81155**

A series of wonderful pools at a clothing-optional resort offering relaxation as its primary activity, are situated on the west slope of the Sangre De Cristo Mountains. Elevation 8,700 feet. Open all year.

Natural mineral water flows out of several springs at temperatures ranging from 85-96°. All pools are supplied on a flow-through basis so that no chemical treatment is needed. The main outdoor cement swimming pool is maintained at 85°. Next to the pool an outdoor soaking pond is built right over a spring, so the water flowing up through the gravel bottom maintains a temperature of 96°. At the top of a steep trail (and well worth the hike) is a series of three soaking pools also built right over a spring The pool temperatures vary from 80-105° depending on the volume of snow melt. Two other pools in the meadows are also spring fed with temperatures varying according to snow melt. There is also a small soaking pool at 83° inside the wood-fired sauna building. The pipe pool (used to be the waterfall) is usually around 96°. Clothing is optional everywhere on the extensive grounds. Watch for poison oak. A map is available to areas that are handicap accessible.

A communal lodge with kitchen, six cabins, and tent spaces scattered through the woods are available for rent. It is twelve miles to all other services in Villa Grove. Visa, Discover Card and MasterCard are accepted.

Note: This is primarily a membership facility, with the premises reserved for members and their guests on holidays and weekends. The public is welcome to visit during the week. Write or phone first for full information.

Directions: From the junction of US 285 and CO 17 take the gravel road County Road GG due east 7 miles to the location.

The clean lines of the spa building echo the peaks of the Sangre De Cristo Mountains in the background.

During summer months when it is too hot to soak in the direct sun, there is a pool under the pagoda to provide protection but still allow for the view.

214   MINERAL HOT SPRINGS SPA
28640 CR 58 EE   719 256-4328
■ **Moffat, CO 81143**

A beautifully appointed, sparkling clean spa located in the north end of the San Luis Valley with spectacular views of the sunsets and moonrises of the Sangre De Cristo Mountains. Elevation 7,747 feet. Open all year for day use. Call for hours.

Natural mineral water flows from several main springs at temperatures ranging from 90-140°, providing outdoor soaking pools with sufficient flow through to require no chemical treatment and to keep water at optimal temperatures. The tower pool, under the old water tower, is five feet deep. There are two other shallower soaking pools maintained at 102-108°. All pools are tiled and protected by glassed-in decks, providing wonderful views. The bathhouse includes private individual tubs with controllable temperatures. Bathing suits required. Some areas are handicap accessible.

Locker rooms, a sauna, massage, wraps and spa treatments, a shop, snack foods and beverages, a gallery of local artisans, gardens, and picnic area are all available on the grounds. Towel, robes and slippers are for rent. A separate pool and deck area is available for groups and private parties. Overnight facilities are planned for the future, and several small rural inns and bed and breakfasts are within a half-hour drive. Credit cards are accepted. It is six miles to all other services.

Location: On Colorado 17, 1 mile south of the junction with US 285, 50 miles north of Alamosa, and 30 miles south of Salida.

Photos top and bottom courtesy of Mineral Hot Springs. Middle photo by Barbara Hanson.

Courtesy of Sand Dunes Swimming Pool

Justine Hill

215   SAND DUNES SWIMMING POOL
■ 1991 County Rd. 63   719 378-2807
Hooper, CO 81136

Expansive views of the Sangre de Cristo Mountains and the Great Sand Dunes Monument surround a hot well swimming pool and baby pool which creates an oasis in the middle of chico bush country. Elevation 7,600 feet. Open all year; hours vary (closed Thursday for cleaning).

Natural mineral water comes up from a 4,200-foot, free flowing artesian well and is piped to a fifty-foot by one-hundred-foot swimming pool with two diving boards and an attached shallow baby pool. The water registers 118° as it enters the main pool and maintains a temperature range between 98-103° depending on the season. A continuous flow through keeps the pools clean although a small amount of chlorine granules are added to the pool at closing. Bathing suits required. Parking spaces, cement entry and sidewalks make the area handicap accessible.

Showers, dressing rooms, a full concessionary, suit and towel rentals are available on the premises. It is three and one-half miles to a restaurant, gas and convenience store. A motel is located approximately ten miles south at the Great Sand Dunes National Monument exit. Campgrounds, RV hookups are available at the Great Sand Dunes, thirty miles away.

Directions: From Alamosa on Colorado 17 go 1 mile north of Hooper and turn east. Continue 1.5 miles and turn north 1 mile to the pool.

216   SPLASHLAND HOT SPRINGS
■ Box 972   (summer)719 589-6307
Alamosa, CO 81101

Large, rural, community-owned plunge in the center of a wide, high valley. Elevation 7,500 feet. Open Memorial Day through Labor Day.

Natural mineral water flows out of a spring at 106° and is piped to a large outdoor swimming pool that maintains a temperature of approximately 94° and to a wading pool for toddlers. The water is treated with chlorine. Bathing suits are required.

Locker rooms, suit and towel rentals, and a snack bar are available on the premises. It is one mile to a cafe, store, and service station and two miles to all other services. No credit cards are accepted.

Location: On CO 17, 1 mile north of Alamosa.

Steve Heerema

A soak in either pool would feel great after the long, grueling hike to get to *Rainbow Hot Springs*. You can plan on camping in the area.

217 RAINBOW (WOLF CREEK PASS) HOT SPRINGS

● **Northeast of the town of Pagosa Springs**

A primitive riverside hot spring at the end of a very rugged five-mile hike in the Weminuche Wilderness, northwest of CO 160. Elevation 9,000 feet, with a 1,000-foot elevation gain from the trailhead. Open all year (subject to flooding). Hard to reach during winter (this is avalanche country).

Natural mineral water flows out of a spring under a rock and cascades down the side of a bluff leaving a rainbow-colored pattern formed by the minerals. It fills two shallow, eight-to-ten person, rock-log-and-mud pools at the east edge of the San Juan River. A high rate of geothermal flow maintains a temperature of more than 100° in these pools. A third sandy-bottom, twelve-inch-deep pool is approximately one-hundred yards upriver. Water at 106° bubbles up from the bottom into this rock-and-mud pool. This pool is useable only during the low water months of July and August. Clothing is optional.

There are no services available except pack-in camping areas scattered along the trail. Two national forest campgrounds are located one and one-half to two miles before the trailhead. Three miles before the trailhead is a trailer park with hookups, showers, propane, cabins, outfitters for horseback riding, fishing, and snowmobile tours. It is seventeen miles from the trailhead to all other services in Pagosa Springs.

Directions: From the eastern end of Pagosa Springs, at the junction of CO 160 and CO 84, drive northeast on CO 160 for 14 miles to a national forest sign for West Fork Road, Trailhead, FS 648. Turn left (north) and drive 3 miles, passing two national forest campgrounds to a parking area and trailhead, following signs for Rainbow Trail. The trail begins with a short steep climb up a 4WD road through Born Lake Ranch. Stay on the trail; you are on private property. After passing a sign saying "Hot Springs 4 miles," bear left when the trail forks. Cross the first of three bridges over the creek after passing a sign for "Weminuche Wilderness." When the trail forks after the third bridge, take the left fork up a very steep trail. Rainbow Trail is marked by red-painted horizontal steel bars extending from trees. At the junction with Beaver Creek Trail, continue on Rainbow Trail. It is approximately 1 mile from here to the springs. After crossing several small rivulets, the trail ascends to a large clearing with fallen logs and campfire rings. The hot springs are just below to the left at river level and are visible at the foot of a rocky bluff. There is no official trail down to the pools.

To reach the pool upriver, continue on the trail through the camping area and down into a meadow where the trail is at river level. The pool is across the river from a seep in the rocks and can be reached by rock-hopping during low water.

Note: Allow three to four hours for the hike in, and about half that time to hike out. Weather changes very rapidly in this area. It is a good idea to check with the San Juan National Forest, Pagosa Ranger District, 970 264-2268.

Source map: *San Juan National Forest.*
GPS: N 37.511 W 106.945

Marjorie Young

Phil Wilcox

THE LEGEND OF PAGOSA SPRINGS

The Great Pagosa Springs is the largest and hottest known geothermal pool in the world. Its depth has been measured to 850 feet without touching bottom. The main spring puts out water at 153°.

"Pahgosa" is the name given the spring by the Ute Indians and means boiling water. Legends tell of a terrible illness that fell upon the Utes. No matter what the medicine men did, the Utes continued to die. In a last desperate attempt to appease the Great Spirit they built a gigantic bonfire along the banks of the San Juan River. They danced and sang around the bonfire until they dropped into an exhausted sleep. When they awoke they discovered a large pool of boiling water where their fire had been. After drinking the water and bathing in it they were cured.

A monument now stands on the site of the bonfire. The minerals from the water have formed a giant tufa mound. Steam rises continually from the mound.

In 1881, Pagosa's first public bath house was built near the springs. Today, the Visitors Information Building near the springs is a replica of the 1888 bathhouse.

218 A   PAGOSA SPRINGS POOL
(THE SPA MOTEL)

PO Box 37   970 264-5910

Pagosa Springs, CO 81147

A nicely maintained motel with swimming pool (dating back to 1938) and bathhouse with modern hot tubs. Located across the San Juan River from downtown Pagosa Springs. Elevation 7,100 feet. Open all year.

Natural mineral water is pumped from a well at 130° and piped to the swimming pool and bathhouse. The outdoor swimming pool is maintained at 95° in winter and 88° in summer. Two indoor soaking pools in separate men's and women's sections are maintained at 108°. The outdoor hot tubs are maintained at 110°. All pools have continuous flow-through, so no chemical treatment is necessary. Each of the two bathhouse sections also has its own steambath. Bathing suits are required in the outdoor pools. In winter the facilities are free to motel guests and open for a fee to the general public. The outdoor pools are handicap accessible.

Rooms, RV spaces, locker rooms, and horse stalls are available on the premises. It is less than three blocks to all other services. Visa, American Express, and MasterCard are accepted.

Directions: In Pagosa Springs on US 160, turn south at the one traffic light in town. One-half block west of the high school, cross the bridge and watch for the motel and pool on your left.

No matter what the season or time of day, the view down the San Juan River from the pools placed along the river and set into the travertine hillsides is beautiful. You can even swim in the river and then climb back into the pools to warm up.

218 B   THE SPRING INN
PO Box 1799   970 264-4168
165 Hot Springs Blvd.   800 225-0934
Pagosa Springs, CO 81147

Lush flower beds accent this resort inn as multiple pools set along the river and into the hillsides offer opportunities for a relaxing soak as you watch the water rushing down the adjacent San Juan River. Elevation 7,100 feet. Open all year.

Natural mineral water flows out of a spring at 155° and is piped to fourteen cement pools of varying sizes and temperatures from 95-112°, all about three feet deep some sculpted into the gently sloping hillside overlooking the San Juan River, several along the paths, and a few along the river bank. A submerged boardwalk with a rope handrail leads you through a large, warm fishpond to a secluded pool located below a tufa mound. All pools have continuous flow-through, so no chemical treatment is necessary. Bathing suits are required. Two of the pools are handicap accessible.

Facilities include suites and motel rooms, massage, a Zen bookstore, sundecks with lounge chairs, and a hike and ski shop. Dressing rooms with showers and lockers are available for day use. Sidewalks are heated geothermally as are the hot water sources at the inn. Other services are within three blocks. Major credit cards are accepted.

Directions: From the one traffic light in downtown Pagosa Springs turn south over the bridge across the San Juan River. The inn is on the right, just past the Visitor Information Center. Phone for rates and reservations.

The three pictures on the right are of various pools found at *The Spring Inn*. The view across the river into the town is particularly lovely in the evening.

Top and bottom photos by Marjorie Young.
Middle photo courtesy of The Spring Inn.

Justine Hill

219   PIEDRA RIVER HOT SPRING

● **West of Pagosa Springs**

A series of shallow primitive pools in a beautiful mountain setting in the San Juan National Forest. Elevation 7,400 feet. Open all year, subject to flooding, mud, and snow.

Natural mineral water at about 110° flows up from the bottom of several ankle-deep, volunteer-built, rock-and-mud pools on the east bank of the Piedra River. Within fifty yards along the east riverbank are additional pools that need to be scooped out before you can soak. The local custom is clothing optional.

No services are available on the premises. There is pack-in camping in the surrounding national forest. It is about seven miles to a campground, cabins, and outfitters for pack trips at the junction of US 160 and FS 622. Three miles east of this junction, at Chimney Rock, are a cafe, gas station, laundry, and store.

Directions: From US 160, 21 miles west of Pagosa Springs, 40 miles east of Durango, and just east of the Piedra River, turn north onto First Fork Rd., FS 622, marked with a national forest access sign. Follow FS 622, a one-lane dirt road (can be muddy) for 6.7 miles to a marked intersection with Sheep Creek Trail (left) and Monument Park Rd. (right). Turn left and park at the clearing and Sheep Creek trailhead. Hike down the steep, rocky trail for about 1 mile to where it widens into a meadow with an old steel cable bridge over the river. Do not cross the bridge; turn right and follow the trail north along the river for approximately 1 mile. The trail, which has been above the river, crosses tiny Coffee Creek, then drops down to a clearing at river level with fallen trees and logs. A sign points to "Hot Springs," to which someone has added "along the river."

Note: The ascent back up to the parking area is fairly strenuous along the steep, rocky trail.

Source map: *San Juan National Forest.*
GPS: N 37.313 W 107.344

The original buildings at *Trimble Hot Springs* go back over one hundred years. Unfortunately, they all burned down. Fortunately, they have been replaced by beautifully cared-for gardens and pools of varying shapes and temperatures, all with year-round magnificent views of the La Plata Mountains.

220   TRIMBLE HOT SPRINGS
6475 County Road 203

970 247-0111

■   **Durango, CO 81301**

Restored historic resort in the scenic Animas River Valley, below the La Plata Mountains. Elevation 6,500 feet. Open all year.

Natural mineral water flows out of a spring at 120° and is piped to the outdoor pools where it is treated with ozone. The Olympic-size swimming pool is maintained at 82°, one of the hydrojet pools is maintained at 100-102°, and the other is maintained at 108-110°. Bathing suits are required.

Facilities include dressing rooms, a workshop and party room perfect for private parties and wedding receptions, snack bar, picnic area, and a fully equipped apartment. Massage and other body skin treatments, aqua aerobics, and yoga classes are available on the premises. It is one mile to a bed and breakfast inn and six miles to all other services. Major credit cards are accepted.

Directions: From the city of Durango, go 7 miles north on US 550, then west 100 yards on Trimble Lane to the springs.

Photos courtesy of Trimble Hot Springs

Barbara Hanson

Courtesy of Wiesbaden Hot Springs

221 A   OURAY HOT SPRINGS
PO Box 468   **970 325-4638**
■ **Ouray, CO 81427**

Large, city-owned swimming pool and visitor information complex. Elevation 7,800 feet. Open all year.

Natural mineral water flows out of a spring at 150° and is cooled as needed to supply three large outdoor pools. The shallow soaking pool is maintained at 100°; the deep swimming and diving pool is maintained at 80°; and the therapy pool is maintained at 105°. All pools have continuous flow-through with a filtration system. Bathing suits are required. There are rails at the pools and the guards are able to help anyone who might need assistance.

Locker rooms, snack house, fitness center, and swim shop with suit rentals are available on the premises. All other services are within six blocks. Visa and MasterCard are accepted.

Location: The entire complex is easily visible on the west side of US 550 in the town of Ouray.

221 B   WIESBADEN HOT SPRINGS SPA & LODGINGS
625 5th St.   **970 325-4347**
PO Box 349 (mailing address)
■ **Ouray, CO 81427**

Charming mountain resort built to complement the spectacular canyon area of Uncompahgre National Forest. Geothermally heated. Elevation 7,700 feet. Open all year.

Natural mineral water flows from three springs at temperatures ranging from 108-130°. All pools operate on a flow-through basis, requiring no chemical treatment. The outdoor swimming pool ranges from 99° to 102°. The soaking pool in the natural vapor cave is maintained at 109-110°, a challenge well worth meeting. The soaking pool in the sauna is maintained at 108°. Bathing suits are required.

A 105° flow-through soaking pool is supplied by a hot-spring waterfall in a private area called "The Lorelei." In this beautifully landscaped space, which may be rented by the hour, suits are optional.

Geothermal heat is used to warm the individually decorated rooms, some with fireplaces and some with kitchens. European mud wraps, aromatherapy wraps, facials, massage, acupressure, reflexology, and a float tank are available on the premises. It is two blocks to a restaurant, store, shops, and service station and eight blocks to overnight camping and RV hookups. Visa and MasterCard are accepted.

Location: Located on the corner of 6th Ave. and 5th St. in the town of Ouray, 2 blocks east of Main Street (US 550). Follow signs.

Courtesy of Box Canyon Lodge

Four outdoor hot tubs with incredible views make this a great place to stay, summer or winter.

221 C BOX CANYON LODGE AND HOT SPRINGS

45 3rd Ave.   **970 325-4981**
■ **Ouray, CO 81427**

Modern, comfortable lodge at the base of 13,000 foot mountains. Situated in a quiet off-highway location adjacent to Box Canyon Falls and the Uncompahgre River. Elevation 7,800 feet. Open all year.

Natural mineral water flows from a spring at 140° and is gravity fed to four outdoor, continuous flow-through redwood tubs requiring no chemical treatment. The four hydrojet tubs are situated on redwood decks that are terraced up the mountainside behind the lodge, offering spectacular views of the city and surrounding mountains. Temperatures in the tubs range from 103-108°. Use of the tubs is reserved for registered guests and bathing suits are required. Major credit cards are accepted.

Several geothermal springs, varying in temperature from 138-156°, are located on the property. In addition to using these springs for the soaking tubs, both the bathing and drinking water is heated via heat exchangers, and, during the winter months, the entire lodge is heated using this natural resource.

Location: Two blocks west of US 550 on 3rd Ave.

221 D BEST WESTERN TWIN PEAKS MOTEL

125 3rd Ave.   **970 325-4427**
■ **Ouray, CO 81427**

Modern, motel in a picturesque mountain town. Elevation 7,700 ft. Open April through October.

Natural mineral water flows out of a spring at 156° and is piped to two pools. The outdoor swimming pool is maintained at 82°, the outdoor waterfall soaking tub at 106°, and the indoor soaking pool at 104°. Pools are reserved for the use of registered guests. Bathing suits are required. There are railings on the pools making them handicap accessible. Major credit cards are accepted.

Location: One block west of US 550 on 3rd Ave.

Marjorie Young

In addition to two outdoor pools, one for soaking and one for swimming, there is also an indoor soaking pool. All the pools use natural mineral water.

This natural hot water pond with temperatures varying from the 90s to 109° now has a cooler pond right next to it to give soakers a choice of temperatures. It's worth a night's stay in the comfortable, clean rooms to experience this pond early in the morning with the steam rising above it, and to enjoy a soak under the stars.

222 ORVIS HOT SPRINGS
1585 County Rd. #3   970 626-5324
Ridgway, CO 81432

Small and charming rustic lodge with multiple geothermal pools, located in a wide mountain valley. Elevation 7,000 feet. Open all year.

Mineral water flows from several springs at temperatures ranging from 112-127° and is piped to a variety of tubs and pools, all of which operate on a flow-through basis requiring no chemical treatment. All pools are available to the public for day use as well as to registered guests.

There are four private rooms with tiled soaking pools that have a water temperature of 102-108° and are drained and cleaned every day. Immediately adjoining the sauna building is one outside soaking pool built of stone, which has a water temperature of more than 110°. There is one large, cement, indoor soaking pool (three feet deep, twenty-five feet in diameter) that has a temperature of 101°. There is also one large, excavated soaking pond (six feet deep, thirty feet in diameter) that has hot mineral water continuously flowing in from the bottom and the sides. This enlarged natural hot spring maintains a year-round temperature of 103-105°. A cold soaking pool now adjoins this pond. Clothing is optional in all pools except the twenty-five-foot indoor soaking pool during peak hours.

Facilities include six lodge rooms which share two baths. Room rates include unlimited use of sauna and pool facilities. Visa and MasterCard are accepted. It is less than two miles to the town of Ridgway and eight miles to Ouray for all other services. Phone for rates, hours, reservations, and directions.

Photos by Marjorie Young

This pool, located right outside the sauna, is 110°.

TEXAS

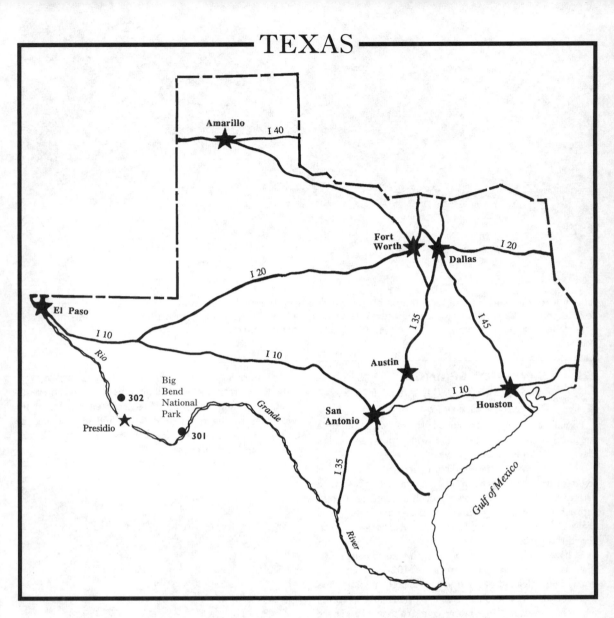

This map was designed to be used with a standard highway map.

MAP SYMBOLS

- ● Non-commercial mineral water pool
- ■ Commercial (fee) mineral water pool
- ☐ Tap water resorts and rental locations

- ⸺ Paved highway
- − − − Unpaved road
- ⋯⋯⋯ Hiking trail

Lynn Foss

301 LANGFORD (BOQUILLAS) HOT SPRING

It looks like you and the sun have to get up early to beat the crowds.

● **Big Bend National Park, Texas**

Historic masonry hot pool in the ruins of an old resort on the banks of the Rio Grande. Located near the Rio Grande Village Campground in Big Bend National Park. Elevation 1,800 feet. Open all year.

Natural mineral water flows out of the ground at 105° into a large, shallow soaking pool a few feet above river level. Following the rains, and when the river level rises above four feet the springs become submerged. So, bring a shovel as it is up to you to dig out the tubs. Swimming in the river is not recommended because of pollution and currents. Bathing suits are required.

There are no services on the premises. It is six miles to a store, service station, overnight camping, and RV hookups and twenty-eight miles to a motel and restaurant.

Directions: From Big Bend National Park Headquarters, drive 16 miles toward Rio Grand Village Campground. Turn right at Hot Springs sign, then drive 2 miles on dirt road to the end and walk .25 miles downriver to hot spring. The last mile of dirt road is very narrow and not accessible by motor home or large campers.

Source map: *Big Bend National Park.*

GPS: N 29.178 W 102.953

A guide to Indian pictographs is available at the trailhead. Be sure to see the colorful murals which still decorate the indside of the old resort hotel rooms.

This property is in the middle of a very primitive and beautiful section of the country characterized by deep canyons and distinctive geology, and is surrounded with such Texas landmarks as the Candelaria Rim, the Davis Mountains, and Capote Falls (Texas' highest). Also nearby are the Big Bend Ranch Park, Big Bend National Park, Chinati Peak (for which the hot springs is now named), and a new national park on the Mexican side of the Rio Grande.

302   CHINATI HOT SPRINGS
915 229-4165

■   **East of Ruidosa, TX**

Historic oasis in the Chihauhuan Desert just below the Chinati Mountains in the northern Big Bend region of Texas. Elevation 3, 500 feet. Open all year; call for information and reservations.

Natural mineral water comes out of a spring at 109° and is piped to three private rooms in a bathhouse, each with a one- or two-person tub, and a larger creekside outdoor pool. The tubs are drained and refilled after each use, so no chemical treatment is necessary. In fact, the water is so pure it is used as tap water on the premises. The major chemical concentrations in the water are lithium and arsenic (healthy minerals in small amounts).

Current facilities include a bathhouse, several rustic adobe cabins, and a ranch house. There are also grassy areas for camping and for picnics. It is 50 miles to Presidio and the nearest available service station or grocery store. A series of outdoor group baths, food service, a retreat facility with additional accommodations, a healing center, and individual retreat cabins are planned for the future

Write or phone first for information, rates and reservations, or see our web site at synchronicity-found.com.

Directions: From Presidio take US 170 north through the small town of Ruidosa. In less than a mile you will see a cattle guard across the highway. Just before you get to this cattle guard there will be another cattle guard on your right. Turn right and cross the cattle guard. You are now on the road leading to the hot springs. It is about 7 miles to the fork in the road that you want. Pass the first fork on the left, which is a sharp backward turn. Follow the next left fork which makes a sharp 30-degree angle. From here it is about 3 miles to the gate which will be on your left. Wind down the hill and through the gate on your left which will be unlocked if you have phoned ahead. The main house will be on your right. Do not park on the grass. You can park in the road or pull in on the driveway if there is room. There should be signs along the way to help. You should plan on about three-quarters of an hour from Presidio to the hot springs (approximately 50 miles).

It is possible to come directly from Marfa to the hot springs along Pinto Canyon Road (#2810), but the road is very rough after the pavement ends and that area is generally deserted. It may be 15 minutes shorter travel time, but it is probably not worth the wear and tear.

GPS: N 30.038 W 104.598

HISTORY OF THE CHINATI HOT SPRINGS

"My intent is to protect and care for this very magical resource, and to make it available to the public for recreational, educational and healing purposes..."
Richard Fenker

(Information taken from the bulletin published by the Tangram Corporation, 1701 River Run Road, Ste. 800, Fort Worth, TX 76017.)

Indians, early settlers, soldiers and area residents from both sides of the border have used the healing waters for hundreds of years.

Mr. and Mrs. W. L. Kingston acquired the volcanic springs in 1898. They built the original cabins and bathhouse in in 1936 making the "Kingston Hot Springs" available to the public. The resort was closed in May 1990 when it was sold to Donald Judd, a local artist, who purchased the property for private use only.

Richard Fenker and the Tangram Corporation purchased the property from Judd's estate in April 1997 are are currently restoring it for general use. The springs were formerly known as Kingston Hot Springs or Ruidosa Hot Springs.

The hot spring plans ultimately call for use by scientists and students in many disciplines.... It also will be linked with organizations interested in the Big Bend area and used as a retreat facility or a center for study...

This door leads to one of the the private baths. Spring water rises and is gathered in a reservoir behind the post at the corner of the porch roof.

All photos courtesy of Chinati Hot Springs

NEW MEXICO

COLORADO

US 64

US 64   US 285

402 A-B

401   ★ Taos

US 64

US 666

NM 44

I 25

403 A-C

NM 4

404 A-B

☐ 405

406

Santa Fe   ★   ★ Las Vegas

US 84

I 40

Albuquerque   ★

US 285

I 40

ARIZONA

US 60

US 60

I 25

Grande

River

US 60

US 380

US 285

414

NM 12

Rio

413 A-B

US 180

412   ● 411A-B

410 A-B

NM 35

★ Truth or Consequences

409

NM 152

407 A-F

Silver City   ★

US 70

NM 90

408

US 180

I 25

★ Deming

I 10

TEXAS

I 10

TEXAS

MEXICO

This map was designed to be used with a standard highway map.

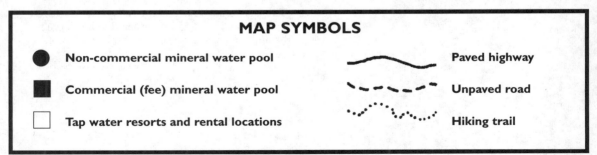

MAP SYMBOLS

●   **Non-commercial mineral water pool**

■   **Commercial (fee) mineral water pool**

☐   **Tap water resorts and rental locations**

〜   **Paved highway**

- - -   **Unpaved road**

····· **Hiking trail**

401   OJO CALIENTE RESORT
**Box 468   505 583-2233
Ojo Caliente, NM 87549**

Rustic adobe resort, originally built in the early 1900s, has been remodeled in a Spanish motif. Located in the foothills of Carson National Forest, forty-six miles north of Santa Fe. Elevation 6,300 feet. Open all year.

Natural mineral water flows out of five different springs with different temperatures and mineral contents. An outdoor, sandy-bottom, iron mineral-water soaking pool is directly over the source of the spring, with a pool temperature up to 105°. An indoor soda pool has piped in water measuring up to 104°. The sun beating on the roof creates a natural steam room, and a sign inside indicates "Quiet Zone." Taps are available at both pools for a drink of the healing mineral water. The outdoor swimming pool and spa contain traces of arsenic with cold water added to maintain a temperature of 85° year round in the pool and 106° in the spa. For the eighteen and older crowd there are three new geothermal mineral and mud pools. The iron and soda pools have continual flow-through and are drained three to four times a week requiring no chemicals. The swimming pool and spa are treated with chlorine. Children are limited to the big and little arsenic pools. A private arsenic tub can be rented with access afterwards to the other mineral pools.

There are separate men's and women's bathhouses, and one that is coed. Water temperatures in the indoor tubs can be adjusted by adding cold water. Bathing suits are required in all the pools, except in the indoor tubs. One indoor tub is handicap accessible, as are all the pools.

Massage, sweat wrap, herbal wraps, salt glows, and herbal facials are offered. Towels and bathing suits can be borrowed. The bathhouses have showers, lockers, and dressing areas. Also available is a dining room (Poppy's Cafe), lodging in the adobe hotel or cottages, camping, a gift shop, volleyball and shuffleboard courts, and horseback trail rides to archaeological sites. Major credit cards are accepted.

Directions: From Santa Fe go, 46 miles north on US 285. Watch for signs.

Each of the pools at the resort has its own specific concentration of minerals. The pool above has a concentration of iron, the one below, soda.

The new adult-only area has three soaking pools and a mud pool which makes your skin feel wonderful.

Photos by Marjorie Young

Justine Hill   Emma Neil

Whether you are with a group of friends watching a moose cross the river, or soaking by yourself, the pools at *Black Rock Hot Springs* are enjoyable in the late summer and early fall when the waters of the Rio Grand River have receded enough to allow access to the pools. There are years when this doesn't happen at all.

402 A   BLACK ROCK HOT SPRINGS

West of the town of Arroyo Hondo

Two mud-bottom rock pools located on the west bank of the Rio Grande Gorge, just a few feet above river level. Elevation 6,500 feet. Open all year; pools may not be open until summer, and the road is subject to flooding.

Natural mineral water flows up through the bottom of the inland pool, maintaining the pool temperature at 97° except when high water in the river floods the pool. The adjacent pool, closer to the river, is much cooler due to more mixing with river water. The apparent local custom is clothing optional.

There are no services available except pit toilets near the John Dunn Bridge. This is also the staging area for kayaking and float trips down the river. It is three miles to a store, cafe, service station, etc., and nine miles to RV hookups. Note: Unpaved roads may become impassable during wet weather.

Directions: From NM522 in Arroyo Hondo, take either County Rd. B-002 at Herb's Lounge and Mini-Mart just north of the river or County Rd. B-005 just south of the river. At .2 mile they join. Continue for .7 mile to where the pavement ends. Bear left over a tiny bridge. At .1 mile bear right, and continue .1 mile farther on. You are now on a two-lane gravel road above the south bank of the Arroyo Hondo River. At .4 mile since you entered the two-lane road, cross a bridge over the tiny creek and bear right. (The very rough road to the left heads toward Stagecoach [Manby] Hot Springs.) Drive for 1 mile, cross another bridge over the river, and .1 mile farther cross the John Dunn bridge, a steel bridge over the Rio Grande where the Arroyo merges. Just past the bridge are pit toilets and a swimming beach to the right. To get to the hot springs, turn left after the bridge and head uphill. Park at the flat clearing in the horseshoe of the turn and walk straight ahead on a path that leads down to the pools near the river, approximately .25 mile (a 5- to 10-minute walk).

The bather above is leaning against the remains of an old bathhouse along the stagecoach route. Just south of the springs, remains of rocky walls are visible where a bridge used to span the river on the route. The old stagecoach road can be seen from the parking clearing. Look across the gorge for a route that cuts diagonally in switchbacks down to the river. Small stones decorate the edge of the retaining wall.

402 B STAGECOACH (MANBY) HOT SPRINGS

Southwest of the town of Arroyo Hondo

Three shallow, sandy-bottom rock pools at river's edge, near the ruins of a bathhouse that was an old stagecoach stop on the east bank of the Rio Grande Gorge. Elevation 6,500 feet. Open all year; subject to road flooding.

Natural mineral water flows out of the ground at 97° directly into the one-foot deep rock pools, which are large enough for three to four people. The lower pool is only slightly above low water in the river, so the temperature depends on the amount of cold water seeping in. Two larger, shallow 80° pools are a few feet away near a sandy beach. The apparent custom is clothing optional.

There are no services available, but overnight camping is not prohibited on the sandy beach. Overnight parking is also not prohibited in the flat parking clearing and surrounding areas at the top of the trail. It is nine miles to a store and service station. Note: Unpaved roads may become impassable during wet weather.

Directions: The suggested route begins at the blinking light (a landmark from which locals give directions) north of Taos and south of Arroyo Hondo where NM 64 heads west toward the Rio Grande Bridge and the Taos Municipal Airport. Follow NM 64 from the blinking light for 4.2 miles (.3 mile west of the airport). Turn right (north) onto an unpaved, graded two-lane road that has a posted speed limit of 20 mph. Drive for 4.5 miles to a fork and bear left onto a badly rutted road. Go .3 mile to a large parking clearing. A wide path leads down from the southwest end of the parking clearing to the springs. Although the trail goes down from the ridge to river level, it is very gradual and not strenuous (a 15- to 20-minute walk).

Source maps: USGS Arroyo Hondo.
GPS: N 36.508 W 105.722

Photos by Justine Hill

NM 126, five miles to a campground, seven miles to an AYH youth hostel, and seventeen miles to RV hookups. Services are also located south of the pools in Jemez Springs.

Directions: From the town of Jemez Springs, go 7 miles north on NM 4 to a large parking area on the east side of the highway 2 miles past "Battleship Picnic Area." From the town of Los Alamos, drive west on NM 501 to the intersection in La Cueva with NM 126 and NM 4. Then go south on NM 4 for 1.5 miles to the large parking area on the east side of the road. From the parking area, a rocky clearing is visible across the river to the northeast. The trail begins at the south end of the parking pull out. A sturdy wooden footbridge across the Jemez River replaces a log crossing. The trail continues up a steep slope to the springs. The parking pullout is posted "No parking after 10 PM." During snow and rain, the slope can become very slippery.

GPS: N 35.849 W 106.627

---

403 A   SPENCE HOT SPRING
(see map on next page)
North of the town of Jemez Springs

A unique group of several sandy-bottom pools on a steep hillside with a spectacular view of surrounding mountains. Located in the Santa Fe National Forest on the east side of the Jemez River. Elevation 6,000 feet. Open all year.

Natural mineral water at 109° flows up through the sandy bottom into a rock-bordered pool large enough for ten people. There is a pipe for draining and cleaning. A series of pipes send the water to two pools just below, which have gradually cooler temperatures. The first is a shallow, one-foot deep sandy-bottom pool between huge boulders with a 100° water source inside a cave. The second is smaller and cooler. Air temperature and wind affect the temperature in these shallow pools. There is also a pipe here for draining and cleaning.

Hike uphill for fifty feet, cross a clearing, then follow the runoff around some large boulders uphill and to the left of the three lower pools for two other pools.

Another pool is about two hundred feet straight uphill from the lower pools. Hike across the clearing and continue uphill, following the runoff. This primitive knee-deep, squishy bottom, sand-and-rock pool is large enough for two to three people. The water source which flows out between the rocks measures 109°. The apparent local custom is clothing optional.

There are no services available. It is 1.5 miles from north of the parking area to a store, gas, restaurant and lodge in La Cueva at the intersection of NM 4 and

Thanks to the many volunteers who show up at *Spence Hot Spring* to help keep this very special place with its many pools and beautiful water in pristine condition. There has been some discussion about closing the pools because of inappropriate behavior—please do your part to make sure this doesn't happen.

Photos by Marjorie Young

Camping overnight gives you a chance to soak in all of the pools at *McCauley Hot Spring*, the large one above and one of the smaller ones, below.

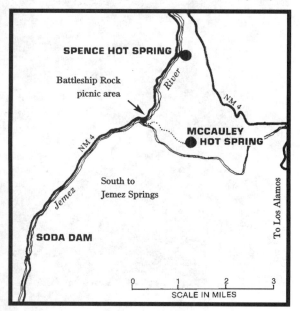

Photos by Erica Janes

SPENCE HOT SPRING

Battleship Rock
picnic area

River

NM 4

MCCAULEY HOT SPRING

NM 4

Jemez

South to
Jemez Springs

To Los Alamos

SODA DAM

0   1   2   3
SCALE IN MILES

403 B MCCAULEY HOT SPRING
(see map)

North of the town of Jemez Springs

Very large, shallow, warm pool whose waters flow down into several deeper smaller pools in a gorgeous mountain clearing. Elevation 7,300 feet. Open approximately May through October due to rain, mud, and snow conditions.

Natural mineral water flows out of the ground at 95° directly into a two-foot-deep pond, forty feet in diameter. Pool temperature measures between 85-90°, depending on air and wind conditions. A second, rock-and-log pool, three feet deep, is approximately fifty feet downhill in the creekbed runoff, where water cascades into two separate places in the pool, accessed by a log and rock bridge. From here it falls down to another pool, four- to five-feet deep where the temperature is a degree or two cooler. The guppies and neon tetras that live in the pool will entertain you by nibbling on your body hair. The apparent local custom is clothing optional.

There are no services on the premises, except level areas for pack-in camping. It is 3.5 miles to a store, gas, restaurant, and lodge in La Cueva at the intersection of NM 4 and NM 126, five miles to a campground and AYH youth hostel, ten miles north to San Antonio campground and seventeen miles to RV hookups.

Directions: From the ranger station at the north end of Jemez Springs, go 4 miles north on NM 4 to Battleship Rock picnic area, which is open 6AM to 10PM only. A day-use fee is charged. Starting from the firepit gazebo in the picnic area, follow FS trail 137, called East Fork trail. Just past the gazebo, the trail immediately forks. Follow the right fork along the river. Stay on the main trail (despite many spurs) that gradually ascends in switchbacks. Hike approximately two miles until you hear the gurgling creek, which is runoff from the warm spring. A large clearing with campfire rings is off to the right just before you reach the pond. This trail is moderately strenuous, especially at this altitude. Alternate directions: At the intersection of NM 126 and NM 4, turn right, staying on 4. Go 5 miles and park at Jemez Falls campground and hike in the two miles to the springs from the marked trail head.

GPS: N 35.820 W 106.627

Lynn Foss

404 A BODHI MANDA ZEN CENTER MOTEL AND HOT SPRINGS

Box 8   **505 829-3854**

■   **Jemez Springs, NM 87205**

A four-unit motel a few minutes stroll away from the riverbank hot pools. Operated by the Bodhi Manda Zen Center and located in the town of Jemez Springs. Elevation 6,300 feet. Closed between September and December 15 for retreats.

Natural mineral water flows out of the ground at 169°, then into three rock-and-sand soaking pools where natural cooling results in varying temperatures. The pools are two-to-three feet deep. The river next to the pools serves as a cold plunge. Bathing suits are required. Call first if you wish to use the pools. No drop-ins, please.

It is one block to a store and cafe and seven miles to a service station. Phone ahead for current information, rates, directions, and reservations.

403C   SAN ANTONIO HOT SPRINGS

North of the town of Jemez Springs

A gem of a hot spring with a series of rock-edged pools built against the hillside of San Diego Canyon in the stunning wooded setting of the Santa Fe National Forest. Elevation 8,000 feet. Open May to October due to weather conditions.

Natural mineral water flows in the low 100s, directly into the rock and cement upper pool, then cascades over rocks and through pipes into two lower pools. People have scooped out just enough of the silty, rocky bottom in the lower pools to create places deep enough to soak up to your waist. The upper pool is somewhat deeper.

There are no services available. However, if you like to fish, the river at the base of the parking lot is a good place to do it . All other services are in La Cueva at the junction of NM 4 and NM 126, or eleven miles south in Jemez Springs.

Directions: From the intersection of NM 4 and NM 126, follow NM126 to FS 376 north, which will be on the right. Take FS 376, a rutted dirt road, 5 miles. The parking area is off to the right. After you park, cross the wood bridge and follow the fairly obvious trail uphill for approximately 10 minutes to the pools. The trail is quite steep and can be very slippery if wet.

GPS: N 35.938 W 106.646

Justine Hill

Marjorie Young

A soak is a great way to celebrate a birthday with friends!

404 B   JEMEZ SPRINGS BATH HOUSE, INC.
Box 105   **505 829-3303**
062 State Hwy 4
Jemez Springs, NM 87205

A pleasant, well-maintained bathhouse located in the park on the main street of Jemez Springs. Elevation 6,200 feet. Open all year.

Natural mineral water flows out of a city-owned springs at 155-158° and is piped to a cooling tank and then to the bathhouse. There are eight private rooms, each containing a one-person bathtub. Curtains can be pulled so that couples can soak next to each other. A private outdoor cedar tub is available to groups of up to six. Cool and hot mineral water are mixed to provide the desired water temperature. Tubs are drained and refilled after each use, so no chemical treatment of the water is necessary. Clothing is optional. Children under five not permitted in tub areas. Indoor tubs and facilities are handicap accessible.

Massage, wraps, facials and other beauty services are available on the premises, as is a store selling local crafts, beauty supplies, cold drinks, and pastries. Towels can be rented. Major credit cards are accepted. It is one block to a store, lodgings, and restaurant, ten miles to a service station. Phone for rates, reservations, and directions.

The Bath House

Mineral Baths · Massages · Gifts

Courtesy of Ten Thousand Waves

405   TEN THOUSAND WAVES
PO Box 10200   **505 982-9304**

❑   **Santa Fe, NM 87504**

An intriguing blend of American technology and Japanese hot-tub traditions offers a range of soaking possibilities. Located three and one-half miles up Artist Road (Ski Basin Road) with desert and mountain views.

Eight privately enclosed outdoor tubs and one indoor tub with two balconies are available. Four of the nine tubs include saunas, and one includes a steam room. A communal wood tub and sauna large enough for twenty-five people and a separate women's pebble-bottom tub with sauna are also available. The tubs use gas-heated well water and a purification method of ultraviolet light, ozone, and hydrogen peroxide and are maintained at a temperature of 104-106°. Bathing suits are required in communal tubs. Handicap accessible.

Eight casitas known as Houses of the Moon are available for rent nearby. Kimonos, sandals, soap, shampoo, towels, and hair dryers are provided. Private lockers are available in both the men's and women's dressing rooms. A juice and snack bar is on the premises. Various other treatments offered include massage, aromatherapy, herbal wraps, salt glows, watsu (in-water massage), East Indian cleansing treatments, and facials. Visa, MasterCard, and Discover Card are accepted. Phone for rates, reservations, and directions.

406 MONTEZUMA HOT SPRINGS

● **Northwest of the town of Las Vegas**

The once-abandoned ruins of a major turn-of-the-century hot-springs resort bathhouse. Located just across the Gallinas River on the property of the lavish Victorian "Montezuma's Castle," now Armand Hammer's United World College. Elevation 6,450 feet. Open all year.

Natural mineral water flows out of several artesian springs at 94-113° into three clusters of concrete soaking pools of various sizes and depths up to six feet, resulting in a wide range of temperature choices. Continuous flow-through (fifteen gallons per minute) eliminates the need for chemical treatment of the water. Volunteers are fastidious about keeping the pools clean, draining and scrubbing them every two weeks. One cluster of pools (the hottest) has been newly redesigned, sculpted, and landscaped into the hillside; a second group of two pools is near a coffin-looking concrete block; the third sit near the old bathhouse. The whole area around the pools can be very wet and marshy. The pools are just steps from the road. Bathing suits are required.

There are no services available on the premises. It is six miles to a store, cafe, service station, etc., in Las Vegas.

Directions: From I-25 take exit 65W in Las Vegas, cross over I-25, turn right on Business 25 to Mills Ave. Turn left on Mills for 1.5 miles to Hot Springs Rd., marked with a sign to Montezuma and United World College. Turn right (this is NM 65) for 5 miles until you see the castle on the hill. A sign along the right side of the road on the metal guard rail indicates "Hot Springs Baths." Park along the shoulder of the road. Several openings in the fence lead to railroad-tie steps down to the pools. The five indoor pools are now fenced and closed. The outdoor pools are open to the public year-round at no charge.

These pools are on the grounds of the United World College. Officials request that you keep the area clean, respect the bathing suit requirement, and keep noise levels down. Please do your part so that the college will continue to allow the pools to remain open to the public.

Photos by Justine Hill

TRUTH OR CONSEQUENCES

The hot springs at Truth or Consequences produce two and one-half million gallons of water per day, have the largest mineral-water table in the Southwest, and boast the highest mineral content in the United States.

These were the sacred springs of the Apaches, and Geronimo speaks of spending a peaceful year in the area. Artifacts indicate high usage by the earlier Mimbres Indians. The springs were known to the Spanish as Ojo Caliente de Las Polomas, Hot Springs of the Doves. The crystal clear water is also good for drinking (no unpleasant odor or taste). The town itself sits on the banks of the Rio Grande, just below Elephant Butte, the largest fresh-water lake in the region, offering boating, sailing, and some of the best bass fishing around.

If you haven't visited this area in a while, you will be pleasantly surprised to find that while the area has retained its uniqueness, it also offers such amenities as golf courses, a museum, restaurants, and many small shops.

Many of the indoor tubs at the various bath houses could easily be handicap accessible.

407 A   ARTESIAN BATH HOUSE AND TRAILER PARK
312 Marr   **505 894-2684**
Truth or Consequences, NM 87901

Five single-size and three family-size ceramic tubs at an average water temperature of 108°, are available for rent by the hour. Tubs are refilled for each use so no chemicals are necessary. Each room contains a bench and cold shower.

RV hookups, tenant laundry, and public showers are available on the premises, plus massage by appointment. No credit cards are accepted.

The *Charles Motel* follows the New Mexico tradition of a soak and a warm wrap in their newly refurbished motel, reflecting the style of the forties.

407 B   CHARLES MOTEL AND BATH HOUSE
                                          800 317-4518
601 Broadway   **505 894-7154**
Truth or Consequences, NM 87901

Nine individual baths are cleaned and refilled for each bather, eliminating the need for chemicals. While the hot water comes in at temperatures between 108-111°, cold water is available to cool the water. Following the soak, the bather can be wrapped in a sheet and then a wool blanket by the bath attendants.

Twenty apartment-style motel units, totally remodeled to reflect the period of the 40s, are available for rent nightly or weekly. Massage, reflexology, ayurvedic work, clay packs, facials, and acupuncture are available.

407 C   FIREWATER LODGE
309 Broadway   **505 894-3405**
Truth or Consequences, NM 87901

New owners are involved in a complete renovation of this older adobe villa. Baths with water temperatures between 108-111° are available in large private rooms.

Motel rooms are currently available for short-term or long-term stays. Note: Building will continue with the addition of an outdoor family-size pool. A restaurant will also be added so that bed and breakfast can be offered. Phone for status of construction.

407 D HAY-YO-KAY HOT SPRINGS
300 Austin Ave.   505 894-2228

■   **Truth or Consequences, NM 87901**

Oldest, continuously operated bathhouse in town, completely renovated with a unique and interesting cactus garden to enjoy. Elevation 4,300 feet. Open all year; limited hours May through September.

Individual springs fill three smaller tubs for one-to-two people and two tubs which will accomodate up to six. All of the tubs are indoors, have gravel bottoms, and are three feet deep. Temperatures range between 104-110° based on the spring and the season. No chemical treatment is necessary. Each pool is in a separate, private room with tile floors and benches. Suits are optional in the private spaces.

Massage, sweat wraps, and herbal wraps are available with advance reservations. A separate spring source for drinking water is provided. A wide variety of water sports and two golf courses are close by and all services are available in the town. Reservations recommended.

407 E INDIAN SPRINGS NATURAL FLOWING POOLS, WATER HOLE #1
218 Austin St.   505 894-2018
Truth or Consequences, NM 87901
Motel units, some with kitchenettes.

407 F MARSHALL HOT SPRINGS
311 Marr   505 894-9286
Truth or Consequences, NM 87901

Natural free-flowing hot springs continuously feed two individual, bathtubs and three pools that are six feet square and four feet deep. The larger pools can hold a maximum of four bathers. All pools are in private rooms with gravel bottoms, benches for resting, and are beautifully decoratedwith ancient Mimbres Petroglyphs on the walls. The water is not chemically treated and there is a hand pump for drinking water in the 75+ year old wooden bathhouse, built over the only hot mineral drainage canal in the continental US. Water temperatures range from 106-112°.

Overnight accommodations are a fully furnished vintage studio and 1964 Airstream trailer. Additional rooms are under construction. The gift shop provides essential oils, natural salves, ceremonial items,etc. Massage and other treatments are available. A lovely patio offers shade, a fountain, and a picnic area. Call for status of construction of the rooms, restaurant and seminar facilities.

Courtesy of Riverbend

407 G RIVERBEND HOT SPRINGS
(affiliated with Hosteling International)
100 Austin   505 894-6183

■   **Truth or Consequences, NM 87901**

Three outdoor soaking tubs on a deck overlooking the Rio Grande with a view of Turtleback Mountain. Elevation 4,300 feet. Open all year.

Natural mineral water at 114° is pumped up from a well and cools as it flows through pipes to the soaking tubs. A three-foot deep, five- by seventeen-foot former bait tank is divided into three tubs, each one a degree or two cooler than the last with temperatures ranging form 104-107°. The pools, which are nicknamed "Hot Minnow Baths," are filled twice daily, morning and evening, for registered guests who may use them free of charge. The pools are drained after each use, so no chemical treatment is necessary. Non-guests may rent the tubs for private use during the day. Bathing suits are required. Two outdoor private tubs with private decks and lanai enclosures where suits will be optional are being planned.

Men's and women's dormitories with a shared kitchen, two private units with kitchenettes that will sleep two to four persons, a family unit for two to ten persons, tepee camping, a pontoon houseboat and a small number of RV spaces are available. Laundry, cold drinks, barbecue, local merchant discounts, and morning bakery goods for dormitory guests are offered. Also available are canoeing, hiking, swimming, and host tours. All other services are within five blocks.

Directions: From the north, take exit 79 off I-25. Drive 2.5 miles to the only traffic light and turn left at Third St. Turn left for 1 block, then right on Cedar. Drive five blocks to the hot springs just south of the park along the river. From the south on I-25 take exit 75 through downtown for 2.5 miles, turn right at the First Baptist Church for 1 block, and turn left for 1 block to the springs.

408 FAYWOOD HOT SPRINGS

165 Highway 61   **505 536-9663**
HC 71 Box 1240

Faywood, NM 88034

Halfway between Deming and Silver City, adjacent to City of Rocks State Park, lies a true desert oasis with large trees and parklike surroundings, creating a charming, natural, rustic atmosphere. Elevation 5,000 feet. Open all year.

Natural mineral water flows from the top of a tufa dome at 130° downhill into several outdoor stone and concrete soaking pools in a naturally beautiful desert setting. The water cools to comfortable temperatures between 104-110°. There are both public and private pools. In the private tubs, the user can control the water temperature. The pools have movable shades which are retracted at night for star gazing. The water is pure enough to be used for drinking. Clothing required and clothing optional areas. Handicap access with assistance.

Tent, RV sites, several nicely appointed travel trailers, and a teepee are available for overnight accommodations. Massage is also available. A new cafe, museum, gift shop and gallery are planned for the future. (Phone for the status of construction.) It is fifteen miles to a store.

Directions: From Deming, take 180 north for 24 miles, turn right (east) on Highway 61, and go about 2 miles from the intersection of 180 and 61. A sign and entrance are on the left. From Silver City, take 180 south about 25 miles, turn left on Highway 61, and proceed about 2 miles from the intersection.

In addition to the beautiful pools for soaking, this 1220-acre ranch has areas with beautiful vistas for picnicking, hiking, bird watching, horseback riding, and solitude.

Photos courtesy of Faywood

● **North of Silver City**

Rock soaking pools on the edge of the Gila River located below streams of hot water cascading from the face of the cliffs above and, depending on river level, in overhangs along the river's edge. Elevation 5,200 feet. Open all year; accessible only during low water flow.

Natural mineral water flows out of many rock fissures, twenty to forty feet above river level, at 102°, runs across a steep slope before dropping directly into the pool at the river's edge. During low water, three pools are found under the edge of the rocks, with hot water dripping from the ceiling at temperatures ranging from 98-101°. Clothing is optional.

There are no services at the location. Camping is permitted at the Forks Campground where the trail starts and all other services can be found one and one-half miles north at Gila Hot Springs.

Directions: From the trailhead at Forks Campground, 1.5 miles south of Gila Hot Springs follow the trail 1.5 miles south along the east bank of the main fork of the Gila River. You will need to cross the river 10-12 times. The trail can be very slippery and difficult when wet. Check with the Forest Service about the need for a permit and conditions on the river.

■ **Silver City, NM 88061**

An all-year vacation center providing multiple services, located in the middle of the Gila National Forest. Elevation 5,000 feet. Open all year.

Doc Campbell's Post offers a country store with groceries, snack bar, ice, gas, fishing and hunting licenses, supplies, gifts, laundromat, showers, and most important, knowledgeable advice about the area. Arrangements can be made for wilderness pack trips, fishing and hunting trips, youth group trips, drop camps, and pack stock for backpackers. Reservations for lodging are also made here. Credit cards are accepted at the store.

Lodging includes a spacious apartment with kitchenette, and a completely furnished trailer all using natural hot springs water for drinking, showers, and baths. The RV park has hot and cold taps at all hookups. Hot springs water can be hooked up to your trailer, or you can use the RV Park showers and hot tub. A picnic pavilion offers grill and fire ring, plus a children's playground.

Note: Allow two hours for the forty-four mile drive from Silver City along scenic route NM 15, a two-lane mountain road which twists and winds through the Gila National Forest.

Lynn Foss

Marjorie Young

410 B GILA HOT SPRINGS—RIVER
● CAMPGROUND

Shady, primitive area with hot pools beside the river. Natural mineral water flowing at 150° from the springs on the east bank of the Gila River, is piped to the riverside camping area. The first pool is quite hot at 110° and greenish-orange with algae. The other two pools cool to 105° as the water is air cooled in these shallow pools. The bathing suit issue seems to be decided by those who are camping there, although official policy is bathing suits required. Ground is fairly level so could be handicap accessible with caution.

All that is provided are water spigots with safe drinking water, rest rooms, and trash cans. There are seven rustic campsites for tents and self-contained vehicles only.

Directions: Located right off of NM 15, the main road into the area. Watch for signs on your right (before you get to Doc Campbell's store). There is a small fee.

A perfect place to camp on the way to view the Gila Cliff Dwellings. If you need supplies or directions you can stop at Doc Campbell's Post just up the road. This whole area is surrounded by beautiful wilderness and is well worth a visit.

Top photo courtesy of Gila Hot Springs
Bottom photo by Nancy Moyer

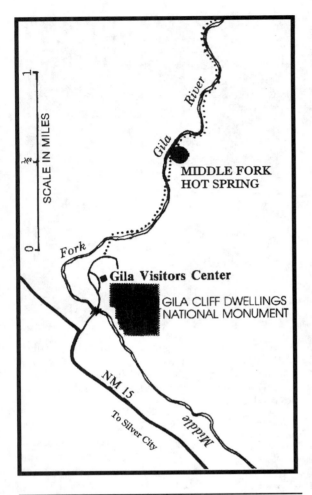

Directions: To reach the trailhead, go to the far end of the visitor center parking lot and turn right. There is a special parking area for hikers up the hill on the left. Walk down the road past the gate to the bottom of the hill. The main trail (157) continues toward the canyon, crossing the river almost immediately. The springs are on the east (right) side of the canyon after the second crossing. The water is almost always very cold and often deep. Check at the ranger station before starting out.

Note: Allow two hours for the forty-four mile drive from Silver City along scenic route NM 15, a two-lane mountain road that twists and winds through the Gila National Forest.

411 A MIDDLE FORK (LIGHTFEATHER) HOT SPRING

(see map)

● **North of the Gila Visitors Center**

A series of shallow rock-and-sand soaking pools on the Middle Fork of the Gila River, one-half mile from the Gila Visitors Center and the Indian Cliff Dwellings. Elevation 5,800 feet. Open all year, subject to high water in the river, which must be forded twice each way.

Natural mineral water flows out of the spring on the east side of the canyon at 130°, directly into several shallow pools next to the river, where the water gradually cools as it flows through the pools. Bathing suits are advisable during the daytime.

All services are back at the Gila Hot Springs Vacation Center.

Photos by Ysobel Luecke

411 B HOUSE LOG CANYON (JORDAN) HOT SPRINGS

Northwest of the Gila Visitors Center

Remote, unimproved hot springs on a tree- and fern-covered hillside in the Gila Wilderness, where the canyon meets the Middle Fork of the Gila River. Elevation 6,200 feet. Accessible only during low water in the river.

Natural mineral water flows out of several springs at 92° and cascades directly into a log- and rock-dammed pool large enough to hold ten people. The apparent local custom is clothing optional.

All services are back at the Gila Hot Springs Vacation Center. Check with the very knowledgeable people here about trails, etc., as they have hiked this area for years. Make sure you have sufficient supplies for whatever trip you take.

Directions: To begin the 8-mile hike, park at the Middle Fork trailhead (trail 157). Follow the trail past the locked gate and straight upstream into the canyon. The trail follows the river for six miles until it joins with the trail from Little Bear Canyon. There should be 14 more crossings (about 2 miles) before you reach the hot springs on the northeast side of the canyon. Continue a bit further after crossing 14 and look for a marshy area with hot water seeps. A mile farther up the Middle Fork beyond Big Bear Canyon, are more warm springs called The Meadows, at the mouth of Indian Creek Canyon.

Note: A wilderness permit is required before entering this area. While obtaining your permit from the ranger at the Gila Visitors Center, check on the adequacy of your provisions and on the level of the water in the river.

Source maps: *Gila National Forest*. USGS *Woodland Park*. (Springs not shown on either map.)

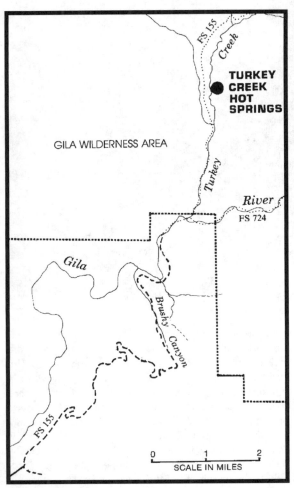

Steve Heerema

412 TURKEY CREEK HOT SPRINGS
(see map)

North of the town of Gila

Several truly primitive hot springs accessible only via a challenging and rewarding hike into the Gila Wilderness. Elevation 5,200 feet. Not accessible during high water in the Gila River.

Natural mineral water (approximately 160°) flows out of many rock fractures along the bottom of Turkey Creek Canyon and combines with creek water in several volunteer-built soaking pools. Temperatures are regulated by controlling the relative amounts of hot and cold water entering a pool. Be careful, as many of these pools are quite hot. The apparent local custom is clothing optional.

There are no services available, but there are a limited number of overnight camping spots near the hot springs. Visitors have done an excellent job of packing out their trash; please do your part to maintain this tradition. All services are seventeen miles away.

Directions: Starting at the end of the 4WD road, Wilderness Trail FS 724 crosses the Gila River several times before reaching Wilderness Trail FS 155, which starts up Turkey Creek Canyon. Approximately 2 miles from the trail junction, FS 155 begins to climb a ridge separating Turkey Creek from Skeleton Canyon. Do not follow FS 155 onto that ridge. (If you encounter switchbacks you've gone the wrong way.) Instead, stay to the right in the bottom of Turkey Creek Canyon, even though there is often no visible trail. Another half-mile will bring you to the first of the springs.

Source maps: *Gila National Forest. Gila Wilderness and Black Range Primitive Area.* USGS *Canyon Hill.* (Note: Springs are not shown.)

GPS: N 33.108 W 108.483

Directions and impressions from Shara Briggs and Steve Heerema, who hiked into this remote area to take the photo above right: After a short walk on what is left of a road that has been washed away, cross the Gila River. Follow the road and cross the river two more times. Then cross Turkey Creek to reach the junction with trail FS 155. Follow this trail, which disappears in the rocky river bed at times. In approximately 2 miles there are campsites near the trail. This is a good place to camp. To reach the springs, follow the trail until you notice a faint trail leading to the right. Take this trail, which will cross a dry creek bed and continue walking upstream for .50 mile. This part of the hike is very rugged and can be slow going. Be prepared and able to cross the creek several times, climb over boulders, and crawl through a cave.

NOTE: The San Francisco Hot Springs are located on private property. At this time the road down to the springs is closed for vehicles. However, the owner is allowing access to the springs. Check in Pleasanton or with the Forest Service as to the current status and legal access.

413 A SAN FRANCISCO HOT SPRINGS —LOWER

● **South of the town of Pleasanton**

Several primitive hot springs along the east bank of the San Francisco River in the Gila National Forest. Elevation 4,600 feet. Open all year.

Natural mineral water flows out of the ground at 110° into a series of volunteer-built, rock-and-mud riverbank pools. People have been fined for nudity.

There are no services available. It is two miles to a store, cafe, and service station in Pleasanton and twelve miles to RV hookups.

Directions: On US 180, 2 miles south of Pleasanton, watch for Forest Service sign with a pair of binoculars indicating viewing site. (When approaching from the south, the signs will be on the left, 1.3 miles after crossing the S. Dugway Canyon bridge.) Turn onto the gravel road which is now gated and walk about 1.5 miles down to the river. The pools are down along the river's edge.

413 B SAN FRANCISCO (BUBBLES) HOT SPRING—UPPER

● **South of the town of Pleasanton**

A series of very enjoyable soaking pools requiring fording the river from Lower San Francisco Hot Springs. Elevation 4,600 feet. Open all year; during high water, fording the river is very dangerous.

Under a spectacular cliff, natural mineral water flows up through the sandy pool bottom at 106°, maintaining the entire five-foot-deep pool at 96-102°, depending on air temperature. The pool cleans itself by flowing out over a small volunteer-built dam. Other nearby geothermal water outflows feed a series of small volunteer-built pools that maintain a temperature of 106°. The apparent local custom is clothing optional.

Directions: From Lower San Francisco Hot Springs, hike downstream approximately .5 miles, crossing the river three times.

414 FRISCO BOX HOT SPRING

● **East of the town of Luna**

Shallow, concrete soaking pool with spectacular views, located in a scenic canyon at the end of a rough road and a rugged but beautiful one and one-half mile trail. Elevation 6,800 feet. Open all year, subject to high water.

Natural mineral water flows out of a spring at 100° and is piped to a four-foot by eight-foot by twenty-inch-deep concrete box located above river level. The apparent local custom is clothing optional.

There are no services available on the premises. There is a walk-in camping area just north across the river from the hot spring. Overnight parking is permitted on level land just east of the private property gate. It is ten miles to groceries and gasoline and twenty miles to all other services.

Directions: Start at the Luna Ranger Station to obtain current information on weather conditions, river level, and a Gila National Forest Map. From US 180 in Luna, drive north on FS 19 (signed Bill Knight Gap Road) and turn east on FS 210 (signed Frisco Box Road) to a private property gate. Pass through the gate, carefully closing it after you, and continue east until this very rough road becomes impassable. Park and hike an additional 1.5 miles east, fording the river six or more times. There is a large elevation change on the hike, and it is often quite windy so take care. On the south bank, look for a pipe and sign for Frisco Box Spring. Follow a well-worn, slightly uphill path 75 yards to the concrete box.

We hope that some compromise can be reached so that it is clear to all that soaking at *San Francisco Hot Springs* is legal.

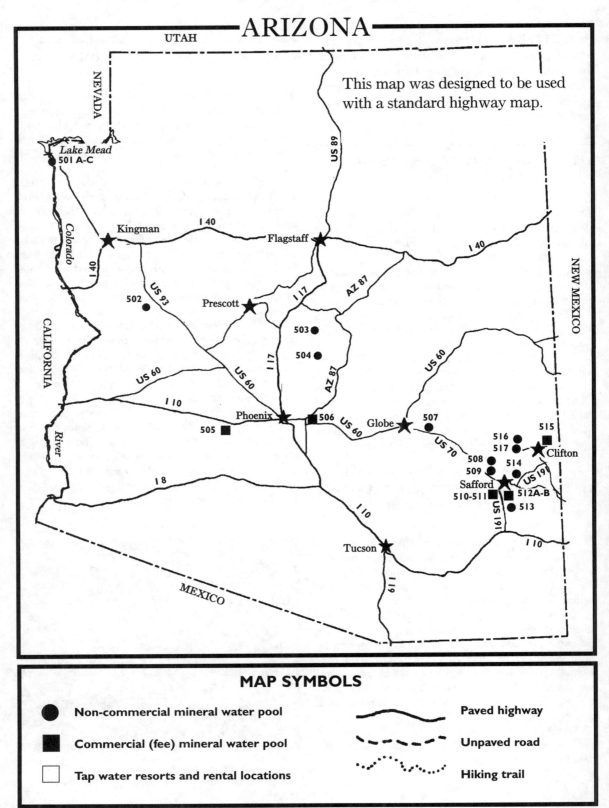

ARIZONA

This map was designed to be used with a standard highway map.

UTAH

NEVADA

Lake Mead
501 A-C

Colorado

CALIFORNIA

Kingman

I 40

Flagstaff

US 89

I 40

NEW MEXICO

US 93

502

Prescott

I 17

AZ 87

503

504

US 60

I 40

US 60

AZ 87

US 60

I 10

Phoenix

506

Globe

507

US 70

516

517

515

Clifton

505

River

508

509

514

US 191

512A-B

Safford

510-511

513

I 8

I 10

US 191

Tucson

I 10

I 19

MEXICO

MAP SYMBOLS

● Non-commercial mineral water pool

■ Commercial (fee) mineral water pool

□ Tap water resorts and rental locations

〜 Paved highway

--- Unpaved road

⋯ Hiking trail

HOT SPRINGS OF THE LOWER COLORADO

Over many centuries, flash floods have carved hundreds of spectacular canyons that lead into the Colorado River. In three of these canyons, downstream from Hoover Dam, natural mineral water flows out of rocky sidewalls at temperatures up to 125°, then gradually cools as it tumbles over a series of waterfalls between sandy-bottom pools. The water is sparkling clear, with no odor and a pleasant taste. In all three of these canyons, volunteers continue to build rock-and-sand soaking pools, even though most of them are washed away every year by the floods. Elevation 800 feet. You can reach these pools all year; however, the extreme heat during the summer months may make this area unpleasant. It is also highly recommended that you check at Willow Beach regarding floods and high water during the rainy season.

Land routes to these springs range from the difficult to the impossible. Most visitors rent an outboard-powered boat at the Willow Beach Marina, which is located at mile marker 52, eight miles downriver from Arizona (Ringbolt) Hot Springs. Willow Beach also has a ramp for launching your own boat, gas for boats, and a store for supplies. There are no overnight facilities at Willow Beach. It is twenty miles to all services in Boulder City, Nevada. The access road to Willow Beach connects with US 93, thirteen miles south of Hoover Dam on the Arizona side of the river.

Rafters and kayakers can obtain a special permit from the Lake Mead National Recreation Area to put in just below Hoover Dam, float to the various hot springs, and take out at Willow Beach.

The National Park Service maintains pit toilets at the entrances to Gold Strike and Arizona.

Note: The amount of water being released from Hoover Dam is controlled by the Bureau of Reclamation and may change from hour to hour, substantially affecting the water level in the river. Therefore, it is important that you secure your boat or raft in a manner that will withstand such changes.

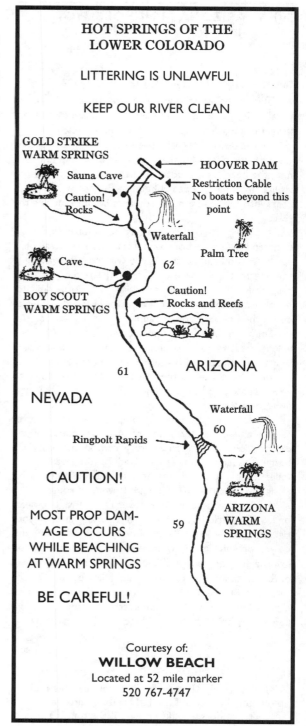

HOT SPRINGS OF THE LOWER COLORADO

LITTERING IS UNLAWFUL

KEEP OUR RIVER CLEAN

GOLD STRIKE WARM SPRINGS

Sauna Cave

Caution! Rocks

HOOVER DAM

Restriction Cable No boats beyond this point

Waterfall

Palm Tree

62

Cave

BOY SCOUT WARM SPRINGS

Caution! Rocks and Reefs

61

NEVADA

ARIZONA

Waterfall

60

Ringbolt Rapids

CAUTION!

MOST PROP DAMAGE OCCURS WHILE BEACHING AT WARM SPRINGS

BE CAREFUL!

59

ARIZONA WARM SPRINGS

Courtesy of:
WILLOW BEACH
Located at 52 mile marker
520 767-4747

501 A ARIZONA (RINGBOLT) HOT SPRINGS

(see map)

● **Near Hoover Dam**

This is the most popular of the three hot springs because it is closest to Willow Beach and downstream from the turbulent water of Ringbolt Rapids. It is one-eighth mile downriver from mile marker 60, and two small warning buoys can be seen on a large submerged rock near the beach at the bottom of this canyon. There is no visible stream at the beach because the hot water disappears into the sand a hundred yards before reaching the river.

The long narrow canyon has beautiful rock formations and a few sections that require some scrambling ability. As you head upstream, you will often be walking in the streambed as well as climbing over sharp rocks, so be prepared with appropriate footwear. Barefoot is definitely not recommended. There is a ranger-installed metal ladder at the one major waterfall.

Source springs in the upper canyon flow at 106°, and volunteers have built a series of sandbag or rock-and-sand soaking pools, each with a slightly lower temperature than the one above. The geothermal water is cooled down to approximately 95° by the time it flows over the twenty-five-foot waterfall.

There is a large amount of camping space in the lower canyon and on a dry sandy plateau just south of the canyon mouth. When you enter the canyon from the river, bear left when the trail splits inland from the beach. A pit toilet is near the camping area. This is the only spring along the river that has a practical overland route.

Hiking directions: From Hoover Dam, drive southeast on US 93 to mile post 4.2 and a dirt parking area on your right, at the head of White Rock Canyon. Follow this canyon downhill, through the wash, to the river. Then follow the edge of the river .25 miles south to the lower end of Ringbolt Hot Springs canyon and hike upstream to the springs. Distance 2.9 miles, with an 800-foot elevation change. The trail is rated moderately strenuous, so allow at least 2.5 hours each way. Watch for Bighorn sheep.

After landing on the beach, walk between the rocks to the hot shower and the ladder that leads you to another wonderful soaking pool at the top. If you continue through the pool at the top, you will come out on top of the rocks and have a wonderful, panoramic view.

Photos on pages 82-83 left by Justine Hill

Hot water seeping out of the rocks fills this soaking pool.

501 B GOLD STRIKE HOT SPRINGS
(see map)

● **Near Hoover Dam**

The beach at the bottom of this canyon is within sight of the warning cable stretched across the river just below the dam. One hundred yards up the canyon from the beach, natural mineral water flows out of cliff seeps at 109° into a series of volunteer-built soaking pools.

As you head farther up the canyon, you will often be walking in the stream bed as well as climbing over sharp rocks, so be prepared with appropriate footwear. Barefoot is definitely not recommended

The canyon includes several beautiful waterfalls, which can be bypassed only with some strenuous scrambling along smooth rock walls. Near the bottom of the first large falls is a sandy-bottom pool with a water temperature of 100°.

From the river, the landmark for this canyon is a pit toilet in the sandy area at the wide canyon mouth. In the river near the canyon mouth, there are some large underwater rocks that cause rapids. There are also large rocks in the shallow water close to shore, making it difficult to navigate into this canyon entrance. Space for overnight camping at the beach is very limited. If you do choose to camp, set up at the far inland edge of the sand, or the changing river levels may flood your site.

Note: Hiking overland to this spring is not recommended. It is extremely difficult and dangerous.

501 C BOY SCOUT HOT SPRINGS
(see map)

● **Near Hoover Dam**

A large cave, shaped like a human ear, can be seen on the west riverbank just upstream (north) from this canyon, whose entrance is protected by a land spit that blocks visibility from the south. When coming from the north, look for the bend in the river on the left past mile marker 62. Ahead is a layered rock formation. The canyon entrance and small beach sit in front of you before the river veers left. Landing on the gently sloping sandy beach is easy, but a sudden drop in river level could leave your boat many yards from the water.

The wide sand-and-gravel canyon mouth has a trickle of 70° water and plenty of camping space for a group. As you head upstream, the canyon narrows. You will often be walking in the streambed as well as climbing over sharp rocks, so be prepared with appropriate footwear. Barefoot is definitely not recommended. Remains of previously constructed cement dams and pipes are visible as you walk upstream into the canyon. There are several pools and waterfalls with temperatures up to 104° in the narrow upper canyon. The apparent local custom is clothing optional.

Note: There is no safe overland hiking trail to this hot spring.

Be sure to wear shoes in order to reach some of the pools located farther up the canyon.

Photos by Justine Hill

502   KAISER WARM SPRING

● **Southeast of Kingman**
Between Wikieup and Nothing

A primitive rock-and-mud pool in a beautiful serene desert canyon with nearby cold creek pools. A fairly easy mile-and-a-half walk through a sandy canyon with minor elevation change. Elevation 2,400 feet. Open all year, but recommended only October through April due to extreme summer heat. This area is also prone to flash floods.

Natural mineral water at about 100° bubbles up through the sandy creekbed along Warm Spring Canyon. The six- to eight-person, volunteer-built pool is approximately eighteen inches deep. Runoff flows through openings in the rock-and-mud wall into the creek. Take along a stiff brush to remove the algae from the rocks. Approximately 150 yards further down the canyon, cold Burro Creek emerges, surrounded by large flat pink and purple sandstone boulders that are ideal for sunning. Clothing is optional.

There are no facilities at the springs. There is plenty of BLM land along US 93 where overnight parking is not prohibited. Pack-in camping is also possible on BLM land in the canyon. It is seven miles from the trailhead to Burro Creek Campground, which has restrooms and RV dump, but no hookups. All other services are eleven miles from the trailhead in Wikieup. Fourteen miles south of the trailhead Nothing, Arizona has gas, AAA garage and towing, and the "T'Aint Much Store."

Directions: From Kingman drive 60 miles southeast on US 93, a portion of which is also I-40. After Wikieup, watch for mile markers. At .1 miles past mile marker 135, look for a gated dirt road just before the impressive Kaiser Canyon Bridge. This rocky road is the trailhead. As this is a very dangerous stretch of US 93, park well off the highway.

Hike the rough rocky "trailhead" just north of the bridge (close the gate). The creekbed is visible below. Hike for approximately 1.5 miles (30 minutes) until the canyon bends sharply to the left. Within 100 yards you will see warm seeps in the sandy canyon floor. Just ahead on the left is the soaking pool. Continue another 150 yards to reach the cold pools in Burro Creek. With a 4WD (high clearance vehicle) you can follow a jeep trail that leads down to within .50 to .75 miles from the springs from Cholla Rd., the third dirt road north of the bridge, .5 miles north of the bridge.

Source map: USGS Kaiser Spring.
GPS: N 34.563 W 113.497

Directions: From the north end of the campground look for a sign marked "River Crossing for Hot Springs, I mile." Follow this trail north, across a wooden bridge at the power plant and along the river until it heads inland up a hill for a short jog to a two-lane, dirt jeep road marked "hot springs road." Follow this road until you see a trail down to the river on your left marked with stone pilings. The hot springs are across the river, visible from the jeep road. Look for palm trees across the river and a stone wall along the riverbank. Depending on the river level, it may be necessary to ford the river twice, first to an island and then to the springs.

Note: These directions keep you on public land. Any attempt to cross fences puts you in real danger of entering private property and getting shot.

Source maps: *Coconino National Forest.* USGS *Verde Hot Springs.* GPS: N 34.357 W 111.710

Photos by `Bill Pennington

503   VERDE HOT SPRINGS

● **Near the Town of Camp Verde**

Small cement soaking pools, all that remains of an historic resort which burned down years ago, are decorated with artwork and historic paintings, including one of the springs resort as it appeared in its heyday. Located on the west bank of the Verde River in a beautiful, high desert canyon. Elevation 2,800 feet. Open all year, subject to river level and bad-weather road hazards.

Natural mineral water flows out of several riverbank springs at 104° and into a small indoor cement soaking pool. A larger outdoor cement pool is built over another spring and averages 98°. Twenty feet below, at low-water level, are several more springs that feed volunteer-built, rock-and-sand pools. Fifty feet upstream from the large cement pool is a 104° pool in a riverbank cave. The apparent local custom is clothing optional. Conscientious visitors have done a superb job of packing out all trash. Please respect this tradition.

There are no services available on the premises, and it is more than twenty miles to the nearest store, service station, and market. Parking and camping are permitted only in a Forest Service campground one mile south of the Childs Power Plant. Therefore, it is a one and one-half mile hike to the river ford at Verde Hot Springs. Check at the ranger station in Camp Verde regarding road conditions and river level before attempting to reach this site.

When the Verde River level is high after heavy rains or spring runoff, be sure to check at the ranger station before attempting to cross the river.

Camilla Van Sickle and Bill Pennington, owners of El Dorado, and inveterate travelers who contribute greatly to this book.

Sheep Bridge Hot Spring: The thick bullrushes surrounding the tub provide a nice screen for the tub and some shade during the hot summer months.

Prepare to be cordially greeted by the very hospitable people at *El Dorado Hot Spring* and to enjoy the desert vistas during the day and the brilliant stars at night. The goal here is to keep the hot springs and surroundings natural while providing the basic ammenities.

504   SHEEP BRIDGE HOT SPRING

● **Southeast of Prescott**

Cement tub on a ledge above the Verde River, surrounded on three sides by a dense growth of bulrushes. Elevation 1,400 feet. Open all year; be aware of flooded roads.

Natural mineral water flows out of a spring at 99° and is piped to a masonry pool close to the river. Other natural pools may be found, depending on water level, below the tub. The apparent local custom is clothing optional.

There are no services available on the premises. A level camping area is seventy-five yards upstream. It is fifty miles to all other services in Black Canyon City.

Directions: It is possible to reach this spring via a very difficult 4WD (high clearance vehicle recommended) route from Carefree. However, the following is the recommended route: From I-17 north of Black Canyon City, take the Bloody Basin off-ramp and drive southeast on FS 269 for 37 miles. This road crosses several streambeds that are usually dry. The first 16 miles to Summit (elevation 4,500 ft.) is a good gravel road. The remaining 21 miles is a poor dirt road, but it is passable by a high-clearance 2WD vehicle. From a parking area at the bridge, walk 75 yards upstream to the soaking tubs. An alternate, perhaps easier route goes from Carefree through Seven Springs

To locate the campground, drive .3 mile back up from the bridge and look on the north side of the road for the remains of a building foundation. A steep path (4WD only!) leads 150 yards down to a level camping area by the river. The soaking tub is 75 yards downstream from this area. There is a shady camping area south of the bridge on a flat area near the river.

Source maps: *Mazatzal Wilderness, Tonto National Forest;* USGS quads, *Brooklyn Park, Bloody Basin, Chalk Mountain.*

505   EL DORADO HOT SPRING

PO Box 10   623 393-0750
■ Tonopah, AZ 85354
HotSpring@El-Dorado.com

Large amounts of crystal clear, odorless, tasteless hot mineral water are helping to create a desert oasis surrounded by picturesque mountain views on three sides. Elevation 1,123 feet. Open all year; call for summer hours.

Natural mineral water at a temperatures of 112° is pumped from a subterranean spring to a variety of indoor and outdoor pools. Some pools have shade, misting nozzles, and cooler water for relaxing soaks in hot weather. Several of the pools in private areas can be rented by the hour. Water from the spring is diverted to a 1,500 gallon cooling tank which soakers can use to adjust the tub and shower temperatures. Misting nozzles help keep things cool. Runoff is used to irrigate the plants which are creating the oasis. No chemicals are necessary. Common areas free of alcohol, tobacco and pets. A toilet and two soaking pools are handicap accessible. Dump station and water available.

Reflexology, aromatherapy, and massage are by appointment only. Sleeping cabins will be added soon. Most other services are available one-tenth of a mile away in Tonopah. Meals from world famous Alice's Restaurant can be delivered to soakers poolside. Major credit cards are accepted. E-mail or phone ahead for information.

Directions to El Dorado: Take exit 94 off the I-10 between Phoenix and Quartzsite and go south on 411th Ave. Turn right on Indian School Road (Texaco Star Mart on the corner) and go west 0.1 miles. El Dorado is on the left (south) side of the road at number 41225, surrounded by ever-growing bamboo.

At *El Dorado Hot Spring*, whether your choice is a bathing suit or nothing at all, there is a pool for you, as well as plenty of room to park overnight. Be sure to visit the bamboo and cactus gardens

506 BUCKHORN MINERAL WELLS
5900 East Main St.   602 832-1111
■ **Mesa, AZ 85205**

An historic, older motel-spa offers many traditional hot mineral water treatment services. Elevation 1,200 feet. Open all year on a very limited basis.

Natural mineral water is pumped from two wells at 130° and 140° and is then run through a cooling tower. Facilities include separate men's and women's departments, each containing 12 small, individual rooms with cement tubs. A whirlpool pump is mounted on the side of each tub. The temperature of the tub water may be varied by controlling the proportions of hot and cold water added. Tubs are drained, cleaned, and refilled after each use so that no chemical treatment is required.

Massage, sweat-wrap therapy and motel rooms are available on the premises with an adjoining cafe and small shopping center. Other stores and restaurants are located across the street. Service stations and RV spaces are available within one-half mile.

No credit cards are accepted. Phone for rates, reservations, and directions.

While waiting to soak, enjoy the world's largest collection of Indian grinding stones.

Photos by Marjorie Young

Courtesy of El Dorado Hot Spring

Justine Hill

Marjorie Young

507　SAN CARLOS WARM SPRINGS

● **East of Globe**

A series of pools in the slow-flowing San Carlos River on the San Carlos Apache Reservation. Located in a tree-covered canyon with an abundance of wildlife. A permit is an absolute requirement. Elevation 3,500 feet. Open all year; pools may be under water during high runoff.

Natural mineral water bubbles up from several spots in the bottom of the river at temperatures between 85-95°. Warm spots can be found both upstream and downstream, but most are above the ford in the river. You can also follow the trail of green algae to where the warm spots are. Clothing optional would be all right during low use times, or head upstream for more private areas, but suits seem to be the order of the day on weekends and holidays.

There are three campgrounds on the reservation (make arrangements at the Recreation Department). Gas is available one mile west of the Recreation and Wildlife Dept. along US 70. The business center on the Reservation has a market. All other services are 20 miles away in Globe.

Directions: From Globe, take AZ 70 and go 20 miles east to the San Carlos Recreation and Wildlife Department, where you must stop and buy a permit. From the headquarters, continue east 4 miles to Hwy 8. Turn left (north) and continue 15 miles. Turn left on an unmarked gravel road (Indian Hwy 3). At four-way intersection turn left onto Road 1500 (marked with small sign by the fence) for 3.5 miles to where the road ends at the river. It is possible during low water for 4WD vehicles to cross the river and explore the other side.

508　WATSON WASH HOT WELL

● **Northwest of the town of Thatcher**

Stone tub with foot bath surrounded by willows in a primitive setting. Elevation 3,000 feet. Open all year, subject to flash floods.

Natural mineral water flows out of a well casing at 102° and directly into a volunteer-built stone tub large enough for six or eight people. The overflow creates a foot bath that should be used to remove the surrounding sand before getting into the tub. The tub can be drained and refilled, and locals seem to do a good job keeping it clean. Since this area is also used as a party spot, be prepared to pack out more trash than you packed in. Even though "No swim suits" is carved in the cement, clothing optional is the local custom only in the evening or during the week. Defer to the preference of those soaking first.

There are no services available on the premises. The surrounding BLM land allows for fourteen days of free camping. Undeveloped picnic sites are along the road. It is six miles to a store, cafe, service station and other services. Steps lead into the pools, which are handicap accessible with assistance.

Directions: From US 70 at the west end of Thatcher, go north on Reay Lane 3.2 miles to the "Y" intersection, which is Safford-Bryce Road. Turn left and drive .25 miles to the first wash across the road. Turn right and drive up the unimproved wash bottom .5 miles to the hot tub, going left at the first "Y" and right at the second. Most portions of the road are rough gravel, with some areas of hard-packed earth and a few sandy spots, all of which are passable in a standard passenger vehicle, except during or just after heavy rains.

509   THATCHER HOT WELL

As of 1997 the city capped off the flow of hot water. It is now NUBP (not useable by the public).

510   ESSENCE OF TRANQUILITY
■ 6074 S. Lebanon Loop   520 428-9312
Safford, AZ 85546   877 895-6810

Courtesy of Essence of Tranquility

A series of soaking tubs surrounded by mesquite, tamarask and palm trees. Elevation 2,990 feet. Open all year. Tubs are rented by the hour or for day use; call for open hours.

Natural 108° mineral water flows out of a 1,632-foot well into into six themed stone and concrete soaking pools. Fresh water at temperatures ranging from 100-106° flows constantly through the pools which require no chemical treatment. No bathing in tubs, a shower is available. Clothing is required in the open tub and on the grounds, but is optional in the private tubs. Facilities are handicap accessible with assistance.

Primitive campsites and tepee rentals are available by reservation. Includes the use of the kitchen, common room and tubs at no extra charge. Various forms of body work are available by appointment and include tub use. No credit cards, no drugs, no glass containers, no food available on premises, and only minimal amounts of alcohol is premitted. There is a convenience store within one-half mile, and it is five miles to town.

Directions: Starting in Safford at the intersection of US 70 and US 191, go south 6 miles on US 191. Turn right at Lebanon Rd. and follow road .5 mi to a 90-degree curve onto Lebanon Loop. Continue .6 miles further. Establishment is on the right.

From I-10 go north on US 191 approximately 25 miles to milemarker 115. Turn left on Cactus Rd. Approximately 1/4 mile west, turn right (north) on Lebanon Loop. The establishment is .25 miles on the left. Park in front.

511   KACHINA MINERAL SPRINGS SPA
■ Route 2, Box 987   520 428-7212
Safford, AZ 85546

Justine Hill

Therapy-oriented bathhouse, recently remodeled, located in the suburbs south of Safford. Elevation 3,000 feet. Open all year.

Natural mineral water flows out of an artesian well at 108° and is piped into private-room soaking tubs where water temperature measures around 104-106°. There are six large, tiled, sunken tubs. They are drained, cleaned, and refilled after each customer so that no chemical treatment is necessary. An addition to the old bathhouse has two large soaking pools, a hot one at 104°, and a cold one, large enough for eight to ten people. No bathing suits are needed in the private tubs.

Facilities also include an exercise room, sweat wraps, massage, reflexology. A free hot-pool soak comes with each therapy service. No credit cards are accepted. Phone for rates and reservations.

Directions: From the intersection of US 70 and US 191 in Safford, go 6 miles south on US 191, then turn right on Cactus Rd. for .25 miles.

Marjorie Young

Justine Hil

512 A ROPER LAKE STATE PARK
Route 2, Box 712   520 428-6760
■   ### Safford, AZ 85546

A small, neatly constructed outdoor soaking pool in a popular state park surrounded by rolling desert hills. Elevation 3,100 feet. Day-use fee. Open all year, 6 AM to 10 PM.

Geothermal mineral water flows from an artesian well at 99° directly into a stone-and-cement pool large enough for six to eight good friends. The water flows through continuously, so no chemical treatment is needed. There is a fifteen-minute limit when other people are waiting. Bathing suits are required. Access to the tub is ramped, with stairs and a handrail leading into the tub.

Facilities at the state park include camping and RV spaces, rest rooms, changing rooms, day-use picnic ramadas, a swimming beach, two stocked lakes for fishing, a boat ramp, and nature trails. A mini-mart and gas are available four miles north and all other services are approximately 6 miles away in Safford.

Directions: From Safford, drive south on US 191 for 6 miles, turn left (east) at the sign for Roper Lake State Park, and continue .5 mile to the park entrance.

512 B DANKWORTH PONDS

●   ### Located in Roper Lake State Park

A shallow, warm, sandy-bottom ditch which has been widened to allow for soaking. Day-use fee.

Warm artesian water continually bubbles up out of the ground and flows through the ditch and out into the bullrushes. The one-foot deep warm ditch is ideal for children. Bathing suits are required.

There are nearby shaded picnic tables, barbeque grills, restrooms, and trash containers.

Directions: From Safford continue three miles south of the Roper Lake State Park turnoff, watch for State Park picnic area sign on the east side of the road, just past mile marker 113. Turn right (east) for .1 mile.

Lynn Foss

Marjorie Young

513   HOT WELL DUNES

● **Southeast of Safford**

Two fenced-in soaking pools and one shallow pond surrounded by hundreds of acres of Bureau of Land Management (BLM) desert sand dunes open to, and popular with, off-road vehicles. Elevation 3,450 feet. Open all year, subject to flash floods.

Geothermal mineral water flows out of an artesian well at the rate of 200 gallons per minute and a temperature of 106° into two fenced soaking tubs. Overflow from the tubs spills into an adjoining shallow sand-bottom pool that provides soaking at a lower water temperature. Bathing suits are required.

A few developed tent or RV camp sites, fire grills, trash can, and vault toilets are available on the premises. Two weeks of camping are permitted on the level ground in this desert area, except where indicated right near the tubs. You will need to bring all your own supplies, including water. It is thirty-two miles to all services in Safford.

Directions: There are several access roads to the area but only the following one is recommended for standard passenger vehicles. From Safford, follow US 70 east for 7 miles to the Agricultural Inspection Station for vehicles entering from New Mexico. At .3 miles east of the station, turn right (south) onto an unmarked gravel road (Haekel Rd.). When road forks at 1.5 miles, take left fork. Continue south for 25 miles and turn left at the sign for Hot Well Dunes.

514   BUENA VISTA HOT WELLS

■ **East of Safford, North of San Jose**

Soaking areas in the bottom of an irrigation canal are shared with the fish, and the people fishing and farming in this rural agricultural area. Elevation 3,000 feet. Open all year.

Hot mineral water flows through open pipeways at temperatures between 130-150° and drops into an irrigation canal. There are no pools per se, and warm areas are found by walking up and down the canal area to a comfortable spot. Since the bottom of the canal is sandy, it is possible to scoop out a soaking pool. Bathing suits are a good idea as there seem to be a fair number of people around.

There are no services at the site. All services can be found about ten miles back in Safford.

Directions: From Safford, drive 7 miles east on US 70 and turn left onto San Jose Rd. After 2 miles, the road splits. Take Buena Vista Rd. to the left about .8 miles and make another left onto a dirt road. This road crosses the irrigation ditch, and there is parking to your right. There is also pullout parking right before you cross the ditch, and a path leads down into the canal, probably the easiest way to get into the water.

515 POTTER'S AZTEC BATHS BED AND BREAKFAST

PO Box 8443   520 865-4847
● Clifton, AZ 85533

A flood in 1996 washed out the hot well on the property of Potter's Aztec Baths, so at press time the hot tubs are not usable, but the bed and breakfast is still operational with plans to dig a new well.

Justine Hill

Primitive seeps along the San Francisco River on the Potter property have been used for years by volunteers who build simple rock-and-mud pools that get washed out and rebuilt every year. They are located a quarter-mile south of the B&B where the three branches of the San Francisco converge. The pools collect the slow seeping hot water which mixes with cold river water. Move the rocks around to adjust the pool temperature.

Potter Ranch management doesn't mind if the public uses these pools, but please call ahead to let them know you are coming, and for directions. And please stay on the trail to protect the eroding, twenty-five foot high riverbank.

516 GILLARD HOT SPRINGS

● Near the town of Clifton

Remote hot springs along the Gila River in the Black Hills area of southeastern Arizona's Greenlee County. Located at the end of a six-mile drive on unpaved roads and a one-mile walk through a sandy wash. Elevation 3,500 feet. Open all year, subject to road washouts due to heavy rain.

Natural mineral water seeps from underground at over 183° along the northeast bank of the Gila River. Following each year's high water and spring runoff, the primitive rock-and-mud pools must be redug. Water temperature is controlled by mixing in cold river water. Due to the slow rate of flow, it may take some patience to achieve the proper soaking temperature. Clothing is optional.

There are no facilities on the premises, but there is plenty of BLM land where camping is permitted. There are also areas for car camping along Old Safford Road near the Gila River. North of the bridge, a road heads down to the river where you can park under the trees. From here it is three miles to the hot springs by the river. Fifty feet downstream from the hot springs is a deep swimming hole. Oozy river mud makes natural mudbaths.

Directions: Drive 35 miles northeast of Safford, AZ on US 70 and US 191 to Three Way (where Hwys 191, 75, and 78 meet). Or, from US 70 in Lordsburg, NM, drive 55 miles northwest through Duncan to the Apache ranger station at Three Way. From Three Way, continue north toward Clifton on US 191 for 5.5 miles. When the divided highway ends, make an immediate left (west) on Black Hills Back Country Byway (also called Old Safford Rd.). Drive 2.1 miles to a primitive dirt road on the right with a sign to Gillard Hot Springs. Turn right onto this unmaintained road for 1 mile to a three-way intersection. Follow the middle fork for .3 mile to a sandy wash and hike up twenty feet to the washed-out road on the right of the wash. Follow it for 1 mile down to the river. The seeps are on the northeast bank near the end of the road. Look for hot steam rising.

Note to Gillard Hot Springs: There may be washouts and detours due to flooding. The rough and sandy road can be maneuvered by passenger vehicles with a knowledgeable desert driver. A 4WD is recommended.

Source map: USGS *Apache-Sitgreaves National Forests* (springs not shown).

Justine Hill

The rough, difficult roads and the distance to get to the springs practically guarantees you a private soaking spot at *Gillard Hot Springs* (above) and *Eagle Creek* (below).

517   EAGLE CREEK HOT SPRING

● **Near the town of Morenci**

Hot water seeps up from the ground in several spots high on a ridge above Eagle Creek in the remote high desert of Eastern Arizona. Reached via a two-mile hike with river crossings and steep scrambles up a rocky bluff. Elevation 4,000 feet. Open all year, subject to river flooding.

Hot 116° water seeps out of the ground and flows through a shallow gully where it cools substantially until it pours over a precipice as a trickling cold waterfall. A soaking pool could be built at the source, which is currently a watering spot for cattle and wildlife. (The entire Eagle Creek canyon is private Phelps Dodge property. Officially visitors should sign in at the P.D. security desk before entering Eagle Creek.) Clothing is optional.

There are no facilities at this remote location except level areas for pack-in camping and car camping on nearby BLM land. Bring plenty of water or a filter for Eagle Creek water.

Directions: (See directions for #516 as far as Clifton.) From Clifton, follow US 191 to Morenci. Turn right at the first traffic light in Morenci and go 1.5 miles to a "Y" at Mine Rd. Stay on US 191 another 3 miles to a small cemetery on your right. Opposite the cemetery is Eagle Creek Rd. (unmarked), a wide gravel road with yellow highway markers. Follow this road for 5.3 miles to a power plant at the creek. Unless you have a 4WD, park here. You will cross the river back and forth 5-6 times to reach Hot Springs Canyon, on your right.

Walk south past the farmhouse just south of the power plant. Or, with a 4WD, cross the river by the power plant and immediately cross again. With a high-clearance 4WD, depending on water level, you may be able to do the river crossings and park opposite the mouth to Hot Springs Canyon (the first large canyon on your right.) Due to flooding, river patterns and crossings may change seasonally. Best landmarks are the canyon walls. When the river level is low, all crossing can be done on foot. Just before the entrance to Hot Springs Canyon, Eagle Creek opens up into a large 5-foot deep swimming hole.

Hike into the canyon approximately 500 feet. On the right is a 35-foot, warm, trickling waterfall. Scramble up the hill to the left of the falls, approximately 80 feet to the top of the ridge. From here look down to the northwest. The dark green areas have the seeps. If you make a sharp left as you start to climb and look uphill you will find a small warm-water cave.

Source map: USGS *Copperplate Gulch.*
GPS: N 33.046 W 109.440

NORTHERN CALIFORNIA

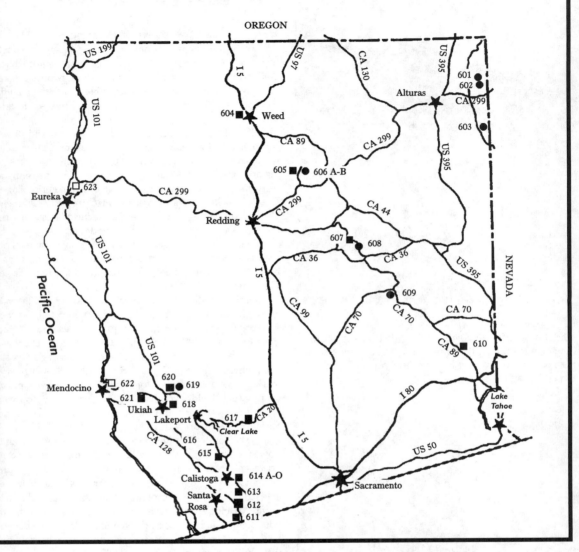

This map was designed to be used with a standard highway map.

MAP SYMBOLS

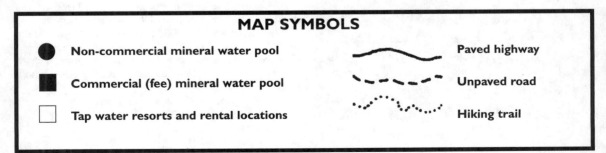

● Non-commercial mineral water pool

■ Commercial (fee) mineral water pool

□ Tap water resorts and rental locations

⎯⎯⎯ Paved highway

- - - Unpaved road

····· Hiking trail

Justine Hill

The pools at *Glen Hot Springs* have been dug out by volunteers in wide portions of the ditches and runoffs where the water has cooled to a comfortable temperature. *Leonard's Hot Springs* is still in need of volunteers to dig the pools there.

601   GLEN HOT SPRINGS
(see map)

● **Near the town of Cedarville**

Undeveloped cluster of hot springs on a barren slope along the east side of Upper Alkali Lake with views of Cedarville and the mountains behind it. Elevation 4,600 feet. Open all year.

Natural mineral water flows out of several springs into a ditch at 180° and cools as it runs toward several volunteer-built soaking pools. Water in the small pool measures 150°, and 111° in the large shallow pool. Runoff continues downhill for two-tenths of a mile to the gravel road where the ditch is one-foot deep and the water temperature measures 107°. Clothing optional.

No services are available on the premises. There is a limited amount of unmarked open space on which overnight parking is not prohibited. It is ten miles to a service station and all other services.

Source map: *USGS Cedarville*.
GPS: N 41.3626 W 120.0613

602 LEONARD'S HOT SPRING
(see map)

● **Near the town of Cedarville**

Abandoned and deteriorated old resort on a barren slope along the east side of Middle Alkali Lake. Elevation 4,500 feet. Open all year.

Natural mineral water flows out of the ground from several springs at a temperature of 150° and cools as it runs toward the lake. A diversion ditch formerly carried this water to the resort, but it now flows through a winding ditch fifty yards southeast of the old swimming pool. The narrow shallow ditch is algae-filled, with decaying old boards along the edge and in the water. Enthusiastic volunteers could clean it out for a pleasant soak at approximately 100°. The local custom is clothing optional.

There is no shade and no services are available on the premises. There is an abundance of unmarked level space on which overnight parking is not prohibited. It is nine miles to a service station and all other services.

Directions: The turnoff for Leonard's is .5 mile east of the turn off for Glen Hot Springs, on the south side of 49 Lane.

Source map: *USGS Cedarville*.
GPS: N 41.3557 W 120.0514

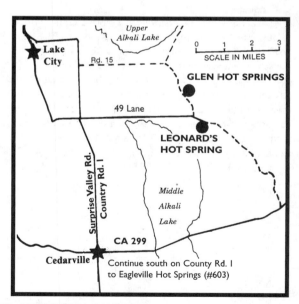

Eagleville Hot Spring provides you with an incredible view whether you are soaking in the redwood hot tub or in the shallow soaking pool.

603   EAGLEVILLE HOT SPRING

● **South of the town of Cedarville**

Shallow, primitive soaking pool and tub with a commanding view of Surprise Valley and surrounding mountains. Elevation 4,600 feet. Open all year.

Natural mineral water flows out of two PVC pipes in the road embankment at 111°. One pipe goes to a volunteer-built rock-and-sand soaking pool, and the other goes to an adjacent five-foot redwood tub. The pools are not visible from the road, so the apparent local custom is clothing optional. Local custom also expects new arrivals to await the departure of those already there.

There are no services available on the premises. It is seven miles to Eagleville and twenty-three miles to Cedarville.

Directions: From Cedarville, on Modoc County Road 1, (Surprise Valley Road), drive south 15 miles to Eagleville. From the post office, drive 7.7 miles. You will pass two houses with a stone fence and lots of "stuff" out front. (If you come to an abandoned house on the east side of the street you've gone .2 miles too far.) Drive one mile further to a pullout on the east side of the road. Continue 75 yards down the embankment to a dead end. Walk 135 yards north to pool and tub. Or, park at the pullout where a short path leads directly down to the pool and tub.

GPS: N 41.1237 W 120.0327

604   STEWART MINERAL SPRINGS
4617 Stewart Springs Rd.

800 322-9223

■   **Weed, CA 96094**

A well-kept rustic retreat available to individuals or groups for special events or seminars. Located on a mountain stream in a green canyon northwest of Mt. Shasta. Elevation 3,900 feet. Open March through November on a reservation basis only.

Natural mineral water is pumped from a well at 40° and is propane heated. There are twelve individual bathtubs and larger tubs in private rooms. Water temperature in each tub is controlled, as desired, by mixing cold and hot mineral water. Tubs are drained and refilled after each use, so no chemical treatment of the water is necessary. Bathing suits are required in public areas.

Facilities include rooms, restaurant (for groups of ten or more), camping spaces, and partial-hookup RV spaces. Massage is available by appointment. A sweat lodge is available for groups. Major credit cards are accepted. It is seven miles to a store, service station, and public bus. Special pickup at the bus depot and at the Weed airport can be arranged.

Directions: Take the Edgewood exit on I-5 north of Weed. Turn north on the west side of I-5 and take the first left onto Stewart Springs Rd. Drive 4 miles to the resort at the end of the road.

The usual custom is to soak in the tub, experience the sauna, and take a dip in this cold mountain spring. This is repeated four times—one for each compass direction.

Phil Wilcox

From the pools you can look up and see bald eagles and cranes swoop down looking for food, and see river otters playing below.

605 HEALING WATERS
196 Hot Springs Rd.   530 337-6602
■ **Big Bend, CA 96011**

The remains of an historical resort being improved and operated by Healing Waters, a nonprofit organization. Located fifty miles northeast of Redding on the tree-shaded south bank of the Pit River. Elevation 2,000 feet. Open all year.

Natural artesian mineral water flows out from three springs at 180°.

(1) Hot mineral baths. Located on the edge of a plateau thirty feet above the Pit River are three interconnected natural stone/cement pools, each large enough for six persons. Faucet-controlled cold creek water is added to each pool to produce whatever temperature is desired by occupants. Each pool has seating at various depths, and all have a superb view of the river. Flushed clean daily. A bathhouse and sauna are under construction. Clothing optional after dark.

(2) Indian Springs. Located about ten feet above the level of the adjacent Pit River, 180° mineral water flows into a series of secluded, shallow pools created by volunteers from riverbed rocks. Clothing optional. Camping adjacent to the springs.

Campsites are available on the premises. Cabin renovation is taking place; call for status. Fishing, swimming and water sports on adjacent Pit River. Bodywork, yoga and wellness workshops are offered. Saunas under construction. Parking for RVs. It is one-quarter mile to a cafe, store, and service station in the small town of Big Bend. Credit cards are accepted.

Directions: From I-5 in Redding, go 35 miles east on CA 299. Turn north 17 miles toward the town of Big Bend. Turn left on Hot Springs Road just before the Big Bend store and the bridge over the Pit River. Continue .25 miles to the end of the road and check in at the office.

Healing Waters (formerly known as Big Bend Hot Springs) is one of California's best kept secrets. The natural beauty is built in, and under new management, the whole place is being cleaned, renovated and enlarged. Come see what a lot of TLC (tender, loving care) can do.

Jayson Loam

Phil Wilcox

Phil Wilcox

606A HUNT HOT SPRINGS

● **Near the town of Big Bend**

Delightful rock-and-cement soaking tub and several creekside rock pools situated on Kosh Creek close to where it joins the Pit River. Located in a beautiful river valley near Mount Shasta. Elevation 2,000 feet. Open all year; road may not be passable during wet weather.

Natural mineral water flows out of several hillside seeps at 104° and cools on its way through several pools down to Kosh Creek. There are two rock-and-cement pools large enough for four. It is a good idea to bring a bucket for the cold creek water to help regulate the pool temperatures. A varying number of volunteer-built rock pools along the river seem to get the most use as temperature-wise they are easier to regulate. Clothing is optional.

There are no services available on the premises, but there is plenty of wide open space where camping is not restricted. General store, service station, cafe, and ranger station are approximately two miles away in Big Bend.

Directions: From Big Bend store, proceed across Pit River Bridge. About .8 mile, FS 37N02 goes off to the right. Continue straight (FS11) another 100 yards and take the first dirt road to the left. Go right at the fork. From this point the road is quite rough for the 1 mile down to the end (just past the Wright Historical Cemetery on your left). Low clearance vehicles may have a problem.

A wonderful few days could be spent in the area around Big Bend visiting *Healing Waters, Hunt Hot Springs* and *Kosh Hot Springs*.

606B KOSH CREEK HOT SPRINGS

● **Near the town of Big Bend**

Charming volunteer-built rock pool for two on a steep hillside in a beautiful river valley near Mt. Shasta. Situated along Kosh Creek near its intersection with the Pit River. Elevation 2,000 feet. Open all year; may not be passable in wet weather.

Natural mineral water flows out of a rocky cliff above the creek at a perfect 104° and flows directly into the pool below. Clothing is optional.

There are no services available on the premises, but there is plenty of wide open space where camping is not restricted. General store, service station, cafe and ranger station are approximately two miles away in Big Bend.

Directions: (See Hunt Hot Springs 606A). From Hunt climb the steep, well-used trail immediately behind Hunt to the other side of the hill and back down to Kosh Creek. The tub will be visible as you descend.

Several hot source springs are used to feed the swimming pool at *Drakesbad Guest Ranch* which is located in beautiful Lassen Volcanic National Park.

607 DRAKESBAD GUEST RANCH
c/o California Guest Services, Inc.
2150 Main St. #5   **916 529-1512**
■   **Red Bluff, CA 96080**

A rustic mountain ranch/resort, reservations only, with a mineral-water swimming pool, plus horses and guides for riding and hiking. Registered guests only. Located in a superb mountain meadow within the boundaries of Lassen Volcanic National Park. Elevation 5,700 feet. Open first part of June to first part of October.

Natural mineral water flows out of two springs at temperatures between 140-150° and is piped to the pool. The swimming pool is maintained at 95° during the day and 105° at night by mixing the two hot water flows. Minimal amounts of chlorine are added to control algae growth. The lodge is handicap accessible. Bathing suits are required.

Facilities include lodge, rooms, cabins, bungalows, and dining room. Saddle horses and guides are available by the hour. Visa and MasterCard are accepted. Telephone for reservations.

Directions: From CA 36 in the town of Chester, take Warner Valley Road northwest 17 miles to the resort, which is at the end of the road. The last 3 miles are dirt/gravel road.

608 TERMINAL GEYSER HOT SPRINGS

According to information received from the United States Department of the Interior, National Park Service, regulations prohibit soaking in the Hot Springs. And I quote, "The reason for this prohibition is that 'bathers,' both through manipulation of water flow to form pools and by the very act of soaking in the pools, disrupt the natural biologic and geologic processes which the National Park Service is mandated to protect. Persons in hot pools observed by Park Rangers will be issued a violation notice and will be subject to either a fine or a court appearance, depending on the individual circumstances."

609 WOODY'S FEATHER RIVER HOT SPRINGS
PO Box 7   **916 283-4115**
●   **Twain, CA 95984**

Primarily a fishing and hunting resort, this site does have one small soaking pool on the north bank of the Feather River, where you can also pan for gold. The resort is located in the tree-covered upper Feather River Canyon. Elevation 2,700 feet. Open all year.

Natural mineral water flows directly into the cement, sandy-bottom pool at 90-100°. No chemical treatment is added. Clothing is optional in the pool and in the adjoining river.

Facilities include rooms, RV spaces, restaurant, and bar. No credit cards accepted. It is three miles to a store and fifteen miles to a gas station.

Directions: On CA 70, go 4 miles west from the Quincy-Greenville "Y," the junction of Hwy 89 and Hwy 70. Located at mile post 28.

Woody was the owner of the springs. She believed that soaking should be free to all—a tradition still in effect.

610 SIERRA HOT SPRINGS
PO Box 366　　　　530 994-3773
■ Sierraville, CA 96126

A six-hundred-acre resort surrounded by secluded forests, meadows, and streams has been restored and expanded by a nonprofit intentional community. Visitors use of the facilities is welcome. While this is a membership facility, non-resident fees are minimal. Elevation 5,000 feet. Open all year.

On a wooded slope natural mineral water flows out of several springs at temperatures up to 112° into several terraced pools and waterfalls which range in temperature from 98-110°. The Medicine Bath (at 100°) is a natural sandy-bottom rock pool on the edge of a large alpine meadow. The Temple Dome houses a pool with the hottest water There are also cold tile and rock plunges and a large oudtdoor warm water pool with a large sun deck. Private tubs are to be found at the Phoenix Baths. No chemicals are needed in any of the pools. Clothing is optional in all pool areas.

Historic hotel, private lodge rooms, dormitory, and camping spaces are available. Call ahead for massage and other heaing treatments. A restaurant and facilities for cooking your own food are also on the premises. It is two miles to all other services in Sierraville. No pets, alcohol, drugs, and no soap or bathing is permitted. Major credit cards accepted. Phone for reservations.

Directions: From the junction of CA 89 and CA 49 in Sierraville, take CA 49 east for 1.1 miles and follow CA 49 north to Lemon Canyon Rd., which runs along the north edge of the airport; then turn right on Campbell Hot Springs Rd., which runs along the east edge of the airport, and continue into the foothills to the lodge office.

The small airport is within walking distance of the springs.

Jayson Loam

611 SONOMA MISSION INN & SPA
PO Box 1447　　　　707 938-9000
■ Sonoma, CA 95476

Luxuriously restored resort providing multiple beauty and health packages for your benefit and enjoyment in a beautiful, romantic setting. Elevation 100 feet. Open all year.

Mineral water flows out of the source at 135° and is piped to one large outdoor and one large indoor whirlpool tub. Both are lightly treated with bromine and refilled daily. The water is maintained at 102°. The mineral water is also used to fill the two outdoor swimming pools, which are treated lightly with bromine and refilled daily. The large pool is maintained at 82° and the spa pool at 92°. Mineral water showers are also available in the spa. Some areas are handicap accessible.

Beautifully appointed rooms, a gourmet restaurant, a cafe, coed exercise and spa facilities, and tennis courts are available on the premises. In addition, over forty different spa treatments are offered. Call for rates, reservations, directions, and details.

Courtesy of Sierra Hot Springs

612 AGUA CALIENTE MINERAL SPRINGS
17350 Vailetti Dr.   707 996-6822
■   Sonoma, CA 95476

A summertime plunge and picnic grounds in the middle of the Sonoma Valley. Elevation 100 feet. Open summer months only.

Natural mineral water is pumped from a well at 96° and piped to a swimming pool that averages 86° and to a hydropool that averages 95°. The adjoining diving pool and wading pool, averaging 70°, are filled with unheated tap water; both pools are treated with chlorine and are drained and filled every day. Bathing suits are required.

A seasonal snack bar is available on the premises. No credit cards are accepted. It is less than one mile to a store, gas station, and all other services.

Directions: From the city of Sonoma, go 3 miles north on CA 12 and watch for Agua Caliente signs.

613 WHITE SULPHUR SPRINGS RESORT
3100 White Sulphur Springs Rd.
707 963-8588
■   St. Helena, CA 94574

Historic, 330 acre resort surrounded by the beauty of the Napa Valley. Elevation 400 feet. Open all year.

Natural mineral water flows out of several springs at various temperatures up to 95°. It is piped to one outdoor soaking pool that operates on a flow-through basis requiring no chemical treatment and is maintained at 85-87°. Also available is a twenty-person jet tub filled with chlorine-treated spring water and maintained at an average temperature of 103°, and a 20-foot by 40-foot sports pool kept at ambient temperature. All pools are available to the public for day use, as well as to registered guests. Bathing suits are required.

Extensive hiking trails on the wooded premises take you through forested canyons and fern-lined creeks. Other facilities include a sauna, extensive sunning areas, a new health center that offers massage (indoors and out), and herbal and mud wraps. Overnight accommodations include creekside cottages and inn rooms. Fully equipped meeting rooms and kitchen facilities are available. The redwood grove is a perfect setting for weddings, picnics, or family reunions. Visa and MasterCard are accepted. It is three miles to central St. Helena and all other services.

Directions: From CA 29 in the center of St. Helena, drive 3 miles west on Spring St. to the resort.

Photos courtesy of White Sulphur Springs

White Sulphur Springs: After a nice hike in the woods (see picture at right), a soak in the hot pool pictured above would certainly be soothing. A year-round creek with waterfall flows through the middle of the property.

CALISTOGA SPAS

CALISTOGA, CA 94515

All of the following locations are in or near the charming town of **Calistoga**, adjacent to the **Napa Valley** wine country, a wonderful getaway. These facilities are open all year and stores, restaurants, etc., are available in the town.

Each of the locations has its own hot wells, which are used to supply the water to the soaking and swimming pools. Chlorination of the pools is a state regulation. Soaking tubs in bathhouses are drained and filled after each use so no chemical treatment is necessary. Unless otherwise noted, resorts with pool facilities are available for day use except during peak times and holidays. Bathing suits are required in all public areas. Major credit cards are accepted. Phone for details.

---

614 A   CALISTOGA OASIS SPA
■   1300 Washington St.   707 942-2122

Spa facility offering mud and mineral baths, facials and massages with private spaces for couples and individuals. Limited selection of spa and bath products. Located on the grounds of Roman Spa. (See complete listing under Roman Spa.)

---

614 B   CALISTOGA SPA HOT SPRINGS
■   1006 Washington St.   707 942-6269

Resort motel with separate men's and women's bath areas. Offers volcanic ash mud baths, mineral baths, steam baths, blanket wraps, and massage.

Resort has four naturally heated mineral baths: outdoor soaking pool, 100°; outdoor swimming pool, 83°; outdoor wading pool, 90°; and a covered hydropool, 105°. Area surrounding pools has places to lounge and a refreshment stand. Indoor men's and women's bathhouses each contain individual tubs, two mud baths, and three steambaths.

All rooms are equipped for light housekeeping. Aerobic classes, workout rooms, and a conference room are available on the premises.

614 C   CALISTOGA VILLAGE INN AND SPA
■   1880 Lincoln Ave   707 942-0991

Courtesy of Calistoga Village Inn

Offers a wide range of affordable lodging, some with Roman tub or whirlpool in room. Spa offers traditional mud bath, therapeutic massage, salt scrubs, facials, and reflexology.

Spa has an outdoor swimming pool at 80-85°, wading pool at 90-95°, and enclosed hydropool at 100-105°. Indoor men's and women's bathhouses, each contain two hydrotherapy tubs, two mud baths, two steam cabinets, and a sauna.

Facilities include rooms, conference meeting rooms, and an on-site restaurant serving all meals.

---

614 D   CARLIN COUNTRY COTTAGES
■   1623 Lake St.   707 942-9102

Fifteen cottages, seven with a two-person, in-room spa, are decorated with an Irish and Shaker country theme. Pools for registered guests only.

MIneral water outdoor pool is maintained at 90-95° in winter and 85° in summer. Outdoor hydropool is 104°. Cottage pools are controllable to 104°.

Continental breakfast served buffet style; can be taken to the poolside or to your room. Late afternoon refreshments are also provided.

Courtesy of Comfort Inn

Courtesy of Golden Haven

614 E COMFORT INN

■ 1865 Lincoln Ave. 707 942-9400
Spa 707 942-4636

Fifty-four beautifully decorated rooms. Complete spa facilities offered across the street at Calistoga Village Inn and Spa (see above).

Large geothermal outdoor swimming pool is maintained at 85-90°; one whirlpool is 104°. Sauna and steamroom are also available.

Complimentary continental breakfast included with room. Facilities include meeting room and non-smoking and handicap rooms.

614 F DR. WILKINSON'S HOT SPRINGS

■ 1507 Lincoln Ave. 707 942-6257

One of the original locations (since 1946) offering massage, mud baths, blanket wraps and skin care.

Two outdoor mineral pools are 82° and 92°; one tropical-foliage indoor mineral pool is 104°. Indoor men's and women's bathhouses each contain four individual tubs, two mud baths, and a steambath.

Contemporary or Victorian style lodgings.

614 G GOLDEN HAVEN HOT SPRINGS SPA AND RESORT

■ 1713 Lake St 707 942-6793

One of only two spas in town offering coed mud and mineral baths as well as massage. Spa open to the public, you need not be a guest at the resort.

Enclosed mineral water swimming pool is 80°; covered hydropool is 102°. Handicap accessibility dependent on services used.

Rooms, some with private sauna or hydropool, some with kitchenettes, are available.

614 H HIDEAWAY COTTAGES

■ 1412 Fairway 707 942-4108

Seventeen cottages for adults only. Spa facilities at Dr. Wilkinson's (see listing).

Outdoor swimming pool is 82°, and hydropool, is 104°. Reserved for registered guests; no day use.

Various accommodations include some non-smoking rooms some with kitchens. A conference room for up to twenty-five persons is also available.

Courtesy of Indian Springs

614 I INDIAN SPRINGS
■   1712 Lincoln Ave.   707 942-4913

California's oldest continuously operating pool and spa offering mud baths, soaking tubs, steam room, massage, and facials. Three active geysers on the premises supply the hot mineral water.

Outdoor, Olympic-size swimming pool is 90-102°, depending on the season. Men's and women's bathhouses, each contain five one-person mud or mineral water soaking tubs and a steam room. Only this spa uses pure volcanic ash, no additives. Pool is handicap accessible.

Comfortable bungalows have recently been restored. Clay tennis court, shuffleboard, bicycle surreys, croquet, and rose gardens are available on the premises.

614 J LAVENDER HILL SPA
■   1015 Foothill Blvd.   707 942-4495

Two private bathhouses for couples offer a full range of mud and seaweed baths, herbal wraps, aromatherapy, facials, massage, and reflexology. You can also make an appointment to create a personalized perfume just for you. Included is a choice of herbal essentials to enhance the soak.

614 K MOUNT VIEW SPA
■   1457 Lincoln Ave.   707 942-5789

Eurospa offering Fango mud baths for two, massage, facials and body wraps. Private rooms designed for couples.

Outdoor pool and mineral water hot tub.

Elegantly decorated rooms and a wonderful restaurant.

Courtesy of Lavender Hill

Lavender Hill: A garden spa for couples to relax and enjoy.

614 L   NANCE'S HOT SPRINGS
■   1614 Lincoln Ave.   707 942-6211

One of Calistoga's original spas offering mud baths, mineral baths, blanket wraps, and massage.

Indoor hydropool is 103°. Indoor men's and women's bathhouses contain four individual tubs (up to 110°), three mud baths, and two steambaths in each section.

Quality lodging features kitchens and rooms for the handicapped. Glider rentals are available at the adjoining airport.

614 M   PINE STREET INN AND EUROSPA
■   1202 Pine St.   707 942-6829

Luxurious full-service spa surrounded by poolside gardens with a view of mountains and vineyards.

Outdoor unheated mineral water pool and heated whirlpool are 103-105°. Three gas-heated, tap water hydropools allow customers to control temperatures.

Sixteen nicely decorated rooms are available.

614 N   ROMAN SPA
■   1300 Washington St.   707 942-4441

The pools and well-appointed rooms are amidst an exquisite garden setting of arbors, fountains, and flower-filled courtyards. Calistoga Oasis Spa is on the premises. This full service spa offers massage, reflexology, coed mud baths, mineral baths, herbal wraps, and facials. Four mud tubs are 101°, and two single and two double whirlpools allow customers to control temperatures.

Outdoor swimming pool is 92-95°, the outdoor hydrotherapy whirlpool is 104° and the indoor hydrotherapy whirlpool is 100°. There are segregated men's and women's saunas.

Attractive lodgings with each room having TV, air conditioning, and a refrigerator. Suites are available as are rooms with large roman tubs piped with natural untreated mineral water. Most rooms are nonsmoking, some have kitchens, and two rooms are handicap accessible.

Courtesy of Silver Rose Inn

614 O   SILVER ROSE INN HOT SPRINGS AND SPA
■   351 Rosedale Rd.   707 942-9581

A three-star rating ranks this romantic, upscale resort as one of the best. All the intimacy of a bed and breakfast inn. Hot mineral water supplies all the showers. Spa area offers four massage rooms for couples or a massage in your room. Full range of body and facial treatments, mud and herbal soaks, bodywraps, and hydrotherm massage are also available. Facilities for registered guests only.

Two large outside pools are 80-90°, and two outdoor whirlpools are 102°. Two hydrotherapy tubs can accommodate couples or singles. Many facilities are handicap accessible.

Twenty guest rooms are each decorated around a theme. Many rooms offer fireplaces, two-person whirlpool tubs, and private balconies. Breakfast can be enjoyed in the dining area, outside on the terrace, or delivered to your room. Entire inn is non-smoking. After noon hospitality hour and a "California" style breakfast is included.

615 HARBIN HOT SPRINGS
■ **PO Box 782**   **707 987-2477**

Middletown, CA 95461

Surrounded by 1,100 acres of secluded forest, meadows, and streams, this historic resort is constantly being enlarged by a nonprofit residential community in the spirit of preserving the springs as a place to come for rest and renewal. Located in a rugged foothill canyon south of Clear Lake. Elevation 1,500 feet. Open all year.

Two natural hot mineral water springs (one sulphur, one iron) flow out of the earth at 120°, and the water is piped to an enclosed cement pool that has an average temperature of 110-115°, and an adjoining cement pool, fed by the overflow, that has an average temperature of 95-98°. The heart pool, cold plunge, and swimming pool are filled with pure cold water from the same springs that feed the drinking supply. The temperature of the heart pool is maintained at 95-98°. The temperatures of the cold plunge and the swimming pool depend on the weather. All pools operate on a frequent cleaning and flow-through basis combining sand filters, peroxide and ozone injections, and ultra-violet sterilizers. Clothing is optional everywhere within the grounds except in the front office, in the kitchen and dining room, and on the main roads where public access is allowed. Limited handicap accessibility.

Facilities include day use of pools, camping, dorm rooms, several conference buildings for the many retreats and workshops offered, one general store, a books store, a cafe by the pools, an espresso bar, and a vegetarian restaurant with a wonderful view where freshly prepared, mostly organic, meals (breakfast and dinner) are served.

Rooms are beautifully and comfortably decorated, and small cottages are just perfect for a romantic getaway. Movies and daily yoga programs are available. A wide range of massage techniques are offered in the separate massage building. For a special summer treat, indulge yourself in the Harbin Clay Works and create a therapeutic body mask for yourself. State accredited training in massage and Watsu is available on the premises. Visa and MasterCard are accepted. It is four miles to a service station in Middletown. Phone for rates, reservations, and directions.

Marjorie Young

Unwinding from city strees at *Harbin* can mean anything from silent soaks and massages out under the trees to a hike on their extensive grounds and decorating your body with clay.

Erana

Marjorie Young

Phil Wilcox

Courtesy of Wilbur Hot Springs

616 WILDERNESS HOT SPRINGS
PO Box 1558   888-538-2370

■ **Middletown, CA 95461**

Very remote, 294-acre, geothermally-active property in Lake County between Middletown and Lower Lake in the very beautiful Jerusalem Canyon. Groups from two to twelve are offered private camping, hiking and soaking opportunities. Use of the facilities is free with purchase of any massage/healing session. Elevation 1,500 feet. Open all year; road may be impassable in wet weather.

Water from several natural mineral water springs is piped to a seven-person fiberglass tub located alongside a picturesque running stream. The water temperature is about 97°. A propane heater can be used to boost the water temperature if desired. Clothing is optional based on the desires of those present.

A campground with picnic tables and barbeques is located on the premises. Massage and other services are offered. Also offered are guided mountain bike tours and hiking. Plans for the future include a cold pool, swimming pool, workshop building, and a small communal kitchen. Call for status. It is 15 miles to all other services in Middletown, and 14 miles to services in Lower Lake. The rugged 1.5 mile road to the property requires a 4WD vehicle. If necessary, transportation is provided from a gated parking area to the campground.

Phone for information and reservations.

GPS: N 38.5005 W 112.2843

617 WILBUR HOT SPRINGS
3375 Wilbur Springs Rd.   916 473-2306

■ **Williams, CA 95987**

A self-styled "Health Sanctuary" twenty two miles from the nearest town, with an abundance of hot mineral water. The large, soaking pools, sundecks, and restored turn-of-the-century hotel are located in the foothills of the western Sacramento Valley. Elevation 1,350 feet. Open all year.

Natural mineral water flows out of several springs at 140°, through a series of large concrete soaking pools under an A-frame structure, and into an outdoor swimming pool. Soaking pool temperatures are approximately 115°, 105° and 95°, with the swimming pool kept warm in the winter and cool in the summer. The water is not chemically treated. Bathing suits are optional in pool areas, required elsewhere.

Massage, rooms, dormitory, and communal kitchen are available on the premises. Visa and MasterCard are accepted. It is twenty two miles to a restaurant, store and service station.

Note: Please, no drop-in visitors. Phone first for reservations and confirmation of services or uses.

Directions: From Interstate 5 in Williams, go west on CA 20 to the intersection with CA 16. A few yards west of that intersection, take gravel road heading north and west for approximately 5 miles and follow signs to the springs.

618   VICHY HOT SPRINGS RESORT AND INN
2605 Vichy Springs Rd.

707 462-9515

FAX 707 462-9516   vichy@pacific.net

■   **Ukiah, CA 95842**

The only Vichy baths in North America. Historic, beautifully restored resort in the Ukiah Valley foothills of Mendocino County. Famous for its warm and naturally carbonated mineral water which will soon be bottled and sold to the public. Guests are invited to explore the 700-acre ranch where wildlife abounds. Elevation 800 feet. Open all year.

Naturally carbonated mineral water flows out of the million-year-old springs at 90° and through redwood pipes to ten enclosed, two-person concrete soaking tubs from the 1860s. Tubs are drained and filled after each use, so no chemical treatment is necessary. One large, communal soaking tub in which the water is treated with ozone is heated to 104°. The Olympic-size swimming pool contains ozone-treated mineral water maintained at approximately 80° during the summer. All tubs and pools are available to the public for day use and to registered guests at any time.

Facilities include a tree-shaded, five-acre central lawn ringed by country-style cottages and rooms, overnight parking for self-contained RVs, a tree-ringed pond, a running stream, and a thirty-minute hike to a lovely waterfall. Massage and facials and bed and breakfast are available by reservation on the premises. Credit cards accepted. It is five miles to a campground and four miles to the center of Ukiah.

Phone, fax, or e-mail for brochure, rates, reservations, and directions.

Courtesy of Vichy Springs

Built in 1854, this cottage is one of the oldest structures in all of Mendocino County. *Vichy* has hosted such famous persons as Mark Twain, Jack London, Ulysses Grant and Teddy Roosevelt. This historical landmark provides fun and relaxation.

Jayson Loam

Courtesy of Vichy Springs

Courtesy of Vichy Springs

619 CRABTREE HOT SPRINGS

● **East of the town of Upper Lake**

Natural hot pools adjacent to a creek-fed stream with a cold swimming hole for a quick plunge. Located in a remote, beautiful rock canyon in Mendocino National Forest. Elevation 2,400 feet. Open all year; roads impassable during wet weather.

Natural mineral water flows out of the ground at approximately 106° into three volunteer-built pools. The first pool uses sandbags and rock to keep the cold creek water out and accommodates six to eight persons. The second pool built with rock and cement and located about three feet above the creek-fed swimming hole is just right for two and is drainable. The third pool located at the west end of the swimming hole and built of sandbags and rocks, will accommodate ten to twelve people. Depending on air temperature, water varies between 98-104°.

There are no services on the premises, although overnight camping is not prohibited. It is approximately four miles to Bear Creek Campground (uphill from springs and left at "T"). All other services are twenty miles away in Upper Lake.

Directions: From Hwy 20 in Upper Lake proceed east on Main St. Turn right at Second St. and take first left onto Middle Creek Rd. (Ranger station on left at 1 mile.) Note odometer. Continue straight from ranger station on Elk Mountain Rd. Middle Creek Campground is at 7.8 miles. (Good spring drinking water on left at 8.2 miles.) At 11.1 miles, bear right onto dirt road 16N20. Sign says "Warning. Road not maintained for passenger car use," but any vehicles except very low clearance cars are okay. Only 4 WD vehicles in wet weather. AT 15.1 bear right toward French Ridge on 16N01. At 17.9 miles bear left uphill on 17N11 (French Ridge) about 6 more miles and turn left at "T" toward Bear Creek. Park .8 miles further at the confluence of two creeks and walk .25 miles downstream to the springs.

Note: As the springs are on private property, please make a special effort to keep the area clean.

Source map: *Mendocino National Forest.*
GPS: N 39.1743 W 122.4930

Photos by Phil Wilcox

Crabtree is one of the more beautiful series of wilderness pools in California. The surrounding terrain is somewhat fragile so please be careful with vehicles and any other activities so that your presence does not impact the environment.

Phil Wilcox

Phil Wilcox

620 SARATOGA SPRINGS RETREAT
10234 Saratoga Springs Rd.
800 655-7153

■ **Upper Lake, CA 95485**

Beautiful conference center and lodge situated on 260 acres in a private valley heavily treed with old oaks, and black walnut trees in an area of plateaus, hills, and mountains. Elevation 1,400 feet. Open all year. Reservation only.

Twelve cold mineral wells supply water to the resort, the swimming pool maintained at ambient temperatures, and the eight- by seventeen- by four-foot hot pool where the water is boosted by propane heat. The pools are treated minimally with bromine and an ozonation process. Hot soda mineral baths are also available. Bathing suits are optional, depending on those present. A new building is handicap accessible.

Lodge, cabins, rooms, areas for camping, meeting rooms, fully equipped kitchen (you cook, or they do by prior arrangement), sweat lodge, and sauna are all available on the premises. Amenities for conferences, workshops, and seminars are being built, along with several outdoor soaking tubs. All other services are in Upper Lake. Credit cards accepted.

Location: Four miles north of Upper Lake or 21 miles east of Ukiah on Hwy 20.

621 ORR HOT SPRINGS
13201 Orr Springs Rd.   707 462-6277
■ **Ukiah, CA 95482**

A small, tranquil resort nestled in the rolling hills of the Mendocino Coastal Range. Located on a wooded creek under Douglas fir and madrones, thirty-one miles inland from Mendocino. Elevation 800 feet. Open all year. Reservations only.

Natural mineral water flows out of several springs at 100° and is piped to a swimming pool, an indoor soaking pool, and four bathtubs in private rooms. The swimming pool averages 70°. The indoor tub and outdoor soaking pool are housed in a bathhouse built in 1858. Some of the water is heated to 105° and pumped to an enclosed redwood tub that overflows into an adjoining shallow outdoor soaking pool famed for stargazing. All pools operate on a flow-through basis, so no chemical treatment is added. Clothing is optional in all bathing areas. Handicap- (wheelchair) accessible areas being added.

Facilities include a fully equipped kitchen, rooms, hostel-style accommodations, small cottages with kitchens, tent spaces along the creek, car camping, and one dry and one wet sauna. Massage is available by reservation. No pets are allowed, and there is a strict policy regarding the child-to-adult ratio. Visa and MasterCard are accepted. The entire facility can be rented. It is thirteen miles of steep and winding roads to all other services in Ukiah.

Directions: From Route 101 in Ukiah, take the North State Street exit, drive .25 mile north to Orr Springs Road, turn west, and drive 13 miles to the resort.

GPS N 39.1349 W 123.2202

622   SWEETWATER SPA AND INN

955 Ukiah St.   707 937-4140

❏   Mendocino, CA 95460

A peaceful and elegant combination of soothing red-wood hot tubs, steaming saunas, fine woodwork and stained glass. Elevation near sea level. Open all year.

Pools are for rent to the public and use gas-heated tap water treated with bromine. One private enclosure with a sauna can be rented by the hour. The water temperature is maintained at 104°. One communal hydropool is available at a day-rate charge. The water temperature is maintained at 104°, and a sauna is included.

Special features: Sweetwater has a variety of unique lodging options, including ocean view units, cottages, and romantic water tower rooms. One private suite can be rented by the hour and also by the night, and a sauna is included. One deluxe Oriental room with spa, ocean view, fireplace, and private sun deck offers privacy and romance. All room rentals include use of tubs. Bathing suits are optional everywhere except in the front office. Professional massage offering a wide range of body work is available on the premises. Visa and MasterCard are accepted.

Note: The management has access to several other wonderful housing options in the area. Phone for rates, reservations, and directions.

623   FINNISH COUNTRY SAUNA & TUBS

5th and J St.   707 822-2228

❏   Arcata, CA 95521

A charming pond surrounded by grass-roofed Finnish style saunas, private outdoor hot tubs, and a European-style coffeehouse in a small Northern California coastal town. Elevation 50 feet. Open every day except Christmas.

Tubs are for rent to the public and use gas-heated tap water treated with bromine. There are six private Burmese teak wood hot tubs rented by the half-hour and maintained at 104°. The conical tubs have benches all the way around and jets at three different levels. Clothing is optional in private spaces.

Facilities include two private sauna cabins and Caffe Mokka, a coffeehouse serving espresso and juices with live folk music on the weekends. No credit cards are accepted. Phone for rates, reservations, and directions.

Jayson Loam

CENTRAL CALIFORNIA

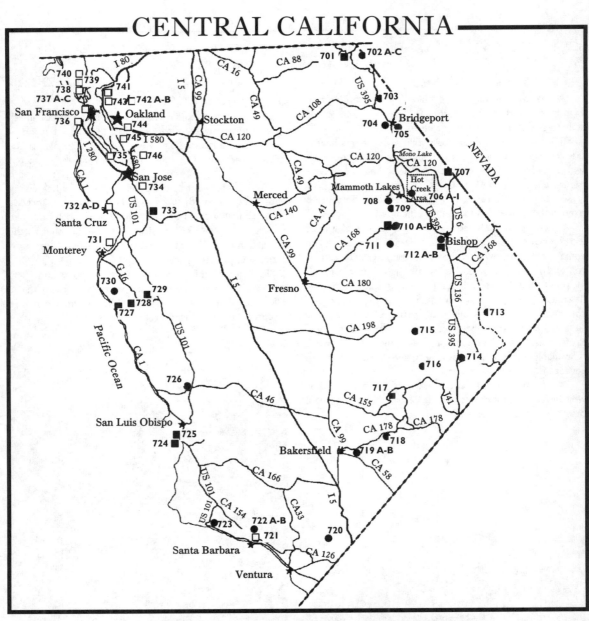

This map was designed to be used with a standard highway map.

MAP SYMBOLS

● Non-commercial mineral water pool

■ Commercial (fee) mineral water pool

□ Tap water resorts and rental locations

⌒ Paved highway

- - - Unpaved road

∙∙∙∙∙ Hiking trail

701   GROVER HOT SPRINGS
Box 188   916 694-2248
■ Markleeville, CA 96120

Swimming pool and soaking pool next to a major state campground and picnic area, located in a wooded mountain valley. Elevation 6,000 feet. Open all year.

Natural mineral water flows out of several springs at 147° and into a holding pond from which it is piped to the pool area. The soaking pool, using natural mineral water treated with bromine, is maintained at approximately 103°. The swimming pool, using creek water treated with chlorine, is maintained at 70-80°. A heat exchanger is used to simultaneously cool down the mineral water and warm up the creek water. Admission is on a first-come, first-served basis, and the official capacity limit of fifty persons in the hot pool and twenty-five in the cold pool is reached early every day during the summer. Bathing suits are required. For handicap accessibility there is a ramp to the pool, although there is not one into the pool.

Campground spaces are available by prior reservation, as with all other California state parks. Cross-country skiers are encouraged to camp in the picnic area during the winter and to ski in to use the soaking pool. The road is also plowed during the winter making for easy access. It is four miles to the nearest restaurant, motel, and service station in Markleeville.

Location: On Alpine County Road E4, 4.5 miles west of Markleeville. Follow the signs.

Photos by Mark Gillespie

In summer, as big as this hot soaking pool is, it fills up very quickly. In winter, skiing or driving in lets you soak almost by yourself.

Three wonderful hot springs with beautiful mountain views are to be found along the banks of the East Fork of the Carson River in Toiyabe National Forest. The springs are accessible during the rafting season, approximately May through July, depending on water flow. Elevation 5,000 feet.

There are no services available at any of the hot spring sites. While the apparent local custom at the pools is clothing optional, please be respectful of those people already there. These springs are not shown on any Forest Service or USGS map but are well known to raft trip guides.

While you can navigate this river yourself if you are an experienced kayaker, for a real treat, one- and two-day raft trips (Class 2 rapids) are available through commercial outfitters. We had a wonderful trip with River Adventures and More (RAM), PO Box 5283, Reno, NV 89513, 800 466-RAFT.

702 A   RIVERSIDE HOT SPRING

● **Near the town of Markleeville**

Approximately eight miles downstream from where you put into the water three small pools are visible from the river on your right (east). Natural mineral water flows into the upper pool at approximately 92° and then continues flowing into the lower pools. The lower tub has been lined with a tarp by some volunteers. During high water these pools are often underwater and need to be rebuilt annually.

Camping is possible near the springs.

Photos by Marjorie Young

702 B   RIVER RUN HOT SPRINGS

● **Near the town of Markleeville**

Natural mineral water emerges from several springs on the hillside at 110° or hotter and cools as it flows toward the river. The temperature of the water drops to approximately 100° by the time it reaches the large shallow pool near an eight-foot cliff at the river's edge. The small upper pools are quite hot and should be approached with caution. When the river water is low, it is possible to stand in your boat under the water coming off the cliffs.

There is a large open area available for camping, but there are no facilities except an outhouse near the springs.

Jayson Loam

Depending on the river level and the amount of water flow you could just shower in your raft, or for a more relaxing soak, walk up to the large pool on the top which overlooks the river.

Marjorie Young

702 C   HOT SHOWERBATH

● **Near the town of Markleeville**

One mile downstream from River Run Hot Springs, a small pullout is visible on the left (west). Follow the warm ooze about 500 yards up into the canyon, where natural mineral water flows out of a spring at 110° and cools to approximately 98° before dropping over a twenty-foot bank into a warm, squishy-bottomed pool.

Marjorie Young

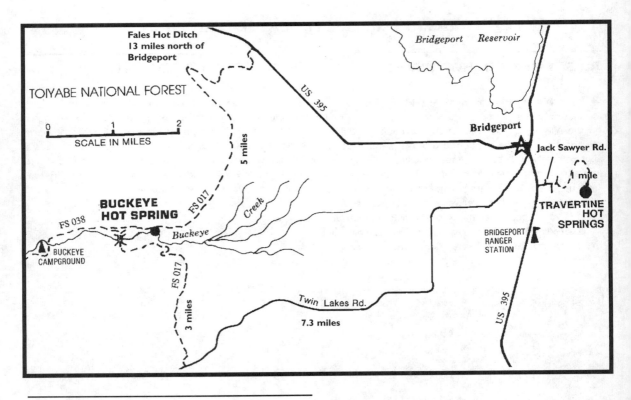

Fales Hot Ditch
13 miles north of
Bridgeport

TOIYABE NATIONAL FOREST

Bridgeport Reservoir

US 395

0   1   2
SCALE IN MILES

5 miles

Bridgeport

Jack Sawyer Rd.

1 mile

TRAVERTINE
HOT
SPRINGS

FS 017

Creek

BUCKEYE
HOT SPRING

FS 038

Buckeye

BUCKEYE
CAMPGROUND

BRIDGEPORT
RANGER
STATION

FS 017

3 miles

Twin Lakes Rd.

7.3 miles

US 395

703   FALES HOT DITCH

● **North of the town of Bridgeport**

A primitive pool on Hot Springs Creek in the sagebrush foothills of the Eastern Sierra. Elevation 7,200 feet. Open all year.

Natural mineral water emerges at 140° from a spring on the property of an old resort, now closed, and flows down Hot Springs Creek, gradually cooling as it goes. Volunteers have dammed the creek to form a thigh-deep, rock-and-sand pool on the east side of the highway .3 mile past the old resort (which is on the west side of the highway). Although the soaking pool is twenty feet below the highway and out of sight of passing vehicles, it is advisable to wear a bathing suit or have it close at hand.

There are no services on the premises. It is seven miles to a Forest Service campground and thirteen miles to all other services in Bridgeport.

GPS: N 38.2103 W 119.2402

Directions: From Bridgeport, drive north on US 395 for 13 miles to a boarded-up, fenced, brown wooden structure that used to be Fales Hot Springs Resort (on the west side of US 395). The gated property just north of the old resort is private and posted "no trespassing." However, from the old resort, drive .3 mile north and park along the shoulder of US 395 on the east side of the road. The creek and soaking pool are 20 feet below the highway (not visible until you park and look over the small cliff).

GPS: N 38.35253 W119.40484

Justine Hill

704 BUCKEYE HOT SPRING
(see map on page 126)

● **Near the town of Bridgeport**

Delightful hot spring in a superb natural setting on the north bank of Buckeye Creek in Toiyabe National Forest. One of the best. Elevation 6,900 feet. Open all year; not accessible by road in winter.

Natural mineral water flows out of the ground at 135°, runs over a large cliff built up by mineral deposits, and drops into the creek. Volunteers have built loosely constructed rock pools along the edge of the creek below the hot waterfall. The pool temperature is controlled by admitting more or less cold water from the creek.

There is another small outflow of hot geothermal water on the bluff near the parking area. Volunteers have dug a shallow soaking pool that maintains a temperature of approximately 100°. It is near the foot of a tree located in the upstream direction from the parking area. The apparent local custom at both pools is clothing optional.

Three hundred yards upstream from the parking area are several acres of unmarked open space on which overnight parking is not prohibited. It is one mile to a Forest Service campground and nine miles to a restaurant, motel, store, and service station in Bridgeport.

There are no services on the premises. There is a parking turnout on the south side of the road on the bluff above the springs.

Directions: (This is the easier route.) At the north end of Bridgeport, take Twin Lakes Road west for 7.3 miles to Doc & Al's Resort. Turn right (north) onto FS 017, a two-lane, graded, washboard road, for 3 miles to the second bridge over the creek, where the road intersects with FS 038 toward Buckeye Campground to the left. Branch off to the right for a few hundred yards up a short hill on the north branch of FS 017 to a large flat parking clearing on a big knoll. The upper pool is a few steps away (slightly downhill and to the right) under a tree, at the crest of the knoll overlooking Buckeye Creek. Several unofficial paths lead down the slope to the pools located along the creek at the foot of a large mound covered over by the mineral deposits.

Source maps: *Toiyabe National Forest; USGS Matterhorn Peak.*

GPS: N 38.23973 W 119.32613

The fellow to the right has relaxation down to a fine art. He put his lounge chair into the small, upper pool in order to soak and read at the same time.

Top photo by Jayson Loam
Bottom photo by Chris Andrews

Along with these soaking pools by the river, there is a small cave (to the left under the overhang) where the water drips off the roof forming a soaking area.

705   TRAVERTINE HOT SPRINGS
(see map on page 126)

● **Southeast of the town of Bridgeport**

An unusual group of volunteer-built soaking pools on large travertine ridges with commanding views of the High Sierra. Located two miles from the center of Bridgeport. Elevation 6,700 feet. Open all year.

The flow of natural mineral water (130-160°) out of several geothermal fissures can be interrupted or shifted to a new outlet by underground movement resulting from local earthquakes. The scalding water is channeled to a series of volunteer-built soaking pools in which the individual pool temperatures are controlled by temporarily diverting the hot water inflow as needed. The upper pool is handicap accessible with assistance. The apparent local custom is clothing optional.

At the upper ten- by five- by two-foot pool, scalding water bubbles up from under large rocks and is directed through a stepped channel with a "bear claw" configuration at pool's edge. The source can be capped to control pool temperature. There is a plug for draining and cleaning the pool, which is done fastidiously by volunteers. Overflow goes into a small adjoining foot bath for rinsing off before entering the pool. Since you can drive right up to this pool it is handicap accessible with assistance.

Three lower rock-and-cement pools, one hundred yards below, are at the foot of a large granite boulder where water seeps up through the rock and gently trickles into the pools at 100°. A primitive 80° rock-and-mud pool nearby is fed by a separate underground source.

There are no services and overnight camping is not permitted. Port-a-potties have been installed. Other primitive amenities include a large deck around the pools covered with old carpets for sunbathing, a wooden bench, and "butt cans." There is no trash collection, so please pack it out. All other services are available in Bridgeport.

Directions: From the Ranger Station .5 mile south of Bridgeport, drive north on Hwy 395 for .2 mile. Turn right on Jack Sawyer Rd., the first paved road on your right. At .4 mile the paved road makes a 90-degree turn to the right. Do not bear right. Continue straight ahead on the unpaved, ungraded road for approximately 1 mile to the pools. On the way you will pass a sign on your left to Bridgeport Barrow Pit; continue straight to the forest service sign on your left. Across from this on the right is a turnoff to a flat camping area. If you continue straight, the second turnoff just ahead on the right leads to the lower pools. Or continue uphill to where the road curves around to the right to reach the upper cement pool.

GPS: N 38.24548 W 119.20539

Photos by Justine Hill

Luis Gonzales

Chris Andrews

Two of the pools, which don't seem to be affected by the constant small earthquakes in the area, have been cemented in, making them more easily available for handicap access. The other pools still have to be rebuilt occasionally based on the latest tremors.

"BIG HOT" WARM SPRINGS

● **Near the town of Bridgeport**
This hot spring is located on private property and has now been closed to the public. People did not follow the simple request to shut the cattle gates to and from the spring. Trespassers will be shot.

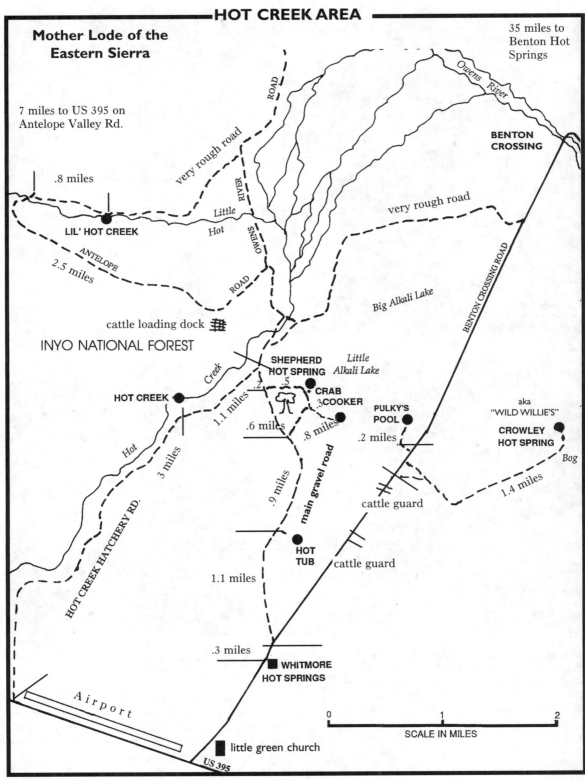

**Mother Lode of the
Eastern Sierra**

35 miles to
Benton Hot
Springs

7 miles to US 395 on
Antelope Valley Rd.

ROAD

very rough road

Owens River

BENTON
CROSSING

.8 miles

Little

Hot

OWENS

RIVER

very rough road

LIL' HOT CREEK

ANTELOPE

2.5 miles

ROAD

BENTON CROSSING ROAD

Big Alkali Lake

cattle loading dock

INYO NATIONAL FOREST

Creek

SHEPHERD
HOT SPRING

.2 .5

Little
Alkali Lake

HOT CREEK

Hot

CRAB
COOKER

.3

PULKY'S
POOL

aka
"WILD WILLIE'S"

CROWLEY
HOT SPRING

Bog

1.1 miles

.6 miles

.8 miles

.2 miles

3 miles

.9 miles

main gravel road

1.4 miles

cattle guard

HOT CREEK HATCHERY RD.

HOT
TUB

cattle guard

1.1 miles

cattle guard

.3 miles

■ WHITMORE
HOT SPRINGS

Airport

0   1   2
SCALE IN MILES

■ little green church

US 395

Steve Heerema

706 A   HOT CREEK

(see map on page 130)

● **East of the town of Mammoth Lakes**

Primarily a geologic observation and interpretive site with some limited use by bathers. Open daylight hours only.

Natural mineral water with a slight sulfur smell emerges from many fissures as steam or boiling water, and several danger areas have been fenced off for safety. Substantial amounts of boiling, geo-thermal water also flow up from the bottom of the creek. A bend in the creek provides a natural eddy in which the mixing of hot and cold water stays within a range of 50° to 110°. Those who venture into this confluence experience vivid thermal skin effects, but they must be careful to avoid the geothermal vents because of the danger of scalding. The trail from the main pool goes upstream 400-500 feet where cold water is diverted around other hot spots in the river. Bathing suits are required.

In the past, night use of this location has resulted in many injuries and some fatalities, so the area may be used only from sunrise to sunset. Citations are issued by the Forest Service to anyone found there after sunset or before sunrise. During the winter, when snow blocks the access road, skiers and hikers may still enter the area during daylight hours.

Facilities include men's and women's changing rooms, pit toilets, and an asphalt parking area with a paved, fenced pathway down to the creek, making the area handicap accessible with assistance. Overnight parking is prohibited. It is ten miles to all services in the town of Mammoth Lakes.

Directions: From US 395, 3 miles south of the Mammoth Lakes turnoff, turn east on Hot Creek Hatchery Road/Airport. At .8 mile, turn right at the sign to "Hot Creek Geothermal Area." From this sign, it is 3 miles to the parking area for Hot Creek. Only the first 1.2 miles are paved. Or, from Benton Crossing Road, take 3S50, the main gravel road, for 2.8 miles. Turn left for .3 miles to the Hot Creek gate and another .8 mile to the parking area.

Source maps: *Inyo National Forest*, USGA *Mt. Morrison*. GPS: N 37.66049 W 118.82834

Bill Franks

Steve Heerema

706 B LIL' HOT CREEK
(see map on page 130)

● **East of the town of Mammoth Lakes**

A very hot flowing creek fed by a 180° geothermal spring. The name Lil' Hot Creek has been given to a large, squishy-bottom soaking pool located just below where the flow from several cold springs cools the hot stream to approximately 107°. The thigh-deep cement-and-rock pool has tiered seats so you can soak at different depths. Pool temperature can be controlled by opening or capping a four-inch plastic pipe that brings the water in from the nearby creek. There's a plug for draining and cleaning the pool. Spillover goes through a tiny channel back to the creek. As you leave, please shut the inflow of hot water so the next ones in will not be scalded.

Plenty of level ground, as well as hideaway spots among the pine trees in the nearby national forest, are available where overnight parking is not prohibited. The apparent local custom is clothing optional.

Directions: There are four routes, depending on your starting point.

1. From the main gravel road (3S50), drive a total of 3.3 miles to the sign for Owens River Road. (This is .7 mile past the turnoff to Shepherd.) You'll pass a cattle loading dock on the left just before Owens River Road. Turn left for .7 mile to Little Antelope Road. Turn left onto Antelope Road for 2.5 miles across a flat open area. At 2.5 miles, at the beginning of the pine forest, is a cattle guard. Make a sharp right just past the cattle guard and follow this very rough, ungraded dirt road for .8 mile to the springs on your right. Whenever the road forks, keep bearing right, following the fence until you come to a flat open area for parking. You'll see steam rising from the creek to your right as you follow the fence. At the parking area, look for a small wooden portion in the wire fence and a cattle-proof entrance. Go through the gate and over log planks across the creek to reach the hot soaking pool.

2. Take Hot Creek Hatchery Road from US 395 for 3 miles to the Hot Creek asphalt parking area. Continue past the parking area for another 1.1 miles to a fork in the unpaved road. Do not bear right, but continue straight ahead for another .1 mile to where the road ends at a wide gravel road. This is 3S50, the main gravel road. Turn left, and on your left you'll see the cattle loading dock mentioned above. Follow directions above.

3. A very beautiful but much longer drive begins at US 395. At the turnoff to Mammoth Lake, instead of heading west toward the lakes, turn east and follow the sign to Little Antelope Valley (not Chalk Hills). At 6.3 miles you will be at the cattle guard at the edge of the pine forest. Turn left onto the ungraded dirt road and follow the fence as described above to reach the soaking pool.

4. For those with 4WD vehicles, or at least with good clearance, continue past the turnoff to Antelope Road another 1.3 miles and turn left. Follow the washboard road 2 miles to the springs, which are now on the left.

GPS: N 37.89027 W 118.84259

Photos by Steve Heerema

It's between you and the cow as to who soaks first.

706 C SHEPHERD HOT SPRING
(see map on page 130)

● **East of the town of Mammoth Lakes**

Natural mineral water flows out of a spring at 107° and through a hose to a twenty by twenty-four inch deep rock-and-cement tub. There are benches in the pool, which is large enough for three or four people. Pool temperature is controlled by diverting the hot water flow from the nearby source pool. The black plastic inflow pipe can be elevated by inserting the iron pipe underneath it. There is a plug for draining the pool, capped with a tennis ball. However, local volunteers prefer emptying the pool with a bucket before scrubbing. A scrub-brush is on site.

There are no facilities except a primitive campfire ring. A posted sign prohibits overnight parking. The apparent local custom is clothing optional.

Directions: From Benton Crossing Road, turn north on 3S50 (the main gravel road) .3 mile past the Whitmore public swimming pool. Drive 2.6 miles to a dirt road on your right. Follow this across an open bog for .5 mile to the pool on your left.

From Crab Cooker, follow the dirt road back the way you came in for .5 mile to a four-way, dirt-road intersection. To reach Shepherd, turn right at this intersection and go .2 mile to the small clearing where the pool is located.

GPS: N 37.66649 W 118.80367

706 D CRAB COOKER
(see map on page 130)

● **East of the town of Mammoth Lakes**

Natural mineral water flows out of a spring at over 120° and through a pipe to a rock-and-cement soaking pool. The pool temperature can be controlled by turning off a valve in the pipe inside the pool when the desired soaking temperature is reached. (Please turn off this valve when leaving so as not to scald the next soakers.) Do not tamper with the pipes in the nearby well, as special plumbing equipment is required to fix them.

There are no facilities on the premises. The apparent local custom is clothing optional.

Directions: Follow the main gravel road for 2 miles from Benton Crossing Road (.9 mile past the turnoff to Hot Tub). Watch for a lone juniper tree on the right side of the road. The road to Crab Cooker is on the right just before this tree. Two separate roads appear to head off to the right, but they merge after a short oval and continue as a rocky, one-lane dirt road for .1 mile to a large white mound of rocks. Follow the road around the left side of these rocks for another .2 mile to a four-way dirt-road intersection. Continue straight for another .5 mile across cow pastures to where the road ends at a flat open area where you will see the pool.

GPS: N 37.66292 W 118.80845

Phil Wilcox

The snow at *Pulky's Pool* didn't deter these soakers. The pool is only one-quarter of a mile from the road, making it an easy walk even with the snow on the ground.

706 E   DAVE'S WARM TUB

● **East of the town of Mammoth Lakes**
As of 1995, there was no longer a tub here and the existing water is only 80° in a shallow, algae-laden seep.

706 F   PULKY'S POOL
(see map on page 130)

● **East of the town of Mammoth Lakes**
Natural mineral water flows out of a spring at 131° and through one pipe to a free-form, rock-and-cement pool up on the plateau, offering a spectacular view of the Sierras. This pool features a very smooth surface and a drain to facilitate easy cleaning. A second pipe admits cold water from a nearby pond allowing for temperature control.

Primitive facilities include a small carpeted deck for undressing and sunbathing, and a cement bench. The area is posted for day use only; no overnight parking is permitted. The apparent local custom is clothing optional.

Directions: From US 395, drive 2 miles past Whitmore Pool over one cattle guard to the second cattle guard. The turnoff to Crowley, 706-G, is just past the second cattle guard on the right (south). For Pulkey's, continue on Benton Crossing Road for another .2 mile to an unpaved road on the left (north). Follow this road as it curves around a large alkali field for .4 mile to a flat parking area and park by fence. The pool is up on the plateau. Caution: Do not attempt to drive to the plateau; even 4WD vehicles have become stuck in the soft ground.
GPS: N 37.66410 W 118.78344

706G CROWLEY HOT SPRING (ALSO KNOWN AS WILD WILLIE'S)

(see map on page 130)

● **East of the town of Mammoth Lakes**

Natural mineral water flows out of a spring and down a small creek channel at 110°, then into a cement pool large enough for 30 people. Construction of such a pool was made possible by the 1983 earthquake, which substantially increased the flow of geothermal water in the creek. No temperature control is necessary because surface cooling keeps the pool temperature about 103° most of the year.

Fifty feet away, at the foot of a large rock outcropping, is a mud-bottom pool at approximately 100°, formed by a dam across the creek. Natural mineral water flows from a separate source near the rock into this knee-deep pool. The pool is large enough for a half-dozen people. The apparent local custom for both pools is clothing optional.

There are no facilities on the premises, but overnight parking is not prohibited in the large parking area.

Directions: From Benton Crossing Road, drive 2 miles past Whitmore Pool. Immediately past the second cattle guard, two rough dirt roads cut off to the right. Take either one (they join up) and drive 1.1 mile to a large rock. Follow the road to the right side of the rock and take an immediate left at the fork. Drive .3 mile to a large level parking area bordered by logs. Do not attempt to drive any farther. To reach the pools, follow the trail from the end of the parking area for approximately 250 yards to where it joins a trail from the opposite direction and a path leading down a small hill to the left. The primitive pool is under some trees near the big rock ahead on your left; the pool with the deck is ahead on the right.

Caution: Do not attempt to drive across the bog to the pool area. Even 4WD's have been trapped.

GPS: N 37.66097 W 118.76776

The top pool is one of the only ones in the area large enough to hold a group. The pool below is much smaller but provides an all-over mud treatment.

Photos by Marjorie Young

706 H HOT TUB

(see map on page 130)

● **East of the town of Mammoth Lakes**

Natural mineral water flows out of a spring at 110° and through a hose to a three-foot-deep rock-and-cement pool. The pool temperature is controlled by diverting the hot water inflow whenever the desired soaking temperature has been reached. There is a plug for draining, and the pool is kept clean by a group of local volunteers. The thigh-deep pool can hold about six people comfortably.

There are no facilities, but there is plenty of level area surrounding the pool, and overnight parking is not prohibited. Campers, please be considerate of others. Park away from the tubs, and keep the noise level down. The apparent local custom is clothing optional.

Directions: From Benton Crossing Road, drive 1.1 miles on 3S50 (the main gravel road) to the second one-lane dirt road on the right. Turn right and go for .1 mile to a clearing, then bear left for another .1 mile to the pool.

GPS: N 37.64712 W 118.80742

706 I WHITMORE HOT SPRINGS

(see map on page 130)

PO Box 1609   760 935-4222

■ **Mammoth Lakes, CA 93546**

Large, conventional public swimming pool jointly operated by Mono County and the town of Mammoth Lakes on land leased from the Los Angeles Department of Water and Power. Open during the day, Monday through Saturday, approximately mid-June to Labor Day.

Natural mineral water is pumped from a well at 90° and piped to the swimming pool where it is treated with chlorine. Depending on air temperature and wind conditions, the pool water temperature averages 82°. An adjoining shallow wading pool averages 92°. Bathing suits are required. Bathrooms, showers, and slide-gate entrance are handicap accessible.

A small access fee includes showers (campers take note) and a barbeque area. A full aquatic schedule is available on the premises. Parking is permitted only during hours of operation. No credit cards are accepted.

Photos on this page by Marjorie Young

located across the street. No camping is permitted anywhere in the town of Benton Hot Springs, which is all privately owned. It is four miles to a campground/RV park and store in the town of Benton, and fifteen miles to a motel, restaurant, and casino north on US 6 at the state line.

Directions: From Bishop, take US 6 north for 36 miles to the tiny town of Benton. Turn west on CA 120 and drive 4 miles until you see the old green and white house on the north side of the street. Or, from US 395 in Lee Vining (Tioga Pass from Yosemite), take CA 120 east for 46 miles to Benton Hot Springs. If you are coming from the series of natural springs outside Mammoth, take Benton Crossing Road south of the Mammoth Airport for 36 miles to where it ends at CA 120. Take 120 east for 3 miles to Benton Hot Springs.

707 THE OLD HOUSE AT BENTON HOT SPRINGS

Rte. 4, Box 58   **760 933-2507**

■ **Benton, CA 93512**

A group of redwood tubs were cut from an old redwood pipeline that used to go to the generating plant. The tubs are on the property of an historic 1860s house now selling arts, crafts, antiques, and collectibles. The tubs are located in an oasis-type setting under cottonwood, Russian olive, tamarisk, and locust trees in high desert and sagebrush-type country along the eastern border of California near the Nevada state line, with views of Montgomery and Boundary Peaks (highest points in Nevada). Elevation: 5,500 feet. Pools are rented by the hour, and reservations are suggested. Open all year.

Natural, soft, silky mineral water flows out of a spring at 135° and supplies water to the entire town of Benton Hot Springs. A cooling/evaporation tank at The Old House provides the only cool water in town. There is no chemical treatment of the water in the tubs. The four tubs, located under the trees, are drained and scrubbed with bleach after each use. Each tub has a hot and cold faucet to adjust water temperature. The five-foot diameter tubs are about three feet deep, have seats inside, and are large enough for four to six people. Bathing suits are optional in the tubs, which are separated by hedges. Owners request that nudity be discreet and only at the tubs.

Facilities include snacks and beverages. A gas pump is

The small wooden hut in the background provides a private place to change and to keep your clothes.

Photos by Steve Heerema

708   RED'S MEADOW HOT SPRINGS

● **In Red's Meadow Campground near Devil's Postpile National Monument**

Tin-roof shed with six cement shower-over bath tubs in six small private rooms, on the edge of a mountain meadow campground. Elevation 7,000 feet. Open approximately Memorial Day to September 20.

Natural mineral water flows out of the ground at 100°, into a storage tank, and then by pipe into the bathhouse. Depending on the use, water temperature out of the shower heads will vary from 90-100°. No charge is made for the use of the tubs, which are available on a first-come, first-served basis.

In summer, all water from the spring is diverted into the bathhouse. During the winter, the cement hot water storage tank is used for soaking and can only be reached by snowmobiles and cross-country skiers.

A Forest Service campground, open during the summer, adjoins the hot springs. It is four miles to a cafe, general store, rustic cabins, and pack station at Red's Meadow Resort, and twelve miles to an RV park and other services in Mammoth Lakes.

Directions: From the town of Mammoth Lakes, take CA 203 west to the end, then follow signs through Minaret Pass to Devil's Postpile National Monument and to Red's Meadow Campground. Note: During the day in summer, private vehicles are prohibited beyond Minaret Pass. A frequent shuttle bus service originates at Mammoth Mountain Inn.

Source map: *Inyo National Forest*. USGS *Devil's Postpile*.

709   IVA BELL (FISH CREEK HOT SPRINGS)

● **South of Devil's Postpile National Monument**

A delightful cluster of volunteer-built soaking pools, some with spectacular views of the wilderness. Elevation 7,200 feet. Open all year.

This location adjoins the Iva Bell camp area which includes numerous camping sites separated by meadows and stands of pines. The two main soaking pools are not visible from the main camping area but are to be found fifty yards east, up and behind an obvious bare rock ledge.

The most popular pool has a nice sandy bottom and is nestled on the back side of this ledge, where a 106° trickle flows out of a fissure slowly enough to maintain a 101° pool temperature in the summertime. A 100° squishy-bottom pool may be reached by following a path thirty yards across a meadow.

From the first pool, another path leads due east for fifty yards to a cozy campsite. From this site, a steep one-hundred-yard path leads up to four more pools, ranging in temperature from 101° to 110°.

The twelve-mile hike (one way) from the road end at Reds Meadow involves an elevation change of 1,000 feet. Detailed directions to such a remote location are beyond the scope of this book. We recommend *Sierra North*, published by Wilderness Press; also consult with the Mammoth Ranger District of Inyo National Forest, 619 934-2505.

Source map: *USGS Devil's Postpile*.

710 A MONO HOT SPRINGS
■ (Summer) Mono Hot Springs, CA 93642
(Winter) Lake Shore, CA 93634
● Northeast of Fresno

A vacation resort offering fishing, hiking, and camping in addition to mineral baths. Located on the south fork of the San Joaquin River near Edison Lake, Florence Lake, and Bear Dam in the Sierra National Forest. Elevation 6,500 feet. Open May to October.

Natural mineral water flows from a spring at 107° and is piped to a bathhouse containing four two-person soaking tubs in private rooms. Tubs have geo-thermal water only, measuring 100-105°. Tubs are drained and refilled after each use, so no chemical treatment of the water is necessary. An outdoor hydrojet pool is maintained at 103-105° and is treated with chlorine. Bathing suits are required except in private rooms. Facilities are available on a day-use basis, as well as to registered guests, and are handicap accessible with assistance.

On the south side of the river directly across from the resort is a series of springs and soaking pools that are open all year, but only to cross-country skiers and snow-mobilers in winter. Water from one spring feeds into a holding tank. From there it is piped across the river to the resort. This tank also feeds a nearby cement soaking tub called "The Coffin" due to its size and shape. A natural, hot water, outdoor shower flows continually from the tank spillover. Along the riverbank are several cement soaking tubs that remain from an historic bathhouse. A rock-and-mud pool is near the cement tubs and another primitive pool, called "The Rock," is next to a large boulder ten feet up the hill from the cement tubs. Pool temperatures are approximately 101°. Bathing suits are advisable in the daytime.

Facilities include a cafe, store, service station, cabins, campground, and RV park. Massage is available on the premises. Visa and MasterCard are accepted.

Directions to the resort: From the city of Fresno on CA 99, go 80 miles northeast on CA 168 to the ranger station at the northeast side of Huntington Lake. Inquire here about road conditions before attempting to drive in. The one lane road is very narrow and winding. Allow at least one hour for this 15-mile stretch.

The cement pools are the remains of an old bath-house locatd across the river from the resort. The pool and buildings below provide a hot soak and a relaxing massage after a day of hiking and fishing.

At 15 miles, you come to the High Sierra Ranger Station. Stop here for info and campfire permits, needed even for cooking in your van. One mile past this station the road forks. Bear left to Mono Hot Springs. At 1 mile, you will cross a small bridge. Continue downhill to a second green bridge. Mono is less than .25 mile past the bridge on your left.

To reach the soaking pools on the south side of the river, park at the pullout just before the green bridge. Proceed through the yellow gate, walking north along the river for approximately 100 yards. "The Rock" is up a small hill to your left, the cement pools a few feet ahead at river level. These pools can also be reached by rock-hopping the San Joaquin River from the resort when the river level is low.

Top photo by Jayson Loam
Bottom photo courtesy of Mono Hot Springs

710 B   LITTLE EDEN

● **Northeast of Fresno**

A primitive, squishy-bottom, thigh-deep pool surrounded by grass and large enough for a dozen people, with a gorgeous view of the surrounding mountains and a real feeling that you are out in nature. Elevation 6,500 feet. Open all year; accessible to cross-country skiers and snowmobilers in the winter.

Natural mineral water bubbles up through the sandy pool bottom at around 100°. Because of its large size, pool temperatures measure only in the nineties. A heavy-duty plastic ladder aids in getting in and out, as the ground around the pool is very slippery. The apparent local custom is clothing optional.

There are no facilities on the premises. Services are less than a mile away at Mono Hot Springs Resort.

Directions: Follow directions given for Mono Hot Springs to the High Sierra ranger station. One mile past the station, park in the turnout just beyond the steel bridge. A steep, unofficial trail to the pool begins on the left (north), approximately 50 feet before the bridge, and goes around a large rock outcropping, through some marshy spots, and down to the pool at the base of the rocks.

The man above was enjoying his first dip in a natural hot spring. The women below had visited this pool many times and thought of it as a favorite.

Top photo by Marjorie Young
Botttom photo by Justine Hill

711 BLANEY HOT SPRINGS

● **Southeast of Florence Lake**

A combination hot spring and mudbath in a grassy High Sierra meadow, 9.5 miles from the road's end at Florence Lake. Elevation 7,600 feet. Open all year.

Natural mineral water oozes up through the squishy bottom of a large pool, maintaining a temperature of approximately 102°, and then flows into a nearby small, warm lake. The apparent custom is clothing optional.

There are no services at this location except nearby backpacker campgrounds. It is ten miles to a store, service station, etc.

The 9.5 mile trail from the road's end has an elevation gain of 1,000 feet and requires fording the South Fork of the San Joaquin River. In the summer it is possible to avoid 3.5 miles of walking by riding the Sierra Queen across the lake. From this part of the John Muir Trail it is only a hike of 1.25 miles down the Florence Lake Trail to reach the springs.

We recommend *Sierra South*, published by Wilderness Press, for detailed directions, or consult the Pine Ridge Ranger District at 209 855-5360.

Nearby is Muir Trail Ranch, which offers rustic log cabin comfort to organized groups on a bring-your-own-food basis. Ranch guests enjoy private rock-and-tile mineral water pools. From the end of the road at Florence Lake, the hiking distance is eight miles. But summer guests can ride the Sierra Queen ferryboat across the lake and then ride ranch horses or four-wheel-drive vehicles the remaining five miles. For information, write the owner, Adeline Smith, Box 176, Lakeshore, CA 93634 from mid-June to October, or Box 269, Ahwanee, CA 93601 in other months.

Source map: USGS *Blackcap Mountain*.

The top pool is the public pool found in Blaney Meadows. The bottom two beautifully designed pools are available to guests at the ranch.

All photos by Bill Ralph

712 A   KEOUGH HOT SPRINGS
Rte. 1, Box 9   619 872-1644
Bishop, CA 93514

Older hot springs resort in the Sierra foothills now set up as a private club requiring membership. It is advisable to phone for current information. Elevation 4,200 feet. Open only when owner is feeling well.

Natural mineral water flows out of the ground at 128° and into the enclosed swimming pool (87-95°) and the wading pool (100°), using flow-through mineral water so that no chlorine needs to be added. Bathing suits are required.

Not services are available on the premises. No credit cards are accepted. It is eight miles to the nearest restaurant, motel, service station and store.

Directions: Go 7 miles south of Bishop on US 395, then follow signs west from US 395.

712 B   KEOUGH HOT DITCH
Near Keough Hot Springs

Runoff from Keough Hot Springs cools as it flows through a series of volunteer-built rock pools in a treeless foothill gully. Elevation 4,100 feet. Open all year.

Natural mineral water flows out of the ground at 128° on the property of Keough Hot Springs, then meanders northeast over BLM land for about a mile before joining with a cold water surface stream. Volunteer-built rock dams create several primitive soaking pools and swimming holes on both sides of the road, each one cooler than the preceding one upstream. The apparent local custom is clothing optional.

No services are available on the premises. The land is posted for day use only, no overnight parking, but reports are that parking for one night is not a problem as long as you leave nothing but tire tracks. Please do not bring any glass objects to the area, since broken glass is the biggest problem at Keough. It is one mile to an RV park and eight miles to a restaurant, store, and service station in Bishop.

Directions: Seven miles south of Bishop on US 395, turn west on Keough Hot Springs Road approximately .6 mile. At the only intersection with a paved road (old US 395), turn north 200 yards to where a cold stream crosses the road. (Note: There is an abundance of level parking space on the north side of the cold stream, but the stream must be forded with care.) Walk an additional 50 yards north to Keough Ditch. Either stream may be followed to where they join, forming a series of warm swimming pools.

GPS: N 37.1534 W 118.2244

These are only two of the soaking areas available to you at *Keough Hot Ditch.*

Photos by Justine Hill

713 SALINE VALLEY HOT SPRINGS
(see photos next page)

● **Northeast of the town of Olancha**

A sometimes crowded, spring-fed oasis located on a barren slope of BLM land in a remote desert valley that has recently been annexed to the western edge of Death Valley. Elevation 1,500 feet. Open all year, but access roads may become impassable during heavy rainstorms.

Natural mineral water flows out of the two main source springs at 107°. Volunteers have installed pipes to carry this water to a variety of cement-and-rock pools for soaking, shampooing, dish washing, etc. By mutual agreement, no one bathes in the source pools. The rate of flow through the soaking pools is sufficient to eliminate the need for chemical treatment of the water. A third (upper) source spring flows into a natural, squishy-bottom pool that maintains an average temperature of 102°. All pools have valves and drains for controlling water flow and cleaning, except the natural upper warm spring. Most of the pools and facilities are handicap accessible with assistance. The apparent local custom in the entire area is clothing optional.

Services on the premises include delightfully decorated two-seater latrines, a shower with sunken porcelain bathtub, a sink for dishwashing, paperback library, central bonfire pit, shade trees, a lawn watered by the natural mineral water, and a goldfish pond to catch the runoff from the pools. There is an abundance of level space on which overnight parking is permitted for up to thirty days in any calendar year. There is an airstrip for small planes. It is more than 55 miles, mostly unpaved, to a store, cafe, service station, etc. Aluminum cans are collected for recycling. Everyone hauls out the remainder of their trash, and the entire area is kept spotless.

Temperatures regularly soar over the 110° mark in the summer, so this desert location with very little natural shade is preferred in the fall and spring. It becomes very crowded on major holidays and three-day weekends. The peace and quiet of the desert can best be enjoyed during the week.

The springs and the area around the springs at Saline Valley continue to be maintained at the highest level due to the continued participation of a group of very loyal and hardworking vounteers. They have formed the Saline Preservation Association which also serves as an interface with the National Park Service and handles any problems that arise. "The Source," a newsletter published by SPA is available by writing to 5322 Centinela Ave., Los Angeles, CA 90066-6908. Please support them.

Directions: The previously preferred route via Olancha is shown on the map. The unpaved portion of the road in from the south is county maintained. An alternate, and some say better route, starts at the north end of the town of Big Pine, on US 395. Drive northeast on CA 168 for 2.5 miles and turn right (southeast) on Death Valley Road. Drive approximately 15 miles and turn right on Waucoba-Saline Road. Drive 32 miles south to a large painted rock at a triangular intersection on the left (east) side of the road. Turn left (east) for 7 miles to the first group of springs. From US 395 it is approximately a 3-hour drive via either route. All roads in are quite rough and a high clearance vehicle is recommended. Either route may be temporarily washed out by infrequent but severe flash floods. Inquire about road conditions before making the trip. Within the area the 2.2 mile road from the lower springs to the upper springs is very rough.

Note: There is now a full-time caretaker with a cellular phone for emergencies. current road information is available by calling Claude or Claudette at Frenchy's Sign Shop in Bishop 619 873-5078 or Bob or Billie Bently in Big Pine at 619 938-2681.

Source maps: So. CA Auto Club *Death Valley*. USGS *Waucoba Wash* and *New York Butte*.

GPS (lower springs): N 36.80576 W 117.77340

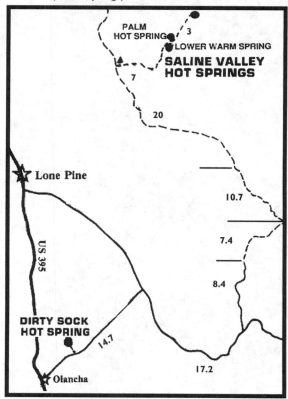

SALINE WARM SPRINGS
CLOTHING OPTIONAL USE AREA

Collage photos by Justine Hill and Phil Wilcox

144

Chris Andrews

Someone must have finally rinsed their socks as this is the first time I have ever seen the water blue and people actually in the pool.

714   DIRTY SOCK HOT SPRING

● **Near the town of Olancha**

Large, shallow pool, green with algae (see caption above), in an open desert area. Elevation 3,600 feet. Open all year.

Natural mineral water flows up from the bottom of a circular, cement-edged pool at 90° and flows out at various lower temperatures, depending on wind and air temperature. The murky water gives an uninviting appearance. The apparent local custom is clothing optional.

No services are available on the premises, and there are no remaining buildings. There are many acres of unmarked level space on which overnight parking is not prohibited. It is five miles to the nearest restaurant, motel, service station, and store.

Directions: From the intersection of US 395 and CA 190, go five miles northeast on CA 190. There are no signs on the highway, so look for a narrow, paved road on the northwest side and follow it 300 yards to the spring.

GPS: N 36.1975 W 117.5690

715   KERN HOT SPRING

● **On the upper Kern River**

A small concrete soaking pool offering a truly spectacular view in return for a truly strenuous three-day hike from the nearest road. Elevation 6,900 feet. Open all year.

Natural water flows out of the ground at 115° directly into a shallow soaking pool built at the edge of the Kern River. Water temperature is controlled by adding buckets of cold river water as needed. Bathing suit policy is determined by the mutual consent of those present.

There are no services available except a backpacker campground 100 yards away. The spring is 31.5 miles west of Whitney Portal and 37 miles east of Crescent Meadow. Situated in the mile-deep canyon of the upper Kern River, this spring has magnificent views in all directions. Detailed directions to such a remote location are beyond the scope of this book. We recommend that you purchase *Sierra South*, published by Wilderness Press, and also consult the Tule Ranger District of the Sequoia National Forest, 32588 Highway 190, Springville, CA 93265. 209 539-2607.

Source map: USGS *Kern Peak*.
GPS: N 36.2868 W 118.2428

Dave Bybee

Justine Hill

Courtesy of California Hot Springs

716   JORDAN HOT SPRING

● **Northwest of the town of Little Lake**

Hot water flows meet with cold creek water on Ninemile Creek in the southernmost part of the Golden Trout Wilderness. Elevation 6,500 feet. Open all year.

Natural mineral water flows out of a spring at approximately 120° down to the river where it may be mixed with cold creek water to form casual pools. Permanent pools are not permitted. The old lodge has a caretaker in the summer but there are no longer any soaking pools available.

It is six miles to the nearest paved road at Sequoia National Forest Road 21S03, reached via County Road J41 from south of Little Lake on US 395. The trail has an elevation change of 2,500 feet. Detailed directions to such a remote location are beyond the scope of this book. We recommend that you purchase *Exploring the Southern Sierra, East Side*, published by Wilderness Press, and also consult with the Mt. Whitney Ranger District of Inyo National Forest, Lone Pine, CA 93545. 619 876-6200.

GPS: N 36.1375 W 118.1810

717   CALIFORNIA HOT SPRINGS
PO Box 146   805 548-6582
■   California Hot Springs, CA 93207

Historic resort that has been restored and expanded to offer family fun. Located in rolling foothills at the edge of Sequoia National Forest. Elevation 3,100 feet. Open all year except Thanksgiving and the week before Christmas.

Odorless natural mineral water flows out of several artesian wells at a temperature of 125° and is piped to the pool area where there are two large, tiled hydrojet spas maintained at 100° and 104°. A flow-through system eliminates the need for chemical treatment of the water. There is one large swimming pool containing filtered and chlorinated spring water that is maintained at 85° in the summer and 94° in the winter. Handicap access is at west end of pool. Bathing suits are required.

The restored main building houses the office, delicatessen, ice cream parlor, pizza stand, gift shop, and dressing room facilities. Massage is available on the premises. Full-hookup RV spaces are adjacent to the resort area. Visa and MasterCard are accepted. It is two miles to a motel, store, and gas station.

Directions: From CA 99 between Fresno and Bakersfield, take the J22 exit at Earlimart and go east 38 miles to the resort.

718 A REMINGTON HOT SPRINGS
(see map on page 148)

● **Near the town of Lake Isabella**

A delightful, two-person cement tub, an adjoining river-level tub and a one-person tub higher up on a hillside in an unspoiled, primitive, riverside setting of rocks and trees. Located in the Kern River Canyon down a steep trail from old Highway 178. Elevation 2,200 feet. Open all year, except during high water in the river.

Natural mineral water at 104° emerges from the ground at 3.5 gallons-per-minute. This flow comes directly up through the bottom of a volunteer-built, cement tub and provides a form of hydrojet action, maintaining the pool temperature at 104°. There is a second, larger tub adjacent to the first and further out into the river. It is most often under water during the winter months and during spring run off. Twenty yards uphill is a drainable, one-person rock-and-cement pool that is fed by a smaller flow of 96° water, and has a valve for draining. The apparent local custom is clothing optional. However, don't be surprised by clothed people floating down river in rafts, innertubes, or canoes.

There are no services available on the premises. It is six miles to a motel, restaurant, and service station and two miles to a Forest Service campground.

Directions: From Bodfish (by Lake Isabella) drive west on Kern Canyon Road (old CA 178, now CA 214) to Hobo Forest Service Campground. Continue west 1.5 miles to a large turnout on the right with a telephone pole in the middle. (This is the second turnout with a telephone pole.) Flat areas for camping can be found near the parking areas. From the parking area, two trails head down toward the river, 300 yards below. A steep, narrow dirt trail on the left leads to a flat area along the river where camping is permitted. To reach the tubs, hike down the very steep "4WD trail" to the right to the rock foundation of an old building. Do not attempt to bring a vehicle down this road as it is often muddy and vehicles can get stuck. Also, it is very destructive to the hillside area. Just before this foundation on your left is a footpath with some natural rock steps leading down toward the river. Under a tree on your left, a spur path leads to the shallow rock-and-cement pool. Follow the main path to the cement pools by the river. This is not a good area for children, please be careful. (Consider going to Miracle Hot Springs with the kids.) Help keep this special place beautiful by packing out all trash.

GPS: N 35.3454 W 118.3312

Phil Wilcox

Now you see it, now you don't. The river-level pool, visible in the photo below, is often under water during spring runoff and whenever water is released from the dam.

Lynn Foss

Friends of the Hot Springs is operating to preserve and protect the endangered hot springs and the fragile eco-system in this area. Please join them in this effort. They can be reached at PO Box 782, Lake Isabella, CA 93240-9459. 760 379-7688.

Justine Hill

718 B MIRACLE HOT SPRINGS
(see map)

● **Near the town of Lake Isabella**

Three concrete and rock pools have been reconstructed by Friends of the Hot Springs (the parent organization of Miracle Hot Springs Assocation) and in conjunction with Kern River Tours. The pools are located adjacent to the Kern River in a beautiful, natural setting. The use of the pools is free although there is a charge for parking. The money collected will be used to continue rebuilding and maintaining Miracle. Elevation 2,200 feet.

Natural mineral water comes out at 125° and cools to approximately 110° as it flows into three pools, each one successively cooler. The wind from the river keeps the air temperature in the 80s even when it is much hotter away from the pools. Snow melt keeps the river quite cool even in the summer. One pool, now under construction, will be clothing optional.

Directions: Take Highway 178 from Bakersfield or Ridgecrest. Four miles west of the town of Lake Isabella take Borel Rd. right. Turn right again at Old Kern Canyon Rd. Approximately two miles down the road is the bridge over Clear Creek. Immediately turn right and then left and look for the sign.

While the newly constructed pools may not be exactly the same as the ones above they will be equally nice, offering us all a chance to soak again at *Miracle Hot Springs.*

> Friends of the Hot Springs is operating to preserve and protect the endangered hot springs and the fragile eco-system in this area. Please join them in this effort. They can be reached at PO Box 782, Lake Isabella, CA 93240-9459.
> 760 379-7688.

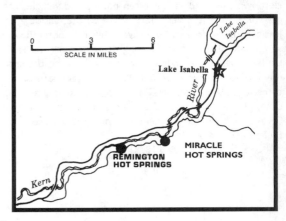

Phil Wilcox

Mark Stover

719   PYRAMID HOT SPRING

● **At the lower end of Kern River Canyon**

A delightful but hard-to-find, natural pool beneath a giant boulder at the edge of the Kern River. Open all year but not accessible during the high water of spring runoff. Elevation 1,900 feet.

Natural mineral water flows out of the ground at 109°, under a giant boulder, and into a sandy-bottom soaking pool large enough for two people, where it maintains a temperature of 103°. The apparent local custom is clothing optional, but the site is visible to vehicles on CA 178.

There are no services available at the location. It is one mile west to a Forest Service Campground (Live Oak) and fifteen miles to all other services in Bakersfield.

Directions: From Bakersfield, go east on CA 178 to the beginning of the Kern River Canyon. Continue 4 miles to a marked turnout on the left, with a six-foot-high, pyramid-shaped boulder at its east end. From the center of the turnout, look across the river slightly eastward to locate a large, cube-shaped boulder on the opposite bank. The pool is under that boulder. To reach it, follow the trail from the east end of the turnout to the large downstream boulder where you can hop across the river. Then follow a faint unmarked path upstream to the pool. Stay next to the river and beware of poison oak.

720   SESPE HOT SPRINGS

(see map)

● **Near the Sespe Condor Sanctuary**

A remote, pristine hot spring located in the rugged, desert mountains of a designated wilderness area. Elevation 2,800 feet. Open all year, subject to flash flooding and Forest Service closures.

Natural mineral water flows out of the side of a mountain at 185°, cooling as it flows through a series of shallow, volunteer-built, river-rock soaking pools. The apparent local custom is clothing optional.

There are no services on the premises. Access is via a nine-mile steep hiking trail from Mutau Flat or via a seventeen-mile hiking trail from Lion Campground. Horses and mules are also allowed on the trails. A Forest Service permit is required to enter the area at any time. Be sure to inquire at the Los Padres National Forest office about fire season closures, flood warnings, and the adequacy of your preparations for packing in and packing out.

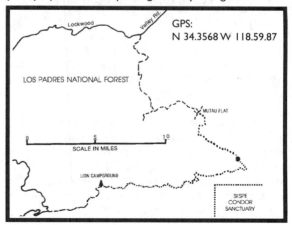

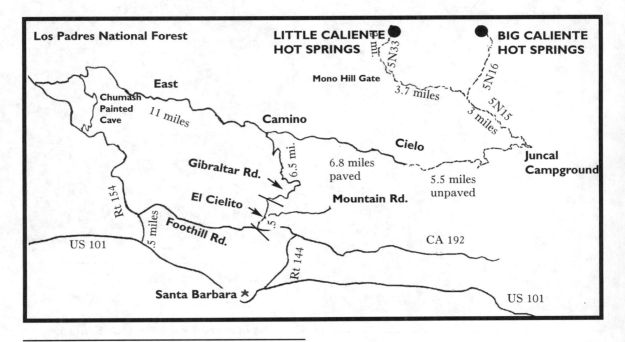

Los Padres National Forest

LITTLE CALIENTE HOT SPRINGS

BIG CALIENTE HOT SPRINGS

Mono Hill Gate

5N33

5N16

5N15

3.7 miles

3 miles

East

Chumash Painted Cave

11 miles

Camino

Cielo

6.5 mi.

Juncal Campground

Gibraltar Rd.

6.8 miles paved

El Cielito

5.5 miles unpaved

Mountain Rd.

Rt 154

.5 miles

Foothill Rd.

.5

US 101

CA 192

Rt 144

Santo Barbara ★

US 101

---

721 THE HOURGLASS

213 W. Cota   805 963-1436

☐   Santa Barbara, CA 93101

Private spa and rental facility located on a creekside residential street near downtown Santa Barbara.

Three private indoor rooms with pools and eight private outdoor enclosures with pools are for rent to the public. Gas-heated tap water treated with chlorine is maintained at 104°.

A private sauna, a juice bar, and massage are available on the premises. Visa and MasterCard are accepted. Phone for rates, reservations, and directions.

---

722 A LITTLE CALIENTE HOT SPRINGS
(see map)

●   **Near the City of Santa Barbara**

Two small volunteer-built pools in a rocky canyon at the end of a wooded, winding, unpaved Forest Service road. Elevation 1,600 feet. Open all year, subject to fire-season and rain/mud closures.

Natural mineral water flows out of a spring at 105° and through a pipe into the upper six-foot by six-foot by eighteen-foot rock-and-cement soaking pool. From here it spills over into the lower slimy-bottom rock-and-mud pool where the temperature cooled a degree or two. The pipe in the upper pool can be detached to stop the inflow and control water temperature. Remains of a

volunteer-built wooden sunning deck and red wooden benches along the lower pool have collapsed due to erosion. The apparent local custom is clothing optional.

No services are available on the premises. It is one mile to a pack-in campground, six miles to a primitive National Forest campground, and twenty-seven miles to all other services.

Directions: See the directions to Big Caliente. At 3.2 miles past Juncal Campground, continue straight at the signed junction. After fording the creek, follow the graded unpaved road uphill for 3.7 miles to Mono Hill Gate. Park here. From the gate it is 1 mile down a gradually descending graded road to Mono Campground (pack-in). It is another mile from here to the hot springs. At Mono Campground, continue straight. When the road forks, bear right at the gunshot wooden National Forest sign. When the path narrows, bear right again across a creekbed where you see primitive wooden steps. Continue a few hundred feet along a narrow path to the springs. The brush becomes gradually greener as you get closer to the springs. Before heading to Little Caliente, it is advisable to check with the ranger station for information on road conditions and where to park. At times parking is near the turnoff to Big Caliente, making the hike more than 6 miles to Little Caliente.

Source map: *Los Padres National Forest.*

722 B BIG CALIENTE HOT SPRINGS
(see map)

● **Near the City of Santa Barbara**

An improved, non-commercial hot spring located in a sparsely wooded canyon reached via ten miles of very windy, rocky gravel road. Elevation 1,500 feet. Open all year, subject to fire closure and road conditions during rainy season. Check with Los Padres National Forest Ranger Station.

Natural mineral water flows out of a bluff at 115°, then through a faucet-controlled pipe to a six-foot by ten-foot concrete pool. Water temperature in the pool can be controlled by diverting the inflow hose or shutting off the faucet. Please close the valve and divert the hose out of the pool when leaving, to prevent scalding others. When the valve is open, hot water showers up into the pool. Continual flow-through keeps the water clean. A galvanized pipe ladder leads into the pool, and concrete decks and benches are on two sides. The apparent custom is clothing optional by mutual consent, although it is advisable to keep bathing suits handy in case the rangers check. Since you can drive right up to the pool, it is handicap accessible with assistance.

A second primitive soaking pool is at creek level below the source spring. From the far end of the parking area, a marked trail leads off toward Big Caliente Debris Dam. Across the creek, water seeps down the mountain from a source spring under a cottonwood tree to the primitive 105° pool at creek level, which fills up with silt and mud and needs to be dredged periodically. This pool can be reached by rock-hopping where a pipe is visible underwater, approximately 100 yards from the trailhead.

Facilities include nearby changing rooms, clean pit toilets across the level parking area, and a picnic table under the trees. A trail from the changing rooms leads down to the cold creek, which has small waterfalls and several small sunning beaches. Several primitive Forest Service campgrounds are within three miles, and it is twenty-five miles to all other services in Santa Barbara.

Directions: Coming from the south on Hwy 101 in Santa Barbara, take Milpas St. exit (Rte 144). Follow Rte. 144 east through city residential streets, and a five-point roundabout, for a total of 6.3 miles, to the end at Rte. 192. Turn left on Rte. 192 (Stanwood Drive) for 1.2 miles to El Cielito Rd. At .3 mile, El Cielito crosses Mountain Drive. Continue straight uphill on El Cielito .5 mile to Gibraltar Rd. Turn right and follow Gibraltar for approximately 6.5 miles to the end at East Camino Cielo. Turn right on very windy East Camino Cielo which is paved for the first 6.8 miles, then unsurfaced for the next 5.5 miles. At Juncal Campground, turn left on 5N15 for 3 miles where the road forks. The right fork (5N16) ends at Big Caliente Hot Springs. (The left fork goes to Little Caliente.)

Coming from the north on Hwy 101, take Rte. 154 exit, heading east for .5 mile to Rte. 192 (called Foothill Rd.). At 4.7 miles is a reservoir (Foothill has changed to Mountain Dr. and again to Mission Ridge). At .4 mile past the reservoir, Rte. 192 makes a sharp left at a fire station and becomes Stanwood Dr. Follow Stanwood to El Cielito Rd. and continue as described above.

Source map: *Los Padres National Forest.*

Lynn Foss

Little Caliente (above) and *Big Caliente* (below) are the only natural hot springs accessible to the public in the Santa Barbara area.

Justine Hill

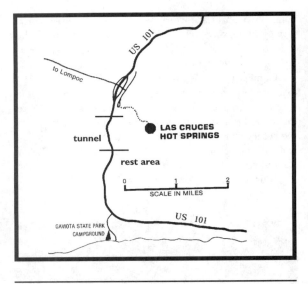

723   LAS CRUCES HOT SPRINGS
(see map)

● **Near Gaviota State Park**

Two primitive, mud-bottom pools on a tree-shaded slope a few miles from the ocean. Elevation 500 feet. Open all year for day use only.

Natural mineral water emerges at 96° directly into a shallow, knee-deep rock-and-mud soaking pool with relatively clear water, large enough for six to eight people. The overflow forms a waterfall over the earthen retaining wall into the larger lower pool, which averages 80° and has a slimy bottom. The water is murky grey. Clothing is optional by the mutual consent of those present.

There are no services available on the premises and overnight parking is prohibited in the parking area at the trailhead where a day-use self-parking fee is charged. Rangers check frequently and cite vehicles without valid parking receipts. It is three miles to a campground with RV hookups and six miles to all other services.

Directions: On Hwy101 approximately 35 miles north of Santa Barbara is Gaviota State Beach on the west with its landmark railroad bridge. From here it is 3 miles to the turnoff for CA 1, west toward Lompoc. Directly across from this turnoff is the small road paralleling the highway and heading south to the parking area for Las Cruces. After Gaviota State Beach you will pass a rest area and go through a tunnel. It is 1 mile past the tunnel to the turnoff.

From the parking area, follow the steep dirt 4WD trail to where it forks at a white sign saying "no horses past this point." Bear right on a narrow trail approximately .75 mile from the parking area to the pools.

Photo to the right is of *Las Cruces Hot Springs*.

Justine Hill

724   AVILA HOT SPRINGS SPA & RV PARK
250 Avila Beach Drive   805 595-2359
■ **San Luis Obispo, CA 93405**

RV resort with natural hot mineral water located in a foothill hollow at a freeway exit. Elevation 40 feet. Open all year.

Natural mineral water flows out of an artesian well at 130° and is piped to various pools. There are six indoor, tiled Roman tubs in which the water temperature is determined by the amount of hot mineral water and cold tap water admitted. These tubs are drained and refilled after each use so that no chemical treatment is needed. The outdoor soaking pool (105°) is drained and filled daily. The fifty- by one-hundred-foot outdoor swimming pool (86°) is filled with tap water and treated with chlorine. Bathing suits are required except in private tub rooms.

Massage, snack bar, RV hook-ups, lawn tent spaces, and a small store are available on the premises. All major credit cards are accepted. It is one mile to a motel, restaurant, and service station.

Directions: From San Luis Obispo, drive south 8 miles on US 101, take the Avila Beach Drive exit (not San Luis Bay Drive), and go north 1 block to the resort entrance.

725 SYCAMORE MINERAL SPRINGS
1215 Avila Beach Dr.   805 595-7302
■ **San Luis Obispo, CA 93401**

Delightful resort offering secluded redwood hot tubs out under the oaks and a private redwood hot tub on the balcony of every motel room. Located on a wooded rural hillside two miles from the ocean. Elevation 40 feet. Open all year, twenty-four hours per day.

Natural mineral water is pumped from a well at 110° and piped to the tubs on the hillside and on the motel balconies. Each tub has a hot mineral-water faucet and a cold tap-water faucet. Each tub also has its own jet pump, filter and automatic chlorinator. The swimming pool is filled with tap water treated with chlorine and maintained at 89°. A 102° natural-looking rock spa that will hold thirty people is located next to the pool. Bathing suits are required except in those outdoor tubs that are screened by shrubbery. Some pools and areas are handicap accessible.

Facilities include a restaurant , motel rooms and suites with hot tubs on the balcony (complete with a full breakfast), new deluxe suites with spas and fireplaces, a one-bedroom cottage with its own hot tub in a private enclosure, dressing rooms, meeting space, and a gift shop. Several varieties of massages and facials are available. A half-hour soak in one of the outdoor tubs is included in each appointment. On request, directions to a nearby clothing-optional state beach will be provided. Major credit cards accepted. Phone for rates and reservations.

Directions: From US 101 8 miles south of San Luis Obispo, take the Avila Beach exit, then go 1 mile west on Avila Beach Dr. and watch for the resort sign on the south side of the road.

726   FRANKLIN LAKES HOT SPRINGS

● **Near the Town of Paso Robles**

Soaking tub, swimming area, and fishing hole in the rolling hills outside Paso Robles. Be prepared to see many species of waterfowl, muskrat, beaver and even huge turtles. Open all year, sunrise to dusk. Small fee.

A thousand-foot deep well produces 98° water at over 700 gallons per minute. The water goes directly into a twelve by twenty-foot concrete soaking tub which in turn spills into a swimming area and then spills into a large (five acres) stocked fishing lake. The water is high in sulfur and has some sodium bicarbonate.

Picnic tables and toilets are provided and there are plans to build changing rooms and showers. Bathing suits are required. Alcohol is prohibited.

Directions: From 101 southbound at Paso Robles take the 16th St. exit and turn left on Riverside Drive. Go .8 of a mile to 13th St. and turn left. 13th St. becoms Creston Rd. Continue 4.5 miles on Creston Rd. to the hot springs.

From 101 northbound at Paso Robles take the Spring St. exit and go right on Niblick Ave. Go 1.8 miles to Creston Rd. and turn right. Continue 2.3 miles to the hot springs.

GPS: N 35.58993 W 120.64258

Courtesy of Esalen

727 ESALEN INSTITUTE
Workshop, room reservation
408 667-3000

■ **Big Sur, CA 93920**

Primarily an educational/experiential center rather than a hot spring resort. Located on CA 1, 45 miles south of Monterey. Elevation 100 feet. Open all year.

Esalen specializes in residential programs that focus on education, philosophy, and the physical and behavioral sciences. Access to the grounds is by reservation only for those wishing to take workshops or rent an available cabin. The hot springs are also open by reservation for up to 32 people each weekday morning from 1 AM to 3:30 AM at a charge. To make a bath reservation, please call 408 667-3047.

Natural mineral water flows out of the ground at 120° and into a bathhouse built on a cliff face, fifty feet above a rocky ocean beach. Within the bathhouse, which looks to the ocean, are four concrete soaking pools and eight individual tubs. There are also two adjoining outdoor soaking pools. Water temperature is determined within each tub by admitting controlled amounts of hot mineral water and cold well water. This flow-through process, plus frequent cleaning of the pools, makes chemical treatment of the water unnecessary. Clothing is optional in and around the bathhouse. Handicap access is limited; make arrangements in advance.

Facilities include housing and a dining room for registered guests. It is eleven miles to a restaurant, store, and service station. Massage is available on the premises. Visa, MasterCard, and American Express are accepted for registered guests.

728 TASSAJARA BUDDHIST MEDITATION CENTER
Tassajara Springs
Overnight Reservations 415 431-3771
Day Reservations 408 659-2229

■ **Carmel Valley, CA 93924**

Primarily a Buddhist Monastery with accommodations available to the public from early May to early September. Located in wooded mountains southeast of Monterey. Elevation 1,500 feet.

Please, no drop-in visitors. Prior reservations are required. Guests are expected to respect the spirit of a monastic community.

Natural mineral water flows out of the ground at 140° into two large, enclosed soaking pools that average 110° and two outdoor pools at 106°. The water, which is not chemically treated, cools as it flows into nearby streambed soaking areas. The outdoor swimming pool is maintained at approximately 75°. There are also steambaths in the separate men's and women's bathhouses. Bathing suits are required in the swimming pool only.

Rooms and meals are included as part of confirmed overnight reservation arrangements. The use of meditation facilities is also included. No credit cards are accepted. It is 90 minutes to a store, cafe, and service station. The road is steep and dangerous requiring good brakes and low gears.

Susan Harris

729   PARAISO HOT SPRINGS

408 678-2882

■   **Soledad, CA 93960**

A quiet resort for adults, with several acres of tree-shaded grass areas, located on the west slopes of the Salinas Valley. Elevation 1,200 feet. Open all year.

Natural mineral water flows out of the ground at 115° and is piped to three pools: an indoor soaking pool with temperatures ranging from 104-106°, an outdoor soaking pool with temperatures between 100-102°, and an outdoor swimming pool with a temperature of 80°. The swimming pool is treated with chlorine. Bathing suits are required. No cut-offs permitted.

Cottages, RV spaces, overnight camping, a snack bar, and a cocktail lounge are available on the premises. No credit cards are accepted. It is eight miles to a restaurant and service station.

Directions: From US 101, exit on Arroyo Seco Rd., 1 mile south of Soledad. Go 1 mile west to stop sign, then go straight onto Paraiso Springs Rd. Continue uphill for 6 miles to resort at end of road.

730   SYKES HOT SPRING

(see map)

●   **Near the village of Big Sur**

Remote, undeveloped hot spring on the Big Sur River in the Ventana Wilderness portion of the Los Padres National Forest. Elevation 1,110 feet. May be submerged during high water in the river.

Natural mineral water flows out of the ground at 100° from under a fallen tree and into a volunteer-built shallow soaking pool. This location involves a ten-mile hike on the Pine Ridge Trail, and a Wilderness Permit must be obtained from the Forest Service. The spring is near one of the most popular hiking routes, so the distance is no assurance of quiet or privacy during the summer months.

The Forest Service issues a trail map to those holding Wilderness Permits and, on request, will mark the hot-spring location on that map. Check your preparations, including water supply, with the ranger.

Source maps for trails: USGS *Ventana Cones, Partington Ridge* (springs not shown).

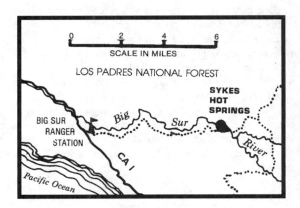

Courtesy of Waterfall Spa

Jayson Loam

731   WATERFALL SPA
1201 La Salle St.   831 393-1725
☐   Seaside, CA 93955

State-of-the-art rental facility located two minutes from downtown Monterey and five minutes from Carmel.

Five beautiful hot pools with waterfalls in private rooms are large enough to hold up to twenty people. The water temperature is maintained at 103° and the water is treated with bromine. In-pool lighting is fiber optic resulting in ever-changing water colors. Every room is handicap accessible.

Facilities include steam and sauna rooms and a full service beauty salon and massage center. Visa and MasterCard are accepted. Phone for rates, reservations, and directions.

732 A   HEARTWOOD SPA
3150A Mission Dr.   831 462-2192
☐   Santa Cruz, CA 95065

A clothing-optional, tree-shaded hot tub rental establishment located on a suburban side street.

A wooden hot tub, cold tub, sauna, and communal sunning areas are available for a day-rate charge. One private tub with a water temperature of 105° can be rented by the hour. All pools use gas-heated tap water treated with chlorine. The private tub area is wheelchair accessible. Bathing suits are optional everywhere except at the front desk.

Massage is available on the premises. The total facility may be reserved for private parties before and after regular business hours. No credit cards are accepted. Phone for rates, reservations, and directions. (Community area open on Sunday evenings for women only.)

Jayson Loam   Marjorie Young

732 B   KIVA RETREAT
         702 Water St.   831 429-1142
☐   Santa Cruz, CA 95060

Trees, grass, and flowers lend a parklike setting to this unusual, clothing-optional, hot-pool rental establishment. Located near the city center.

A single day rate gives entry to the communal grass area, two large hot tubs, a cold-tub plunge, and a large sauna. Adjoining indoor dressing and social rooms are also available. Pools use gas-heated tap water and are treated with chlorine and ozone. Two private enclosures, rented by the hour, have water maintained at 102°. Bathing suits are optional everywhere except in the front entry.

Massage is available on the premises. Major credit cards are accepted. Phone for rates, reservations, and directions.

732 C   TEA HOUSE SPA
         112 Elm St.   831 458-9355
☐   Santa Cruz, CA 95060

Beautiful hot pool and sauna rooms overlooking a Japanese bamboo garden, located in the heart of downtown Santa Cruz and available for rent by the hour.

Four private-space suites, consisting of a shower, changing area, and tub use bromine-treated tap water. The fiberglass pools offer a view of the garden and a sliding glass door can be opened. Two of the suites also offer saunas. Water temperatures are maintained at 104°. Many of the tubs are handicap accessible. Herbal tea and large towels are provided.

Massage is available on the premises. No credit cards. Phone for rates and reservations.

732 D   WELL WITHIN

☐   417 Cedar St.   831 458-WELL
      Santa Cruz, CA 95060

New, beautifully appointed hot pool establishment with Japanese gardens and waterfalls visible from the individual rooms. Located in downtown Santa Cruz and available for rent by the hour.

Four private indoor tubs and two outdoor tubs are maintained at approximately 102°. Two of the indoor tubs and both outdoor tubs have saunas. The outdoor tubs can accommodate up to six persons each and the gate between the two tubs can be opened to hold up to fourteen people. The tubs are treated with bromine. The entire facility is handicap accessible and one of the outdoor tubs is equipped with special railings.

A shower and changing area are found in each room. Towels and herbal tea are included. Massage and skin care services are avilable by appointment. Visa and MasterCard are accepted. Phone for rates, reservations, and directions.

Marjorie Young

Dressing areas in each bathhouse and places to rest. Picnic tables are also available. The current owners are in the process of some major renovations and hope to reopen the resort. Suggested items to bring with you: bathtowel, lunch, drinks, empty container for spring water (up to two gallons per person), bathrobe, sandals, slippers, camera, bathing suit for outdoor tub. No children under three are allowed.

Phone or fax for reservations, and directions.

733   GILROY YAMATO HOT SPRINGS

Phone: 415 434-2180
Fax: 415 333-3550

■

Two indoor bathhouses, an outdoor soaking pool and a few cabins are all that remain of a 242-acre resort first built in the late 1860s. Located in the oak-studded foothills adjacent to Henry Coe State Park the facility offers lovely areas for hiking, picnicking and just relaxing and enjoying the beautiful natural surroundings and wildlife. Designated a state historical landmark. Open by reservation only (do not go without as you will be turned away).

Hot mineral water comes out of a spring at temperatures ranging from 100-105° and is piped directly into the large tiled soaking tubs in the separate men's and women's bathhouses (no suits allowed). The spring also feeds the outdoor cement pool where large rocks are used as seats in the pool. All pools operate on a flow through basis and require no chemicals.

While Gilroy is now famous for its garlic, it was initially the hot springs that brought people to the area. The Southern Pacific Railway provided shuttle service between the train station and the hot springs. Gilroy Hot Springs even had its own post office.

734 GRAND CENTRAL SAUNA AND HOT TUB CO.

376 Saratoga Ave.   408 247-8827

☐   San Jose, CA 95129

One of a chain of urban locations established by Grand Central, the pioneer in the room rent-a-tub business.

Twenty-one private indoor tubs are heated to 102-104° and treated with chlorine. The individual rooms each have a sauna and dressing room. Towels and soap are provided.

No credit cards or reservations are accepted. Phone for hours, rates, and directions.

735 WATERCOURSE WAY

165 Channing Way   415 462-2000

☐   Palo Alto, CA 94301

The beautiful oriental decor creates a comfortable and interesting environment, offering a variety of enjoyable rooms and experiences.

Pools for rent to the public use gas-heated tap water treated with chlorine and muriatic acid. Ten individually decorated private rooms each have a different combination of hot pool, cold pool, sauna, and steambath. Water temperature in the pools is approximately 103°. In one of the rooms, special oils or bath salts can be added to the tub as the water is drained and refilled after each use. To accommodate larger groups, two rooms can be joined.

Facials, spa treatments, and massage are available on the premises. Visa and MasterCard are accepted. Phone for rates, reservations, and directions.

Jayson Loam

736 TROPICAL GARDENS

200 San Pedro Rd.   415 755-8827

☐   Colma, CA 94105

Recreation-oriented rent-a-tub business sharing quarters with a racquetball facility and health club. Located a few blocks south of Daly City.

Ten private rooms have pools that use gas-heated tap water treated with chlorine. Water temperature is maintained at 102-104°. Saunas are included in seven of the rooms.

Other facilities include racquetball and handball courts, a tanning studio, Nautilus conditioning, swimming pool and locker rooms. Massage is available by appointment. No credit cards are accepted. Phone for rates, reservations, and directions.

737 A THE HOT TUBS

2200 Van Ness Ave.   415 441-TUBS

☐   San Francisco, CA 94109

One of the few stress-reduction establishments offering tile tubs and decks in a chrome and glass urban environment. Located on a main street just west of downtown.

Pools in 20 private rooms are for rent to the public. Gas-heated tap water treated with chlorine is maintained at 104°. A sauna, music, and rest area are included. Towels and soap are provided.

Massage and a juice bar are available on the premises. No credit cards are accepted. Phone for rates, reservations, and directions.

737 B FAMILY SAUNA SHOP

2308 Clement   415 221-2208

☐   San Francisco, CA 94121

One of the pioneer stress-reduction centers in San Francisco. Located in the Richmond District.

Two private rooms with pools for rent to the public use gas-heated tap water treated with chlorine. Water temperature is 104°.

Four private saunas are available for rent. Massage and facials are available on the premises. Visa and MasterCard are accepted. Phone for rates, reservations, and directions.

737 C GRAND CENTRAL SAUNA AND HOT TUB CO.

15 Fell St.   415 431-1370

☐   San Francisco, CA 94102

The first of a chain of urban locations established by Grand Central, a pioneer in the private room rent-a-tub business.

Pools in 26 private rooms, each with a sauna, are for rent to the public. The pools use gas-heated tap water treated with chlorine and are maintained between 102-104°. Towels and soap are provided.

Tanning booths are available on the premises. Credit cards are not accepted. Reservations are not accepted. Phone for rates and directions.

738 F. JOSEPH SMITH'S MASSAGE THERAPY

158 Almonte   415 383-8260

☐   Mill Valley, CA 94941

A Marin healing center with two five-foot deep hot tubs nestled under redwood trees, located in a country setting.

Two private enclosures with water temperatures of approximately 104° and treated with chlorine are rented to the public. One of the tubs is available for communal use during the day. A sauna is also for rent. Bathing suits are optional in the tub and sauna areas.

The prayer garden is open for relaxation and meditation. The crystal room also provides a space to meditate. Massage and advanced body therapy classes are available on the premises, as are chiropractic and acupuncture services. Massage classes and workshop space are available. Phone for rates, reservations, and directions.

A lovely garden with a small waterfall and a quiet ambiance sets the mood for a relaxing soak at *F. Joseph Smith's.*

Photos by Marjorie Young

740   FROGS

☐   School Street Plaza   415 453-7647
     Fairfax, CA 94930

One of the first rent-a-tub facilities in the San Francisco Bay area. Located in a Marin County suburb and recently renovated by new ownership.

There are two outdoor hot tubs in private enclosures, plus a large communal hot tub and a cold plunge. There are two saunas (the hottest in the Bay area) and a clothing-optional sundeck.

Voted "best of Marin" for massage therapy, with therapists available until midnight. Phone for rates, reservations, and directions.

739   SHIBUI GARDENS

☐   19 Tamalpais Ave.   415 457-0283
     San Anselmo, CA 94960

An inviting blend of Marin County natural redwood hot tubs and Japanese landscaping. Located on a suburban side street.

Three privately enclosed hot tubs using bromine-treated, gas-heated tap water are for rent by the hour. Water temperatures range from 102-105°. One communal cold pool is also available to customers at no extra charge. Bathing suits are optional inside the pool and sauna spaces.

A private indoor sauna is for rent on the premises. Massage is available. Phone for rates, reservations, and directions.

Courtesy of Albany Sauna

741 ALBANY SAUNA AND HOT TUBS
1002 Solano Ave.   510 525-6262
☐   Albany, CA 94706

Established in 1934 as one of the earliest rent-a-tub establishments in the Bay Area, it has since been extensively remodeled. Located two blocks west of San Pablo Ave.

Three outdoor, privately enclosed pools for rent to the public use gas-heated tap water treated with chlorine and cleaned with diatomaceous earth filtering system. Water temperature is maintained at approximately 105°. There are railings throughout the facility.

Four private rock-steam saunas, individually controlled for temperature with an outside air source for comfortable breathing, are available for rent. Swedish massage, and hair and skin care products are available on the premises. Major credit cards are accepted. Phone for rates, reservations, and directions.

742 A THE HOT TUBS
1915 University Ave.   510 843-4343
☐   Berkeley, CA 94704

One of two urban locations in Berkeley and San Francisco.

Twelve private rooms with pools use gas-heated tap water treated with chlorine. Water temperature varies between 102-104°. A sauna is included.

A juice bar is available on the premises. No credit cards or checks are accepted. Reservations are not accepted. Phone for rates and directions.

742 B THE BERKELEY SAUNA
1947 Milvia St.   510 845-2341
☐   Berkeley, CA 94704

A stress-reduction establishment located a few yards north of University Avenue.

Three private rooms with gas-heated tap water pools are available for rent to the public. The bromine-treated water is maintained at temperatures from 104-106°.

Three private saunas are also for rent. Massage is available on the premises. Credit cards accepted. Phone for rates, reservations, and directions.

743 A AMERICAN FAMILY HOT TUB
88 Trelany Lane   510 827-2299
☐   Pleasant Hill, CA 94523

Suburban rent-a-tub establishment located a few yards west of Contra Costa Blvd.

Twelve private outdoor pools are for rent by the hour. Gas-heated tap water treated with chlorine is maintained at 102-104°. Sauna and massage are available on the premises. Visa and MasterCard are accepted. Phone for rates, reservations, and directions.

743 B SUNSHINE SPA

1948 Contra Costa Blvd.   510 685-7822

☐   Pleasant Hill, CA 94523

Funky, fun-loving rent-a-tub business, that prides itself on its great massages, located in the Pleasant Hill Plaza, fifteen miles east of Oakland.

Pools using gas-heated tap water treated with bromine are for rent to the public. There are seven private rooms, each with an in-ground hot tub, shower, massage table, and mural. Pool temperatures range from 90-102°. Handicap accessible.

Massage is available on the premises. Major credit cards accepted. Phone for rates, reservations, and directions.

744 PIEDMONT SPRINGS

3939 Piedmont   510 652-9191

☐   Oakland, CA 94611

Urban rent-a-tub establishment situated in downtown Oakland.

Four hot tubs, one in combination with a sauna, were built outdoors in private enclosures, complete with redwood decks, changing areas, and showers. Water temperature is maintained at 102-104° and can be cooled down with hoses. All tubs are chlorine treated.

Massage, facials, salt scrubs, and other skin care treatments are available. Phone for rates, reservations, directions, or a brochure .

745 HOT TROPICS

17389 Hesperion Blvd.   510 278-8827

☐   San Lorenzo, CA 94580

Seniors, families, singles, and couples are welcome at this rent-a-tub establishment just a couple of blocks off Hwy 880.

Fourteen private indoor tubs are heated to 102-105° and treated with chlorine. Five rooms are also equipped with saunas, futons, and showers. Seven rooms do not have saunas but do have large skylights that roll open when the weather permits. Special minerals are added to the tubs. Handicap accessible.

No credit cards or reservations are accepted. Phone for hours, rates, and directions.

746 PARADISE SPAS

5168 Mowry Ave.   510 793-7727

☐   Fremont, CA 94538

Suburban rent-a-tub and tanning center located in a shopping center just off Highway 880.

Eight private rooms, including two with special black lighting, come complete with tubs and showers. The water is heated to 102-104° and is chlorine treated. Towels and radios are supplied.

Tanning booths are available. Visa and MasterCard are accepted. Phone for reservations.

SOUTHERN CALIFORNIA

This map was designed to be used with a standard highway map.

MAP SYMBOLS

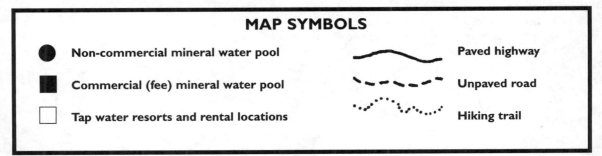

● Non-commercial mineral water pool	～ Paved highway
■ Commercial (fee) mineral water pool	- - - Unpaved road
□ Tap water resorts and rental locations	⋯ Hiking trail

801 A   FURNACE CREEK INN RESORT
Box 1   **760 786-2345**
■   **Death Valley, CA 92328**

An historic resort built around a lush oasis on a barren hillside overlooking Death Valley. Elevation, sea level. Open mid-October to mid-May.

Natural mineral water flows out of a spring at 89°, into two outdoor pools, and through a large, palm-shaded arroyo. The swimming pool maintains a temperature of approximately 85°, and the flow-through rate is so great that no chemical treatment of the water is necessary. Bathing suits are required. Pools are for the use of registered guests only.

Facilities include two saunas, lighted tennis courts, rooms, two restaurants, live entertainment, dancing, and a bar. Major credit cards are accepted.

801 B   FURNACE CREEK RANCH RESORT
Box 1   **760 786-2345**
■   **Death Valley, CA 92328**

A large, ranch-style resort in a green oasis setting. Located in the center of Death Valley, one mile west of Furnace Creek Inn. Elevation 178 feet. below sea level. Open all year.

Natural mineral water is piped from the 89° spring serving the Inn to a swimming pool at the ranch. The rate of flow-through is so great that a temperature of approximately 85° is maintained and no chemical treatment is necessary. Pool use is open to the public as well as to registered guests. Bathing suits are required. Most facilities are handicap accessible; handicap rooms are available.

Facilities include rooms, three restaurants, bar, store, service station, RV hookups, golf course, and lighted tennis courts. Major credit cards are accepted.

Hot mineral water supplies for the large pools at both the inn and the ranch. It is also responsible for the natural oasis setting in an otherwise arid desert landscape.

Photos courtesy of Furnace Creek

802 A SHOSHONE INN
Box 67   **760 852-4335**
■   **Shoshone, CA 92384**

Older resort located on CA 127 in desert foothills near the southern entrance to Death Valley. Elevation 1,600 feet. Open all year.

Natural mineral water flows out of a spring at 93° with such pressure that no pumps are needed to push it through the pipes to the outdoor swimming pool. The rate of flow-through is so great that a temperature of 92° is maintained and no chemical treatment of the water is necessary. A waterfall at the end of the pool cools the inflow for pool use in the summer. Pool use is available only to registered guests. Bathing suits are required.

Facilities include rooms, restaurant, bar, store, service station. RV hookups and overnight camping spaces are available at the Shoshone RV Park (802 B). Major credit cards are accepted.

Location: Shoshone is 28 miles south of Death Valley Junction and 58 miles north of Baker on CA 127.

802 B SHOSHONE RV PARK
Box 67   **760 852-4569**
■   **Shoshone, CA 92384**

Lush, green, tree-shaded RV park one hundred yards north of the Shoshone Inn on the main street (CA 127) in Shoshone.

The natural mineral water outdoor swimming pool described at left is adjacent to the RV park and is for the use of registered guests of either facility and for local residents. Non-guests may use the pool by paying a day-use fee (which is the same as the overnight RV park fee).

Half the hot geothermal well water supplies the RV park's showers, the inn, and the pool; the other half is used for the town water supply. All water must be brought to a rolling boil for at least a minute before being used for drinking or cooking.

No credit cards are accepted at the RV park.

All photos this page by Justine Hill

Shoshone Development, Inc. owns the whole town, population 40.

Justine Hill

803A DELIGHT'S HOT SPA
Box 368   760 852-4343
■   Tecopa, CA 92389

One of the original hot spring spas in the arid, alkali desert east of Death Valley, originally established in the early 1940s. For adults only (ages 21-101). Elevation 1,400 feet. Open all year.

Hundreds of warm mineral springs supply water to the entire region. Delight's has four large, three-foot-deep, private, coed cement tubs that hold two to three people. Water flows from a 285-foot artesian well into three of the tubs. The fourth is fed by a small spring that comes directly into the spring house. where it measures 106°. Pools are open from 5 AM to 9 PM and are drained and scrubbed nightly. A new radical hydroxil system will ensure chemical-free water. Pools have stairs and bars and are handicap accessible with assistance. No suits allowed in the pools.

Facilities include rustic housekeeping cottages with refrigeration (no TVs, radios, or phones), full hookup RV spaces, showers, and rest rooms. Massage, herbal facials, and clay treatments are available by appointment. The clubhouse has a stage, pool table, and fireplace and is large enough for banquets and weddings. Plans are to build new pools and add to existing services. Call for status of construction. It is two miles to all other services in Tecopa.

Directions: From CA 127, 5 miles south of Shoshone or 50 Miles north of Baker, drive east on Tecopa Hot Springs Rd. for 3 miles. A red windmill and sign to the spa are on the east side of the street.

803 B TECOPA HOT SPRINGS
(OPERATED BY INYO COUNTY)
PO Box 158   760 852-4264
■   Tecopa, CA 92389

A county-operated trailer park, bathhouse and campground located on the Tecopa loop off CA 127. Elevation 1,400 feet. Open all year, seven days a week, twenty-four hours a day; free to park users and the general public.

Natural mineral water flows out of a spring at 108° and is piped to separate men's and women's bathhouses. Each one has two gravel-bottom, three-foot-deep soaking pools maintained at 100° and 105°, plus an enclosed outdoor sunbathing area. The indoor pool is twelve by twelve and the enclosed outdoor pool is eight-feet by twelve-feet; both pools have steps and grab bars for handicap access. Posted signs require nude bathing. Mixed bathing is not permitted.

RV hookups and overnight spaces are available on the premises. There is an air-conditioned community center with library, exercise classes, and social activities. No credit cards are accepted. It is two miles to a store and service station.

Justine Hill

803 C TECOPA DESERT POND

● **Near the town of Tecopa**

A cement-bottom tub with cement steps, protected on two sides by wooden barriers. Located on an open stretch of flat white alkali BLM desert. Elevation 1,400 feet. Open all year.

Natural 98° mineral water flows in through a pipe from an artesian well next to the six-foot- by six-foot by two-and-a-half-foot pool, with overflow running off the far side of the pool in a continual flow-through pattern. There's a valve for draining and cleaning the pool. Clothing is optional.

There are no facilities on the premises. Overnight parking for one night is not prohibited on BLM desert. Partying remains are evident near the pool, but the tub itself is kept clean by volunteers. It is one mile to all services in Tecopa.

Directions: Located on the Tecopa loop of CA 127, 5 miles south of Shoshone, 50 miles north of Baker, and 27 miles southwest of Pahrump, NV on CA 178/NV 372. One block south of Delight's Hot Spa on Tecopa Hot Springs Rd. and just north of the county-run Tecopa Hot Springs bathhouse, turn east at the sign saying "Slow, Entering County Park, Co. in Inyo." At .3 mile pass a large duck pond on your left, and the gravel road bears right. Do not bear right, but continue straight ahead on the ungraded, unsurfaced road across the alkali desert. At .2 mile, go to the left of the log barrier and keep driving on the rough road toward the only cluster of green foliage in the area. The tub is at the foot of the small palm tree, a total of .9 mile from Hot Springs Rd. During the rainy season, the road may be impassable.

804 DEEP CREEK HOT SPRINGS
(see map)

● **Near the town of Hesperia**

Beautiful, remote, year-round springs on the south bank of Deep Creek at the bottom of a spectacular canyon in the San Bernardino National Forest. Elevation 3,000 feet. Open all year.

Natural mineral water flows out of several rock fissures at 108° and directly into volunteer-built, rock-and-sandbag pools on the edge of Deep Creek. Water temperature in any one pool will depend on the amount of creek water admitted. The local custom is clothing optional.

There are no services, and overnight camping is prohibited in the canyon near the springs. It is seven miles by a year-round trail to an overnight parking area. There is also a steep, two and one-half mile, slippery trail of decomposed granite down the north side of the canyon from Bowen Ranch, where a fee is charged for admission to the ranch and for overnight parking. From either parking area it is ten miles to all services. Note: The trail from Bowen Ranch ends on the north bank of Deep Creek, which overflows during spring runoff so that it is not safe to ford.

Directions: From I-15, take the Hesperia exit and drive for 8 miles along Main Street to a Y in the road, where Main St. becomes Rock Spring Rd. To reach Deep Creek via Bowen Ranch, continue another 1.1 miles, bear left on Kiowa Rd. for .4 mile, then right on Roundup for 4.2 miles (the last 1.2 miles are unpaved). Turn right (south) on Bowen Ranch Rd., a wide, unpaved, washboard road, and drive 5.5 miles to the ranch. Whenever you come to a fork, bear right to reach the ranch.

Directions to the year-round trail: Follow directions above to Deep Creek Rd. Turn right (south) for 5 miles to the pavement end. Bear left across the open space, heading toward the earthen dam. Park at the southeast end of the earthen dam near the overflow ramp. To reach the trailhead, go up the paved service road next to the overflow. From the top of the service road you can look down to the right and see a bathing beach at the creek and to the left, the trailhead marked with a rusty tin sign. There is short, steep ascent to the trail, which hugs the side of the mountain for 6 miles to the springs.

Source maps: *San Bernardino National Forest*. USGS *Lake Arrowhead*.

All photos by Justine Hill

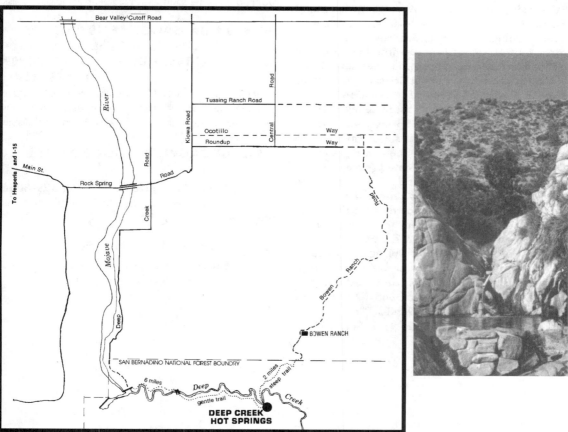

DESERT HOT SPRINGS RESORTS, MOTELS, AND SPAS

Desert Hot Springs has been called "The Mineral Water Capital of the World, " with natural crystal-clear, tasteless, odorless, geothermal water throughout the entire town. Over fifty hotels, motels, spas, resorts, swimming pools, RV parks, and mobile home communities have therapeutic hot mineral water facilities. Most facilities are open all year and require reservations.

All of the establishments listed below are in or near the city of Desert Hot Springs, which is ten miles north of Palm Springs. All of them pump natural mineral water from their own wells and offer at least one chlorine-treated (except where noted) swimming pool and one hydropool. Bathing suits are required at almost all locations. Those places that have indicated that they have handicap access are marked. You may wish to check with other places when you call.

The town of Desert Hot Springs provides all services. Most locations take credit cards, except where noted. For information contact the Chamber of Commerce, PO Box 848, Desert Hot Springs, CA 92240. 760 329-6403. City and zip code for locations is Desert Hot Springs, CA 92240.

805 A   AGUA CALIENTE HOTEL AND MINERAL WATER SPA

14500 Palm Dr.   760 329-5652

Outdoor mineral water pool. Indoor therapy pool. In room pools. Some rooms with kitchens. Handicap access.

805 B   AMBASSADOR ARMS AND HEALTH SPA MOTEL

12921 Tamar Dr.   760 329-1909
                                   800 569-0541

Indoor and outdoor 104° therapy pools 90° outdoor swimming pool, all with fresh mineral water on a flow-through basis. Also 200-250° dry sauna. Kitchens available.

805 C   BROADVIEW LODGE MOTEL-SPA

12672 Eliseo Rd.   760 329-8006

Indoor therapy pool, outdoor swimming pool, sauna. Rooms with connecting kitchens.

805 D   CARAVAN SPA MOTEL

66810 Fourth St.   760 329-7124

Hot mineral spa, outdoor swimming pool.

805 E   DAVID'S SPA MOTEL

11220 Palm Dr.   760 329-6202

Indoor and outdoor hydropool, swimming pool, steam and dry sauna. Massage. Kosher kitchen.

805 F   DESERT HOT SPRINGS SPA

10805 Palm Dr.   760 329-6000

Jayson Loam

Largest full-service spa resort in the area. Seven mineral water soaking pools ranging from 80-106° and the Olympic-size pool are open for day use.

Facilities include a restaurant, bar, and gift shop. Various types of massage, facials, beauty treatments, and classes in water aerobics are available to guests and the general public on a day-use basis.

805 G   DESERT PALMS SPA MOTEL

67485 Hacienda Ave.   760 329-4443

Six pools on two and one-half acres, enclosed indoor and outdoor spas, sauna. Acu-massage. Handicap access.

805 H   DESERT SPRINGS INN

12697 Eliseo Rd.   760 251-1668

A 90° swimming pool, 104° sauna, enclosed sunbathing area. Rooms with kitchens.

805 I   DOM'S FLAMINGO MOTEL & SPA

67221 Pierson Blvd.   760 251-1455

Seven mineral pools and swimming pool. Kitchens available. Restaurant on premises. Handicap access.

805 J   EL REPOSO SPA

66334 W. Fifth St.   760 329-6632

Enclosed hot mineral pool, outdoor swimming pool. Recreation room, apartments with kitchens. Sauna.

805 K   EMERALD SPRINGS RESORT

68-055 Club Circle Dr.   760 329-1151

Indoor therapy pool and outside swimming pool. Some units with kitchens.

805 L   HACIENDA RIVIERA SPA

67375 Hacienda Ave.   760 329-7010

Day use only. Outdoor swimming pool, enclosed hot pool. Water temperatures vary with the season.

805 M   HILLVIEW MOTEL

11740 Mesquite Ave.   760 329-5317

Enclosed hot mineral therapeutic jet pool; large outdoor heated pool.

805 N   HIGHLANDER LODGE

68187 Club Circle Dr.   760 251-0189

Indoor spa, outdoor pool.

805 O   ILONA'S HEALTH & FITNESS AT EMERALD SPRINGS RESORT

68055 Club Circle Dr.   760 329-1151

A 90° swimming pool, 102° outdoor spa, 106° indoor spa, and sauna. Health, fitness and nutrition classes and programs. Handicap access.

805 P   KISMET LODGE
13340 Mountain View   760 329-6451
Swimming pool, hot therapy pool. Handicap access.

805 Q   LAS PRIMAVERAS RESORT AND SPA
66659 Sixth St.   760 251-1677
104° indoor hot tub, 92° outdoor swimming pool, sauna. State-of-the-art outdoor cooling system cools outdoor temperature fifteen to twenty degrees. Luxury units with jet tubs, kitchens. Handicap access.

805 R   LIDO PALMS SPA MOTEL
12801 Tamar Dr.   760 329-6033
Two outdoor pools, large indoor spa, dry sauna. Kitchenettes. Massage.

805 S   LINDA VISTA LODGE
67200 Hacienda Ave.   760 329-6401
104° outdoor pool, two enclosed therapy pools, sauna. Rooms with kitchens.

805 T   LORANE MANOR
67751 Hacienda Ave.   760 329-9090
Enclosed hot tub, outdoor swimming pool. No credit cards accepted. Handicap access.

805 U   MA-HA-YAH LODGE & HEALTH SPA
66111 Calle Las Tiendas   760 329-5420
Two indoor hot tubs, 100° and 102° (one has special handicap access), one body-temperature outdoor hot tub, outdoor swimming pool, sauna. Kitchenettes. Sauna, massage, and reflexology. No credit cards accepted.

805 V   MINERAL SPRINGS
11000 Palm Drive   760 329-6484
Pool, spa, mineral springs waterfall. Rooms with private spas. Bar. Salt rubs.

805 W   MIRACLE MANOR SPA-TEL
12589 Reposo Way   760 329-6641
Enclosed hot pool, outdoor pool. Therapeutic massage, facials.

805 X   THE MIRAGE SPRINGS HOTEL, CASINO AND SPA
10625 Palm Drive   760 251-3399
Eight outdoor hot spas at different temperatures, including an eighteen-inch deep "champagne" bubbling spa and two dry saunas. Whirlpool bathtubs in separate men's and women's areas. Massage. Restaurant, banquet facilities, approved gaming. Handicap access.

805 Y   MISSION LAKES COUNTRY CLUB
8484 Clubhouse Blvd.   760 329-6481
Residential country club with eight-unit motel. Swimming pool, spa, and golf course open to public. Handicap access.

805 Z   MONTE CARLO
67840 Hacienda Ave.   760 329-9058
Small motel with heated pool, spa.

805 AA   THE MOORS RESORT SPA MOTEL
12637 Reposo Way   760 329-7121
Family oriented. Swimming pool and hot therapy pool are wheelchair accessible.

805 BB   PYRAMID OF HEALTH SPA
66-63 East Fifth St.   760 329-5652
A 90° swimming pool and 105° mineral water hydrojet pool. Kitchenettes. Handicap access.

805 CC   ROYAL FOX INN
14500 Palm Dr.   760 329-4481
Indoor and outdoor therapeutic hot pools with hydrojets, large swimming pool, sauna. Rooms with private hot mineral swimming pool. RV park. Exercise room, massage.

805 DD ROYAL PALMS INN BED & BREAKFAST

12885 Eliseo Rd.   760 329-7975

Covered outdoor twelve-foot spa. Seven units.

805 EE SAHARA SPA MOTEL

66700 E. Fifth St.   760 329-6666

Indoor spa, indoor swimming pool, sauna, hot waterfall. Handicap access.

805 FF SAM'S FAMILY SPA HOT WATER RESORT

70875 Dillon Rd.   760 329-6457

One of largest, multi-service resorts with all facilities open to the public for day use as well as to registered guests. Large outdoor swimming pool uses chlorinated mineral water. Gazebo-enclosed wading pool and four covered hydropools use flow-through mineral water, requiring no chemical treatment.

Coed sauna, motel rooms, restaurant, RV hookups, overnight spaces, store, laundromat, playground, exercise room. Barbeque area. Handicap accessible with assistance.

805 GG SAN MARCUS INN

66540 San Marcus Rd.   760 329-5304

Indoor therapy pool, outdoor swimming pool, and sauna.

805 HH SANDPIPER INN & SPA

12800 Foxdale Dr.   760 329-6455

Large swimming pool, therapeutic hot spa, dry and steam sauna.

805 II SKYLINER SPA

12840 Inaja St.   760 251-0933

Mineral pool with spa; covered citrus patio.

805 JJ SPA TOWN HOUSE MOTEL

66540 E. Sixth St.   760 329-6014

Hydro-jet therapy pool. Large mineral pool.

805 KK STARDUST MOTEL

66634 Fifth St.   760 329-5443

Hydrojet pool, swimming pool.

805 LL SUNSET INN

67585 Hacienda Ave.   760 329-4488

Pool, two hydrojet spas, dry sauna, wet sauna. Some rooms with kitchens. Massage.

805 MM SWISS HEALTH RESORT

66729 Eighth St.   760 329-6912

A 100° indoor mineral pool, 104° hydropool, 80-90° outdoor mineral pool, all flow-through, requiring no chlorine. Various kinds of massage. No children or pets. Handicap access.

805 NN TAMARIX SPA

66185 Acoma   760 329-6615

Smaller motel with heated mineral pool.

805 OO TRAVELLERS REPOSE BED & BREAKFAST

66290 First St.   760 329-9584

Outdoor pool and covered spa. No credit cards.

805 PP TROPICAL MOTEL & SPA

12962 Palm Dr.   760 329-6610

Outdoor hydropool, enclosed hydropool, long "lap" mineral swimming pool. Pools, showers, and picnic area available for day-use fee.

805 QQ TWELFTH STREET MOTEL

66725 12th St.   760 329-6997

DESERT HOT SPRINGS RV AND

■ MOBILE HOME RESORTS

No credit cards are accepted except where noted. All locations have as their address Desert Hot Springs, 92240.

MEMBERSHIP RV PARKS

806 A   AMERICAN ADVENTURE
70405 Dillon Rd.   760 329-5371

One swimming pool, three hydropools and a sauna. Family-oriented. Not open to the public for drop-in visits except during the summer.

806 B   CATALINA RV SPA
13800 Corkill Rd.   760 329-4431

Hot mineral swimming pool, therapy pool. Clubhouse with activities. Family oriented.

806 C   TWO SPRINGS RESORT
14200 Indian Ave.   760 251-1102

MOBILE HOME AND RV PARKS

806 D   CALIENTE SPRINGS
70200 Dillon Rd.   760 329-2970

Four hot spas, 168-foot mineral water swimming pool. Tennis courts. Overnighters welcome.

806 E   CORKILL RV AND MOBILE HOME PARK
17989 Corkill Rd   760 329-5976
                        800 982-3714

One swimming pool, one hydropool, one soaking pool, and two cold pools, enclosed and covered.

806 F   COUNTRY SQUIRE PARK
66455 Dillon Rd.   760 329-1191

Swimming pool, spa, clubhouse. Family oriented. Overnighters welcome.

806 G   DESERT HOT SPRINGS TRAILER PARK
66434 W. Fifth   760 329-6041

806 H   DESERT VIEW ADULT MOBILE PARK
18555 Roberts Rd.   760 329-7079

Outdoor swimming pool and two indoor hydropools. Strictly a mobile home park with no RVs and no overnighters.

806 I   DESERT OASIS MOBILE HOME PARK
71850 Corkill Rd.   760 329-7346

Large swimming pool, three enclosed hydropools. RVs also welcome.

806 J   DESERT SPRINGS SPA
17325 Johnson Rd.   760 329-1384

Large swimming pool, hydropool, RV park.

806 K   GOLDEN LANTERN MOBILE VILLAGE
17300 Corkill Rd.   760 329-6633

One outdoor swimming pool, three enclosed soaking pools. Mobile home spaces, RV hookups, overnight spaces. Used mobile homes for sale. Restaurant, store, and service station next-door.

806 L   HEALING WATERS PARK
13131 Langlois Rd.   760 329-5306

One outdoor swimming pool, three therapy pools. Overnighters welcome.

806 M   HOLMES HOT SPRINGS MOBILE PARK
69530 Dillon Rd.   760 329-7934

One outdoor swimming pool, one outdoor soaking pool. RV hookups and overnight spaces.

806 N MAGIC WATERS MOBILE HOME PARK
17551 Mt. View Rd.   760 329-2600

Outdoor swimming pool and indoor hydropool use hot mineral water. Mobile homes, RV hookups, overnight spaces.

806 O MOUNTAIN VIEW MOBILE HOME PARK
15525 Mt. View Rd.   760 329-5870

One outdoor swimming pool, one semi-enclosed hydropool. Mobile homes, RV hookups, overnight spaces.

806 P ROYAL FOX RV PARK
14500 Palm Dr.   760 329-4481

Swimming pool, two hydropools, and two saunas available to registered guests in the RV park as well as to motel guests.

806 Q SAM'S FAMILY SPA (photo below)
70875 Dillon Rd.   760 329-6457

See entry 805 FF for full description.

Justine Hill

806 R SANDS RV COUNTRY CLUB
16400 Bubbling Wells   760 251-1030

Swimming pool, two hydropools. Registered guests only. Nine-hole golf course open to the public.

806 S SKY VALLEY EAST
74711 Dillon Rd.   760 329-2909

One swimming pool, an outdoor hydropool, an enclosed hydropool on separate patio reserved for adults. Adjoining patio with outdoor swimming pool and outdoor hydropool for family use. Men's and women's saunas. Mobile homes, RV hookups, and overnight spaces.

806 T SKY VALLEY PARK
74565 Dillon Rd.   760 329-7415

Two outdoor swimming pools, one outdoor hydropool, two enclosed hydropools, one indoor hydropool. Men's and women's saunas. Mobile homes, RV hookups, overnight spaces.

806 U SPARKLING WATERS PARK
17800 Langlois Rd.   760 329-6551

Mineral water swimming pool, two spas at 100° and 104°. For senior adults. Overnighters welcome.

806 V TAMARISK MOBILE PARK
18075 Langlois Rd.

Covered swimming pool, hot tub. RV hookups. Overnighters welcome. Visa and MasterCard.

806 W VISTA GRANDE SPA
17625 Langlois Rd.   760 329-5424

Swimming pool, two spas. Senior adults. Overnighters welcome.

MOBILE HOME COMMUNITIES

806 X   CORKILL PALMS
17640 Corkill Rd.

Natural hot mineral water pool and spa. Senior adults.

806 Y   DESERT CREST COUNTRY CLUB
69400 Country Club

Swimming pool, spa. Senior adults.

806 Z   DESERT VIEW ADULT MOBILE PARK
18555 Roberts Rd.   760 329-7079

Outdoor swimming pool, two indoor hydropools. Mobile homes only.

806 AA   JOSHUA MOBILE HOME PARK
18080 Langlois Rd.   760 329-3277

Swimming pool, two enclosed hot pools. Senior adults.

806 BB LA POSADA PARK
17555 Corkill Rd.   760 329-7113

806 CC PALM DRIVE TRAIL PARK
14881 Palm Dr.   760 329-8341

806 DD QUAIL HOLLOW MOBILE HOME PARK
15300 Palm Dr.   760 329-2921

806 EE   RAINBOW SPA, INC.
17777 Langlois Rd.   760 329-7165

Mineral water swimming pool, two hydropools at 98-100° and 100-104°. Senior adults.

806 FF   SKY HAVENS MOBILE PARK
14777 Palm Dr.   619-329-5001

806 GG WAGNER MOBILE HOME PARK
18801 Roberts Rd.   760 329-6043

One outdoor swimming pool, two indoor hydropools, two indoor cold pools. Mobile homes and RV hookups. No overnighters.

806 HH WHISPERING SANDS MOBILE HOME PARK
15225 Palm Dr.   760 329-7210

Swimming pool, hydropool.

Photos for *Turtleback Mesa* on next page by Justine Hill

807   TURTLEBACK MESA B&B
PO Box 8038   760 347-5358
■   Palm Springs, CA 92263

Modern spacious adobe located approximately twenty miles east of Palm springs in the Indio Hills, surrounded by rocky Nature Conservancy land in desert tortoise country. Elevation 1,200 feet. Open all year.

Natural 130° mineral water pumped up from 425 feet underground heats the building through radiant floor coils and flows into a large outdoor swimming pool where it mixes with cold city water. The large outdoor jet tub, which can hold twenty-eight to thirty people, is maintained at 105-110°. No chemicals are added to this mineral water which has the same mineral content as the Ouray Caves in Colorado.

Facilities include two rooms with private toilets and a shared shower. Rooms open directly onto the patio and pool area. Sculptures of turtles from cultures around the world turn this bed-and-breakfast into an ethnic art gallery. All other services are ten miles away in Thousand Palms.

Management prefers guests who are comfortable in a clothing-optional environment. Facilities are only available to registered guests. Call for reservations.

808   PALM SPRINGS SPA HOTEL
AND CASINO, RESORT
100 N. Indian Canyon Dr.
760 325-1461
■   Palm Springs, CA 92262

A major destination resort with an elaborate mineral-water spa located in downtown Palm Springs. Elevation 500 feet. Open all year.

Natural mineral water flows out of historic Indian wells on the property at temperatures of 106°. The spa has separate men's and women's sections, each containing 14 marble tubs separately controllable with mineral water temperature up to 104°. These tubs are drained and refilled after each use so that no chemical treatment of the water is necessary. Each spa also has vapor-inhalation rooms, a steambath, and a dry sauna. Bathing suits are required in the outdoor poor area, optional in the bathhouse and solarium. Fees to use the spa are discounted for hotel guests.

Services and facilities on the premises include massage, barber and beauty shop, rooms (handicap accessible rooms are on the ground floor), restaurant and lounge, pool bar, snacks, airport pickup, and group conference rooms. Also available is an Indian-owned gaming casino, open twenty-four hours. All major credit cards accepted. Pool and spa facilities are available to the public as well as to registered guests.

Directions: Take the Indian Canyou Dr.. exit from I-10 and drive south 6.5 miles to the resort.

Jayson Loam

Courtesy of Bashford's

809 A BASHFORD'S HOT MINERAL SPA
10590 Hot Mineral Spa Rd.
760 354-1315

■   Niland, CA 92257

Primarily a winter RV resort for adults, located on a desert slope overlooking the Salton Sea. Elevation 50 feet below sea level. Open October 1 to May 30.

Natural mineral water flows out of an artesian well at 150° and into two cooling tanks from which it is piped to an outdoor swimming pool maintained at 84° and to an outdoor hydropool maintained at 102°. The water in both pools is chlorine-treated. Mineral water is also piped to six outdoor soaking tubs with temperatures from 101-105°. These tubs are drained and refilled after each use so that no chemical treatment is needed. Bathing suits are required.

RV hookups, overnight spaces, and a laundry room are available on the premises, and catfish fishing (no license required) is about one mile away. Discover cards are accepted. It is seven miles to a motel, restaurant, and service station.

Jayson Loam

809 B FOUNTAIN OF YOUTH SPA
10249 Coachella Canal Rd.
760 354-1340   888 8000-772

■   Niland, CA 92257

The largest of the RV parks in this area, located on a desert slope overlooking the Salton Sea. Elevation sea level. Open all year.

Natural mineral water flows out of an artesian well on the property at 137°, is cooled by heat exchangers, and is piped to two pool areas, one of which is reserved for adults. The two outdoor swimming pools range in temperature from 85-90°. The five outdoor hydropools range in temperature from 100-107°. The water in all pools is chlorine treated. Pools are available to registered campers only. No day use. Bathing suits are required.

The facilities include a laundromat, store, cafe, RV hookups, overnight camping spaces, recreation rooms, library, exercise and fitness room, and car wash. Services include massage, beauty and barber shops. Church services and activity programs are also offered. No reservations are taken. If no hookup spaces are available, it is possible to dry camp and get on a waiting list. It is two and one-half miles south to a service station across from the border patrol on CA 111 and four and one-half miles north to a motel and restaurant at Bombay Beach.

Directions: from CA 111, 3 miles south of Bombay Beach, drive east on Hot Mineral Spa Rd. for 1.5 miles, then right onto Spa Rd. for 1.1 miles.

Justine Hill

809 C   IMPERIAL SEA VIEW HOT SPRINGS
10595 Hot Mineral Spa Rd.
760 354-1204

■   **Niland, CA 92257**

The original "Old Spa" location, with the first hot well drilled in this area. Located on a desert slope overlooking the Salton Sea. Elevation fifty feet below sea level. Open all year.

Natural mineral water flows out of an artesian well at 165° and into a large holding and cooling tank from which it is piped to seven outdoor pools. Five hydropools are maintained at a variety of temperatures from 96-104°. Two mineral-water soaking pools are maintained at 96° and 88°. All pools are treated with chlorine. Bathing suits are required.

RV hookups, overnight camping spaces and a store are on the premises. No credit cards accepted. It is six miles to a service station on CA 111 across from the border patrol and seven and one-half miles north to a restaurant and motel in Bombay Beach.

809 D   LARK SPA
HCO-1, Box 10   760 354-1384

■   **Niland, CA 92257**

Mobile home and RV winter resort located on a desert slope overlooking the Salton Sea. Elevation fifty feet below sea level. Open all year.

Well water, gas heated and chlorine treated, is used in an outdoor hydropool maintained at 102°. Bathing suits are required.

Overnight spaces and RV hookups are available on the premises. No credit cards are accepted. It is one mile to a store and service station and four miles to a motel and restaurant.

Directions: From Niland, drive 10.5 miles north to Frink Rd. and turn right (east) for 1 mile. Frink Rd. is 3 miles south of the border patrol station on CA 111.

810   FIVE PALMS WARM WELL OASIS

●   **Near the city of Brawley**

An exotic, true desert oasis surrounded by palm trees and tall bullrushes in the otherwise arid, sparsely vegetated Imperial Valley desert south of the Salton Sea. Elevation 113 feet below sea level. Open all year.

Natural 92° mineral water bubbles up from an artesian well through a three-inch pipe in the middle of a large, clean, sandy-bottom soaking pond that is eighteen inches deep and large enough for a dozen people. In winter, the bullrushes and palms help shade the pool. The custom is clothing optional.

There are no services available except plenty of open BLM desert where overnight parking is permitted with a fourteen-day limit. Caution: Choose your parking space carefully; vehicles have been know to get stuck in the soft sand underneath a deceptively firm crust. Parking is not permitted within a 150-foot radius of the springs, and overnight camping is not permitted within approximately a one-half mile radius of the well so that animals will feel safe to come to the water. Please help by cleaning up any party trash. All services are available in Brawley, approximately sixteen and one-half miles away.

Directions: From Brawley, drive 15 miles east on CA 78, crossing the canal. Take the second dirt road right (.4 miles past the canal). Follow the one-lane road for 1.6 miles to five tall palms, the only greenery in the area. The one-lane, graded, unsurfaced road has some soft sandy spots that can usually be negotiated by normal passenger vehicles.

● Near the town of Holtville

Two cement soaking pools and a large pond, fed by an artesian well, located just off the I-8 right-of-way on the east edge of Holtville. Elevation sea level. Open all year; closed midnight to 5 AM.

Natural mineral water flows out of an artesian well at 125° and splashes on the edge of a six-foot by six-foot by three-foot deep cement cistern. Hot water showers in through holes in an overhead swing-arm horizontal pipe, which can be diverted when the desired pool temperature is reached. A smaller, cement, bathtub-size pool is next to the larger tub. There is very little self-cleaning action, and algae growth is rapid. Volunteer snowbirds regularly scrub the pools with bleach, which also removes the algae smell. Because the pools are visible from I-8, bathing suits are recommended. A four-step ladder makes the tub handicap accessible with assistance. A sign reminds campers that "soap is prohibited in spa/pond." The area is posted for day-use only and the sheriff patrols regularly.

Overflow from the tub goes into a large, shallow, sandy-bottom "olde swimming hole" that used to be stocked with fish. Water temperature measures 90°, and fan palms offer a spot of shade.

Facilities include wooden benches, a cement walkway, trash cans, nearby BLM pit toilets, and a fenced-off parking area where overnight parking is prohibited. A primitive BLM campground with a fourteen-day limit is located twenty yards north of the well, across the road. Camping permits are required September to April and a fee is charged. Free overnight camping is available one mile outside the long-term camping area. All services are in Holtville.

Directions: At the east end of Holtville, take the Van Der Linden exit (CA 115) from I-8. Go north and immediately take the first right turn onto a frontage road paralleling I-8. At approximately 1 mile you will cross over the Highline Canal. Just past the canal on the right (south) is a flat, fenced parking area with pit toilets. The pools are just ahead toward I-8

GPS: N 32.45352 W 115.16181.

POOL AREA RULES
(FOR AREAS WITHIN POST AND CABLE FENCE LINE)

1. Curfew from Midnight to 5 a.m.
2. No Food
3. No Beverages
4. No Pets
5. No Use of Soap

VIOLATORS SUBJECT TO CITATION AUTHORITY
(43CFR 8365.1-6)

Highline photos by Justine Hill

Jayson Loam

Courtesy of Agua Caliente

812   JACUMBA HOT SPRINGS SPA LODGE AND RESORT

Box 371   619 766-4333

■   **Jacumba, CA 92034**

An older motel spa located just off I-8, 80 miles east of San Diego. Elevation 2,800 feet. Open all year.

Natural mineral water with a slight sulfur odor flows out of a spring at 140-150 gallons per minute at a temperature of 97° and is then piped to an indoor hydropool and an outdoor swimming pool. Continuous flow-through maintains a temperature of 95° in the hydropool and 85° in the swimming pool, with no chemical treatment of the water required. Hot mineral water showers are in the spa room. The pools are available to the general public for a use fee. Pools are handicap accessible, with assistance. Bathing suits are required.

Facilities include rooms, the rustic Alpine restaurant, a bar, sauna, tennis and shuffleboard courts, a German "biergarten patio" with Mexican sculpture and pottery, and a lawn area with shade trees. Horseback riding and guided hikes can be arranged. Massage is available on the premises. Visa, MasterCard and American Express are accepted. It is one block to a store and service station and .5 mile to RV hookups.

Directions: Take the Jacumba exit off I-8 and go 3 miles to the tiny town of Jacumba. The spa is located on the north side of Old Highway 80, the main street through town.

813   AGUA CALIENTE COUNTY PARK

For reservations   619 565-3600

■   **Located in the Anza Borrego Desert**

A county-operated, desert campground located in a wildlife refuge area near the Anza Borrego Desert. A wide variety of animals and beautiful spring wildflowers and succulents are native to this area. No pets are permitted at any time! Elevation 1,300 feet. Open September through May.

Natural mineral water flows out of several springs at 96° and is then piped to two pools where it is filtered and chlorinated. The outdoor swimming pool with a water temperature between 90-92° is available for families. The large indoor hydropool is located in a corrugated tin quonset hut. The chlorine-treated mineral water is solar and gas heated to 104°. The hydropool, showers, restrooms, and dressing area are all handicap accessible. Bathing suits are required. Pool facilities are available to the public for day use, as well as to registered campers. Handicap accessible.

Facilities include RV hookups and overnight camping spaces, hiking trails, picnic and barbeque area, horseshoe pits, shuffleboard, and a children's play area. Credit cards are accepted. It is one-half mile to a small general store, cafe and phone, twenty-five miles to a gas station, and thirty-five miles to a motel. There is a nearby airstrip for small planes.

Directions: Take the Ocotillo exit off I-8, 27 miles east of El Centro and 95 miles east of San Diego. Follow Imperial Co. Rd. S-2 for 25 miles into the Anza Borego desert to the sign for Agua Caliente Springs. Bear left .1 mile to the general store and left again for .5 miles to the campground.

Courtesy of Warner Springs

815   THE TUBS
7220 El Cajon Blvd.   619 698-7727
❏   San Diego, CA 92115

San Diego's original rent-a-tub establishment, located on a main suburban street near San Diego State University.

Eleven spa suites for rent to the public use gas-heated tap water that is treated with chlorine and maintained at 102°. Saunas are included in all rooms as are showers, towels and body shampoo. Each suite is equipped with an AM/FM stereo cassette player. The VIP Suite, large enough for 12 persons, has a bathroom and steambath, plus a sauna.

A juice bar is available on the premises. Visa and MasterCard are accepted. Phone for rates, reservations, and directions.

814   WARNER SPRINGS RANCH
31652 Hwy. 79   760 782-4200
■   Warner Springs, CA 92086

Private destination resort in rural northeastern San Diego County. Elevation 3,100 feet. Open all year.

Natural mineral water flows out at 130-140° into an Olympic-size swimming pool where it is cooled to 102°. A cool freshwater pool is adjacent to the hot pool. Bathing suits are required. Handicap accessible.

Facilities include cabins, sauna, spa, equestrian center, golf, tennis, a restaurant, and an airport. Massages can be booked ahead. There are no phones or TVs in the rooms. Major credit cards are accepted. Phone for rates, reservations, and directions.

A California Historic Site

816 CARLSBAD MINERAL WATER SPA
2802 Carlsbad Blvd.   **760 434-1887**
■ **Carlsbad, CA 92008**

Modern mineral water spa and therapeutic baths located on the site of an 1880s health spa and hotel. The original spa (and entire town) was named for the famous Karlsbad health resort in Bohemia which has a similar mineral water content. Open all year.

Carbonated mineral water from an aquifer 1,700 feet deep is recharged from the Cleveland National Forest, sixty miles east of Carlsbad. No chemicals are necessary as a fresh bath is drawn for each customer. Each room is lavishly decorated using an Egyptian-Roman theme.

Services include carbonated mineral water baths, mud or clay facials, total-body clay, aromatherapy, massage, body wraps, and special spa packages.

Phone for rates and reservations.

817 A LAKE ELSINORE HOT SPRINGS MOTEL
316 N. Main   **909 674-2581**
■ **Lake Elsinore, CA 92330**

Older motel and spa located several blocks north of downtown Lake Elsinore. Elevation 1,300 feet. Open all year.

Natural sulphur water flows out of an artesian well at 100° and is piped to three pools and to the bathtubs in all rooms. The outdoor swimming pool is maintained at 104°. All pools are chlorine treated and are available to the public as well as to registered guests. Bathing suits are required.

Facilities include a sauna and a recreation room. Rooms and massage are available on the premises. Visa and MasterCard are accepted. It is five blocks to a restaurant, store, and service station.

817 B HAN'S MOTEL AND MINERAL SPA
215 W. Graham   **909 674-3551**
■ **Lake Elsinore, CA 92330**

An older motel in downtown Lake Elsinore. Elevation 1,300 feet. Open all year.

Natural mineral water flows out of an artesian well at 133° and is piped to two pools and to the bathtubs in every room. The outdoor swimming pool is maintained at 86°, and the indoor hydropool at 105°. The water in both pools is chlorine treated. There is also a dry sauna and outdoor shower. Bathing suits are required.

Rooms are available on the premises. No credit cards are accepted. It is two blocks to a restaurant, store, and service station.

818   GLEN IVY HOT SPRINGS SPA
25000 Glen Ivy Road   909 277-3529
800 454-8772

■   Corona, CA 91719

Large, well-equipped, beautifully landscaped day-use resort and spa located on the dry east side of the Santa Ana mountains seventy miles from Los Angeles. Elevation 1,300 feet. Open all year, except Thanksgiving, Christmas, and New Years. (You must be over sixteen years of age to be admitted)

Natural mineral water from two wells at 90° and 110° is mixed and piped to a wide variety of pools. There are seven sunken hydrojet tubs with temperatures of 104-106°, using continuous flow-through, unchlorinated mineral water. The other pools have automatic filters and chlorinators. An outdoor swimming pool is maintained at 85°, a covered soaking pool at 103°, two outdoor hydropools at 101° and 104°, two outdoor shallow bubble pools at 103° and 100°, a large outdoor floating pool at 90°, and a California red clay-bath pool at 100°. (Guests should bring an old bathing suit to wear in the mud bath as the clay does stain some fabrics.) Bathing suits are required.

Facilities include a new entrance building "Entrada al Paraiso" offering a fine spa boutique, men's and women's locker rooms equipped with hair blowers, a coed dry sauna, and two outdoor cafes. Spa treatments include Swedish, shiatsu, and aromatherapy massage, eucalyptus wraps, apricot body scrubs, European facials, manicures, pedicures and waxings. Advance reservations for these services are highly recommended. Entrance to the spa facilities and restroom are handicap accessible, but no attendants are provided or lifts for the pools. All major credit cards, ATMs and personal checks are accepted.

Directions: Eight miles south of Corona on I-15, exit right onto the Temescal Canyon Rd. Go 1 mile south to Glen Ivy Rd., turn right and follow signs to the resort.

Justine Hill

Club Mud

Glen Ivy: A personal favorite is this pool which you can wade into and cover yourself with red mud. Then you go stretch out in the sun as the mud crackles and tickles producing the softest skin you've ever had.

La Vida, which means "life" in Spanish, is about to get a new infusion of money and will hopefully open this year after being closed since the 1960s.

---

819 LA VIDA MINERAL SPA
6155 Carbon Canyon Rd.
714 996-7200
■ ### Brea, CA 92621

An historic mineral water spa and hotel dating back to the 1930s is being replace by a modern holistic health center, spa and hotel, slated to open in 1998. Located in the rural foothills of northern Orange County, northwest of Brea. Elevation 700 feet.

A pure 111° artesian spring with no sulphur odor pour out of the ground at the rate of 25,000-30,000 gallons per day and will be used to fill the refurbished 1940s swimming pool, as well as a new state-of-the-art spa facility which will be open to the public.

Adjacent La Vida restaurant and bikers bar remains open for business.

Call for current status of new hotel and spa.

Courtesy of Neptune's Lagoons

Courtesy of Puddingstone

820 NEPTUNE'S LAGOONS
2784 W. Ball Rd.   714 761-8325

❑   Anaheim, CA 92804

Modern, suburban pool-rental facility near Disneyland and Knott's Berry Farm. Open seven days.

Private-space hot pools using gas-heated tap water are treated with chlorine. There are six indoor fiberglass pools with water temperatures maintained at 99-101°. Three of the rooms have saunas.

Each room has a hydrojet tub with bubble controls, a dimmer for lights, air conditioning, relaxation bed, shower, towels, hair dryer, tape player, and sky light. TV and VCR are available. Handicap accessible.

All major credit cards are accepted. Phone for rates, reservations, and directions.

821 PUDDINGSTONE HOT TUBS
1777 Camper View Rd.   909 592-2222

❑   San Dimas, CA 91773

A unique, modern rent-a-tub facility that offers both privacy and a spectacular view. Located in Bonelli County Regional Park overlooking Puddingstone Reservoir, twenty-five miles east of Los Angeles.

Fifteen outdoor pools (twelve private and three deluxe) using chlorine-treated tap water heated by a combination of propane and electricity, are for rent to the public by the hour. The tubs can hold up to six people. The very large unheated community pool has a 360° view with spacious decking, fire pit and barbecue, a food serving area, and a bandstand. It can be reserved for large groups and parties. The smaller tubs offer a beautiful view, tub temperature controls, and a three-sided enclosure for privacy. All facilities are handicap accessible.

A wedding gazebo is available on the premises and intimate picnic-style meals for two can be ordered ahead along with "special occasion" packages with flowers and balloons. You are welcome to bring a picnic basket. An RV park, golf course, picnic area, horse stables, boat rentals, and Raging Waters recreation area are available in the adjoining regional park. Phone for rates, reservations, and directions.

Located off I-10, Fairplex exit.

822 BEVERLY HOT SPRINGS
308 N. Oxford Ave.   213 734-7000
■   **Los Angeles, CA 90004**

A modern, Korean-style, indoor spa built over a hot water artesian well a few miles west of downtown Los Angeles. Elevation 300 feet. Open all year.

From a well drilled in the early 1900s, mineral water flows out at a temperature of 105° and is piped to large, tiled, soaking pools equipped with hydrojets in the women's section (first floor) and the men's section (second floor). Each section also has a pool of cooled mineral water. All pools operate on a continuous flow-through basis so that no chemical treatment of the water is necessary. Bathing suits are not required in pool rooms.

Facilities include a dry sauna and a steam sauna in each section, plus a restaurant and beauty salon. Shiatsu massage, cream massage, and body scrubs are available on the premises. Visa and MasterCard are accepted. Phone for rates, reservations, and directions.

Courtesy of Splash

823   SPLASH, THE RELAXATION SPA
8054 W. 3rd St.   213 653-4412
❑   **Los Angeles, CA 90048**

Eighteen beautifully decorated, romantic, very private suites located in an urban Los Angeles location.

All rooms feature a chlorinated hydrojet tub with controls for bubbles, water temperature, and cool-off mists. Also included are dimmer controls for room and tub lights, air conditioning, relaxation bed, and fully equipped dressing room with shower and herbal soaps and towels. Many of the more exotically decorated suites offer additional amenities such as saunas, waterfalls, aquariums, skylights, etc.

Gift certificates, in-suite catering, corporate memberships and overnight stays are available. Group discounts for private parties are also available, as well as help in arranging the party.

Major credit cards are accepted. Phone for rates, reservations, and directions.

Courtesy of Beverly Hot Springs

BAJA CALIFORNIA
BAJA NORTE

Map for **BAJA SUR** is on page 195

Tijuana Hwy 2 Mexicali

Ensenada

905

901

910

911 902

906

907

908

909

912

913

San Felipe

903

904

Hwy 1

Hwy 3

Hwy 5

Pacific Ocean

Gulf of California

914

Guerrero Negro

Hwy 1

Baja Norte

Baja Sur (map on page 195)

Many of the hot spring locations in Baja are situated in very remote desert areas. The directions are often quite involved and depend on roads that are washed out during rains. Alternate routes often need to be used. For specific directions and road information, we suggest you contact **Rob's Baja Tours, PO Box 4003, Balboa, CA 92661. 714 673-2670.** Rob also provides special guided trips that relieve you of having to worry about any of this.

All photos in this section by Rob Williams except those on page 186 by Justine Hill.

This map was designed to be used with a standard highway map.

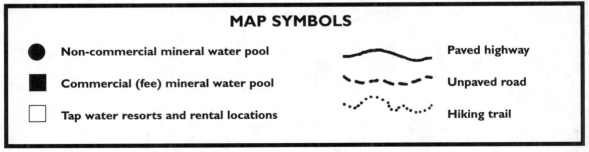

MAP SYMBOLS

● Non-commercial mineral water pool

■ Commercial (fee) mineral water pool

☐ Tap water resorts and rental locations

——— Paved highway

– – – Unpaved road

· · · · Hiking trail

901 GUADALUPE CANYON HOT SPRINGS

■ **Southwest of Mexicali**

Beautiful mineral water soaking pools, waterfalls, and campsites in a remote palm canyon on the east slope of the Sierra Juarez Mountains. Elevation 1,300 feet. Open all year, but summer temperatures often reach 110°. For campground reservations call Rob's Baja Tours at 714 673-2670.

Natural mineral water emerges from several springs at 125° and flows through man-made aqueducts to pools and flush toilets. More than twenty drainable soaking pools, built of rocks and cement, are scattered through palm forests and piles of boulders. Bathing suits are required except at night.

A limited number of campsites at Campo 1, each with its own parking area, palapas, pool, and picnic table, can be rented by the day, week, or month. Reservations require two weeks notice. This Campo has new rest rooms and some newer tubs. There is no electricity or telephone at this location. All services are sixty miles away in Mexicali, but there is a restaurant and a small store that sells cold beer and soft drinks. Ancient Indian caves, cascading waterfalls, and thick palm forests are within hiking distance. Other palm canyons in the mountain range may be explored for primitive hot springs, but the use of an experienced guide is recommended.

Directions (via Tecate): From San Diego go East on Hwy 94 approximately 40 miles. Turn south on Tecate Road (188) and go 1.3 miles to the border crossing (open 6:00 AM to midnight). Four blocks past the border, turn left on Mexico Hwy 2. Travel east 41 miles to La Rumorosa (last chance for gas). Just east of La Rumorosa you will begin the winding descent to the desert. At approximately 65 miles (200 yards past the K28 marker) there will be signs for "Cannon De Guadalupe." Turn right onto a graded dirt road. This dirt road has a great number of "washboards" and some bad dips. Ten miles down the road you will see signs for The Canyon at Rancho Ponderosa. (Ignore any signs that say to turn left. This is an alternate route only in dry weather). At 27 miles, turn right at the sign for the canyon. This last part is 7 miles of good but winding dirt road. The last mile is rough (take it slow). Campo 1 is on the left across the road from a sign which says "BIENVENIDOS."

The warm mineral water in the swimming pool is 85 degrees–just perfect for a hot summer day.

Pools can be found in caves or out in the open where a group of friends can enjoy a beautiful desert sunset.

The pool on the left is a brand new swimming pool. The one above was originally built as a horse trough and is only eighteen inches deep. The runoff from the main spring forms a small hot water fall (below) where you could sit and enjoy a shower.

902 PALOMAR CANYON HOT SPRINGS

● **Southwest of Mexicali**

Small wilderness hot springs in a remote palm canyon on the east slope of the Sierra Juarez Mountains, 45 miles from the nearest paved road. Elevation 1,500 feet. Open all year, but summer temperatures often reach 110°.

Natural mineral water bubbles out of three small source pools at 98° and then sinks into the sand as it flows down the canyon. A small cement pool at 96° is good for bathing but only eighteen inches deep. A large rock-and-cement pool at 85° degrees has just been built. At this remote location, the apparent local clothing custom is the mutual consent of those present.

There are no facilities or services, but there is an all-year cold water stream in the canyon and excellent camping locations for backpackers. Four-wheel drive is required on the last few miles of the access road, and the springs are a two-hour hike up the canyon beyond the end of the road.

Directions to such a remote location are beyond the scope of this book. The use of a guide service is recommended.

903   VALLE CHICO HOT SPRINGS

● **Southwest of San Felipe**

A remote, primitive hot spring in a barren canyon in the eastern escarpment of the Sierra San Pedro Martir. Elevation 1,500 feet. Open all year, but summer temperatures often exceed 110°.

Natural mineral water bubbles out of a large source pool at 144° and flows across the canyon into an all-year cold water stream. Volunteers could build a soaking pool at that confluence but have not yet done so. At this remote location, the apparent clothing custom is the mutual consent of those present.

There are no services at this location.

Directions to such a remote location are beyond the scope of this book. The use of a guide service is recommended.

In such remote areas it is not unusual to find the hot water simply flowing across the ground. This area could use volunteers to build more permanent pools.

A series of three soaking pools is revealed for a few hours each day at low tide. Located between the volcanic rocks, the pools need the cool ocean water to make the water temperatures comfortable.

The tiny pueblo of Puertecitos does provide such necessary services as gas, vehicle repair, a small store, campsites, a restaurant, fishing, and boat ramps.

904 PUERTECITOS HOT SPRINGS
On the Gulf of California

● **South of San Felipe**

Geothermal water bubbles up from under volcanic rock along the edge of the Sea of Cortez and collects in waist-deep soaking pools that are under water during high tide and useable only several hours each day during low tide. Elevation sea level. Open all year, although summer air temperature can soar above 110°.

Natural mineral water flows up through the gravel bottom of the soaking pools that have been blasted out of the volcanic rock. Two rectangular pools are large enough for a dozen people each; a third round pool can accommodate six people. Pool temperatures vary widely, depending on the mix of geothermal water and sea water. There is only a brief time each low tide when the mixture makes it possible to soak. Bathing suits are recommended.

There are no services at this location. It is .25 miles to all services in the tiny pueblo of Puertecitos. Services include gas (honk your horn 8 AM to 8 PM for service), vehicle repair, a four-room hotel, small store for provisions, and campgrounds all along the Sea of Cortez south from San Felipe.

Directions: From the round-about at the Pemex Station just past the arches in San Felipe, follow Hwy 5, which is the road toward the airport. At 6.4 miles take the turnoff toward Laguna Chapal, Percebu, and El Faro. Pay careful attention to signs along this road warning of "vados" (dips), which are deep, steep, and imperceptible until you are upon them. It is 53 miles from the round-about in San Felipe to the town of Puertecitos, where the paved road ends.

In Puertecitos, just before the Pemex station, turn left toward the pink entranceway marked "Private Property: Puertecitos Hot Springs, boat ramp..." The owners collect a fee of $1.00 per person to go to the springs. At .2 miles past the gate, on the left is "Taller Panama," a large tin building where the dirt road veers to the right up a hill past the boat ramp. Follow this road for .6 miles to a cul-de-sac and turn around. The hot springs are in the tide pools on the right below a green building. There are parking turnouts on both sides of the road. There is a cement walkway through the volcanic rock down to the pools.

To Tecate

LA MISION

Rio San Miguel

Guadalupe

GUADALUPE

905 Russian Valley Hot Springs

EL SAUZAL

ENSENADA

△ Cerro de Ensenada

906 Las Rosas Hotel and Spa

Arroyo de Ensenada

Bahia de Todos Santos

PIEDRAS GORDAS

910 Marconi Warm Springs

OJOS NEGROS

Punta Banda

907 Punta Banda Hot Springs

Rio San

AGUA CALIENTE

911 Agua Caliente Hot Springs

Carlos

908 Cantu Hot Springs

GATE

EJIDO URUAPAN

912 Uruapan Hot Springs

909 Rancho Gilberto Hot Springs

(RUINS)

★ SANTO TOMAS

Continue southeast to: 913 Valle La Trinidad

This map shows in more detail those springs in or near Ensenada. Use this map with a detailed road map.

As arid as this land appears, less than a quarter of a mile away is a lovely cold stream and waterfall.

905   RUSSIAN VALLEY HOT SPRINGS
(see map on page 195)

● **South of Tecate**

Several undeveloped wilderness hot springs near a beautiful waterfall in a remote valley that was named for an historic Russian settlement. Elevation 1,500 feet. Open all year.

Natural mineral water flows from two main source springs at 125°. In one sandy-bottom pool, the geothermal water bubbles up from below and is cooled by evaporation to maintain the pool temperature at approximately 110°. The other source spring flows out of a sandy bank into a rock-lined pool where it is mixed with creek water and the temperature is controlled by moving rocks to admit cold water. In this remote location, the apparent local clothing custom is the mutual consent of those present.

There are no services on the premises, but there is a delightful cold pool and waterfall beside the access trail a quarter mile from the springs. All services are twenty five miles away in Ensenada.

The hot springs area is located fifty miles south of Tecate and ten miles east of Hwy 3. See map at right for detailed directions.

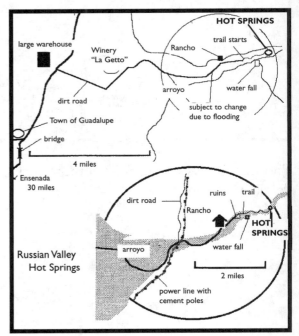

906   LAS ROSAS HOTEL & SPA

(see map on page 195)

Post Office Box 316

011-52-61-74-43-10

❏   Ensenada, Baja California, Mexico

A charming, upscale, small hotel/resort on the magnif-icent shoreline north of Ensenada. Elevation sea level. Open all year.

Tap water, heated with propane, is used in a seaside pool maintained at 80° and in a hydrojet spa maintained at 104°. Bathing suits are required. Pools are available for day use except during the busiest summer months. Inquire by telephone to determine current status.

Rooms, restaurant, fitness center, and racquetball court are available on the premises. It is two miles to all other services in Ensenada. Visa and MasterCard are accepted.

Directions: From Tijuana, take the Hwy 1 toll road south for 60 miles to Las Rosas, which is two miles north of Ensenada.

907   PUNTA BANDA HOT SPRINGS

Estero Beach   (see map on page 195)

●   **On the Punta Banda Peninsula**

A unique opportunity to literally dig your own hot spring pool at low tide on an easily accessible beach south of Ensenada. Elevation sea level. Open all year.

Natural mineral water (up to 170°) bubbles up through many yards of beach sand. During high tide swim-mers can feel the extra warmth in the surf. During low tide it is possible to dig pools in the beach sand. These fill with a soakable combination of hot mineral water and cold sea water. Bathing suits are required.

Parking is available in the adjoining trailer camp, which offers its tenants hot mineral water piped from geother-mal wells on the premises. It is eight miles to all other ser-vices in Ensenada.

Directions: From Ensenada, drive south on Hwy 1 to Hwy 23 Maneadero. Turn right on the paved road for approximately eight miles to the Agua Caliente Trailer Camp. This beach is also known as La Jolla and is near the Baja Beach and Tennis Club.

Soakers travel thirteen miles of very scenic, improved, dirt road, climbing to 2,000 feet before crossing the Punta Banda ridge and dropping to a remote beach on the Pacific Coast.

908 CANTU HOT SPRINGS
(see map on page 195)
● **South of the Punta Banda Peninsula**

A small pool at the edge of the ocean on a remote rocky beach just past Rancho Cantu. Elevation 20 feet. Open all year.

Natural mineral water flows from a small, 90° stream down an arroyo to a shallow, hand-made pool about 100 yards from the beach. You may need to do some further digging to enlarge the pool to your specifications. Due to the remote location, clothing is optional.

There is free camping on the windswept bluffs, fifty feet above the beach. There are no services on the premises, and it is thirty miles (one hour driving time) back to Ensenada. This is a good area for fishing, diving, and surfing.

Directions: Take Hwy 23 .5 miles past La Jolla Beach and turn left onto graded dirt road. There is a sign for Ej. Cantu. The dirt road winds up the mountain and crosses over the top, then drops down to the Pacific Coast. Note the kilometer markers (small cement posts on the side of road).

909 RANCHO GILBERTO/ ST. TOMAS HOT SPRINGS
(see map on page 195)
● **South of Ensenada**

Hot water comes up in several locations in a small stream which flows down into a valley near Santo Tomas and is surrounded by farming areas and tree-covered hillsides. Elevation 500 feet. Open all year.

Natural mineral water flows up from the streambed at 100° in several places. You will need to dig your own pool and place rocks and sand around the edge to hold the water. Temperatures are regulated by mixing hot water with cold stream water. Bathing suits are required.

There are no services on the premises, but overnight parking is available at the farmhouse one-hundred yards away. It is fifteen miles to a campground at La Bocana Beach and four miles to a store and restaurant.

Directions: From Ensenada, travel 20 miles south on Highway 1. Turn right on the dirt road with a sign for La Bocana. Drive 4.1 miles on graded dirt road toward the ocean. Rancho is on the left side, no sign.

The only way to find out where the hot water comes up in this stream is to feel for it. Then, build yourself a pool to soak in.

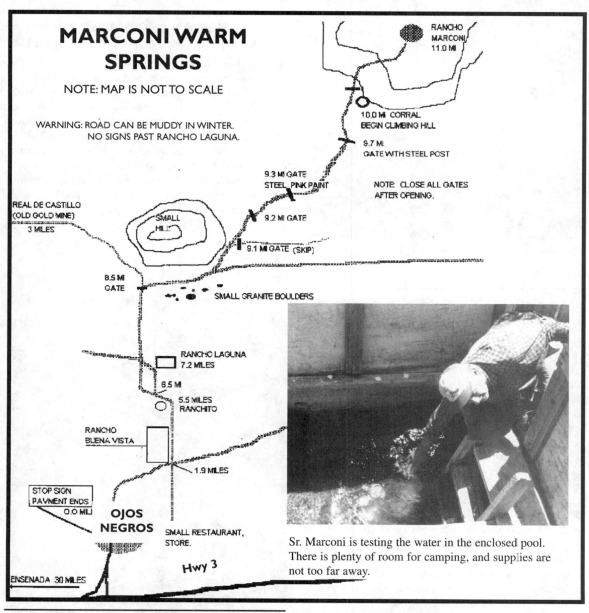

MARCONI WARM SPRINGS

NOTE: MAP IS NOT TO SCALE

WARNING: ROAD CAN BE MUDDY IN WINTER.
NO SIGNS PAST RANCHO LAGUNA.

RANCHO MARCONI 11.0 MI

10.0 MI CORRAL
BEGIN CLIMBING HILL

9.7 MI
GATE WITH STEEL POST

NOTE: CLOSE ALL GATES
AFTER OPENING.

9.3 MI GATE
STEEL PINK PAINT

9.2 MI GATE

9.1 MI GATE (SKIP)

REAL DE CASTILLO
(OLD GOLD MINE)
3 MILES

SMALL HILL

8.5 MI GATE

SMALL GRANITE BOULDERS

RANCHO LAGUNA
7.2 MILES

8.5 MI

5.5 MILES
RANCHITO

RANCHO
BUENA VISTA

1.9 MILES

STOP SIGN
PAVMENT ENDS
0.0 MLI

OJOS
NEGROS

SMALL RESTAURANT,
STORE.

Hwy 3

ENSENADA 30 MILES

Sr. Marconi is testing the water in the enclosed pool.
There is plenty of room for camping, and supplies are
not too far away.

910   MARCONI WARM SPRINGS
(see map on page 195)

● **East of Ensenada**

Located in the foothills of the Sierra Juarez Mountains at the norther end of the Ojos Negros Valley. Elevation 1,500 feet. Open all year.

Natural mineral water at 80° fills one enclosed six-foot by four-foot by three-foot deep pool. Considering the hot summers in the area, this water temperature should feel quite good. Clothing may be required outside the enclosed area even though there are very few tourists. However, this is a farming community.

There is one shelter for camping plus many open areas where camping is permitted. There is a $10 charge per night per car. The nearest food and gas are in in Ojos Negros, and all other services are found in Ensenada.

Directions: take Hwy 3 east of Ensenada for 30 miles and turn left at the sign to Ojos Negros. Pavement ends one mile later in the center of town. It is 11 miles to the springs (see detailed map above).

Relaxing, waiting for the pool to refill with fresh water.

911 AGUA CALIENTE HOT SPRINGS
(see map on page 195)

■ **East of Ensenada**

An older commercial hot springs "resort" located in an arid valley five miles south of Hwy 3. Elevation 1,500 feet. Open all year, but the bar and restaurant are open only during April through August.

Natural mineral water flows out of several springs at temperatures ranging from 80 to 108°. The warmest source spring supplies 108° water to the bathhouse tubs, which are drained and filled after each use. It also flows directly into a large concrete outdoor soaking pool which maintains a temperature of 97°. Water from the coolest spring is piped to a large swimming pool at a temperature of 75° which is drained and filled every week. No chemical treatment is added. Water from a third spring at 97° is piped to the motel rooms, bar, and restaurant as tap water. Bathing suits are required except in individual tubs.

Motel rooms with bar and restaurant service operating during spring and summer months only. It is sixteen miles to all other services in Ensenada.

Directions: (Do not attempt in wet weather.) From Ensenada, drive east on Hwy 3 to marker KM 26. Watch for "AGUA CALIENTE" sign and turn right on a 5-mile dirt road that ends at the resort. Not recommended for trailers or low clearance vehicles.

As there is no telephone or mailing address, it is not possible to secure reservations. It is very crowded during Easter vacation.

912 URUAPAN HOT SPRINGS
(see map on page 195)

■ **South of Ensenada**

A well-worn combination bathhouse and laundry in a green fertile valley at the base of coastal scrub foothills two miles from Hwy 1. Elevation 500 feet. Open all year.

Natural mineral water flows out of many pastureland springs at temperatures ranging from 118 to 138° and is piped to a cistern that supplies a fifty-year-old building with five individual bathtub rooms and five outdoor washing machines. Clearly, the tubs are for cleanliness bathing, not recreational soaking, and clothing is optional only in private spaces.

913 VALLE LA TRINIDAD/RANCHO LOS POZITOS

(see map on page 195)

● **Southeast of Ensenada**

Sandy bottom pools, semi-developed, at the headwaters of a stream in an open valley. Surrounded by small hills, low mountains, and agricultural lands in the midst of old ranchos. Elevation 2,800 feet. Open all year.

Natural mineral water flows up from the bottom of the first pool at 105°. This eight-foot square pool has a sandy bottom, brick walls, and tin roof. The second pool is lined with rocks and located in the middle of the stream. In the third, water flows into a six-foot square brick pool. Bathing suits are required.

Overnight parking is permitted at the farm hous about one-hundred yards away. It is five miles to a store, restaurant and other services.

Directions: Go east from Ensenada on Highway 3 about 60 miles. Turn right toward Valle De Trinidad on paved road. After 1 mile turn right onto dirt road at church. Continue 2 miles toward west end of valley and follow dirt road about 5 miles with some signs for San Isidoro. Look for Rancho Los Pozitos, Family Arballo.

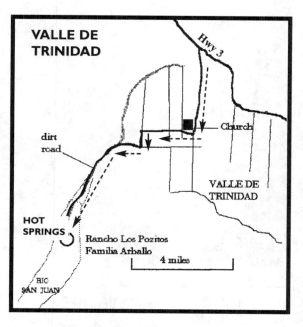

While it is always fun to soak in the middle of nature, having a pool with a bit of covering to offer protection from the sun is welcome in this hot, arid valley.

914   MISSION SAN BORJA HOT SPRINGS

The hot spring water was mixed with water from several cold streams to water the fields when the mission was in use in the 1800s.

● **East of the town of Rosarito**

A small, historic source pool on the grounds of a well-preserved mission in a remote and enchanting part of the Sierra La Libertad. Elevation 2,200 feet. Open all year.

Natural mineral water at 96° flows out of a rock-lined source pool built by the missionaries in the early 1800s. It is located at the edge of the mission cornfields, a five-minute walk southeast from the main building. The runoff from the spring was commingled with a nearby cold stream to water the mission's fields. Bathing suits are required.

There are no facilities or services, but camping is permitted anywhere among the ruins of the old mission buildings.

Directions: At Rosarito, from Hwy 1, turn east on a dirt road for 21 miles. There will be no sign for the mission, but there are two ranchos on the way, and the road ends in a remote valley where the mission is located.

BAJA SUR

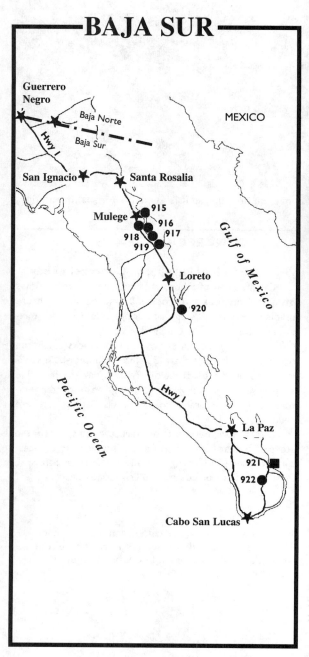

Guerrero Negro

Baja Norte

Baja Sur

MEXICO

San Ignacio

Santa Rosalia

915

Mulege

916

918 /917

919

Gulf of Mexico

Loreto

920

Pacific Ocean

Hwy 1

La Paz

921

922

Cabo San Lucas

915   MULEGE MISSION WARM SPRINGS

● **Near the town of Mulege**

Warm water springs found in the middle of a stream creating a jungle-like oasis complete with fan palms and ponds surrounded by desert and a view of the mountains. Elevation 50 feet. Open all year.

Natural mineral water bubbles up through the sand into the cool streambed at 90° creating an interesting effect as you sit in the stream. Bathing suits are required.

There are no services on the premises. It is two miles to a campground and one mile to all other services in Mulege.

Directions: Park at the mission and walk down hill. Cross stream in front of the dam. Continue 100 yards downstream; gas bubbles can be seen rising in the stream. Suggestion: On Hwy 1 at Mulege, ask for Arcadio Valle Somora at the ABC Bus Station and hire him to guide you.

This squishy-bottom pool at Santispac Beach is located above the tide line, so it is available for soaking all day.

916   SANTISPAC BEACH

●   South of Mulege, on Concepcion Bay

Two squishy-bottom soaking pools built by volunteers near a mangrove swamp on the edge of the bay. Elevation sea level. Open all year.

Natural mineral water oozes up through the rock-encircled mud bottom of one source spring, maintaining a temperature of 106° except when flooded by high tide. A second source spring, on slightly higher ground, has been excavated by volunteers to create a squishy-bottom pool that maintains a temperature of 102°. Bathing suits are required.

Santispac beach is a popular RV and camping destination on the Sea of Cortez. Camping is $5 per car per night, and there is a small restaurant on the beach. All other services are ten miles north in Mulege.

Directions: From Mulege, drive 10 miles south on Hwy 1 and turn left into the commercial parking and camping ground. Drive to the far right side of the cove, to a small area for parking, and walk approximately 100 yards on a dirt trail around the mangrove swamp to the two pools.

917   CONCEPCION BEACH

●   South of Mulege, on Concepcion Bay

On the edge of a beautiful bay, very hot water flows from rock fissures into rock-and-sand pools which are usable only when the high tide brings cold water for mixing. Elevation sea level. Open all year.

Natural mineral water flows out of cracks above the high tide line at more than 135° into volunteer-built soaking pools on the beach below. Twice a day the high tide supplies enough cold water to bring the pool temperatures down to tolerable soaking levels. Bathing suits are required.

Directions: There are no direct routes down the steep cliffs that border this beach. Therefore, it is necessary to hike south along the tide pools from Santispac Beach (see 916) or north from Los Cocos Beach.

Since these pools require cold ocean water to cool them down to a soakable temperature, it would be a good idea to bring along a tide table to figure out when to expect a high tide.

●   **South of Mulege, on Concepcion Bay**

A small permanent soaking pool in a fantastic setting on the edge of Concepcion Bay. Elevation sea level. Open all year.

Natural mineral water seeps into a tide pool at the base of a cliff. Volunteers have built a rock-and concrete wall around the tide pool, which maintains a temperature of 86° at low tide. Small shrimp have been observed in the warm, partly salty water. Bathing suits are required.

The camping fee at El Coyote Beach is $10 per night, but there is no additional fee for using the hot spring. There are no other facilities at the beach, but there is a restaurant at Rancho El Coyote across the highway. All other services are seventeen miles away in Mulege.

Directions: From Mulege, drive 17 miles south on Hwy 1 to the El Coyote Beach commercial campground. Park and follow a rocky trail 100 yards to the pool.

Waiting for the tide to go out so that you can build a pool where the hot water seeps up through the sand.

919   BUENA VENTURA HOT SPRINGS

●   **South of Mulege, on Concepcion Bay**

Build your own pool in Concepcion Bay as hot water flows up through the sand at low tide on this beach twenty-five miles south of Mulege. Elevation sea level. Open year round.

Natural mineral water at 100° pushes up through various spots in the sand at low tide, just waiting for someone to build a small soaking pool with the available rocks. The apparent local custom is clothing optional.

The Playa Buenaventura Hotel and Restaurant is nearby. It is twenty-five miles to all other services in Mulege.

Suggestion: See Mike at the Playa Buenaventura Hotel and Restaurant for boat rentals and for progress on future plans to build a hot pool.

920   AGUA VERDE HOT SPRINGS

●   **Near Agua Verde, south of Loreto**

Two pools in the Sea of Cortez, surrounded by a volcanic, rocky coastline and panoramic ocean views. Elevation sea level. Open all year.

Natural mineral water percolates up through the sand into two large eight-foot and ten-foot rock pools. The temperature at low tide in the upper pool is 110° and 105° in the lower pool. High tide covers the pools. The apparent local custom is clothing optional.

There are no services available on the premises, but overnight parking is permitted (watch the tides). It is two hundred yards to the nearest campground and thirty miles to all other services. This is a very good area for snorkeling.

Directions: Go 29 miles south of Loreto and turn at sign for Agua Verde. Go another 12 miles and take first turn onto the beach. Go north on beach 1 mile. You must wait for low tide to drive to the site.

Along with some of the best diving, spectacular views, and an oceanside campground, there are two large soaking pools available at low tide.

921   HOTEL BUENA VISTA RESORT
PO Box 574   800 731-4914
■   **La Paz, Baja California Sur, Mexico**

This full destination resort is located on the coast between the Baja desert and the Sea of Cortez, southeast of La Paz. Elevation sea level. Open all year.

Natural mineral water flows up from several wells at 180° into pools that are drained and refilled once a week. The large swimming pool, with a swim-up bar, is maintained at 80°, and a smaller swimming pool is 80-100°. There is also a hydropool. All three use an ion filtration system. Also hot water seeps up on the beach next to the hotel at low tide. The pools are open to the public for day use for a charge. Bathing suits are required.

Luxurious rooms, tennis courts, gift shop, a restaurant, and entertainment on Saturday nights are available on the premises. The hotel also has its own fishing fleet. Deep sea fishing is legendary in this area. Major credit cards are accepted. Phone for rates, reservations, and directions.

922   AGUA CALIENTE (SANTIAGO) HOT SPRINGS

●   **Near the town of Santiago**

Mountains and trees surround two small hot pools located in a canyon with fresh-water streams and cold pools. Elevation 900 feet. Open all year.

Natural mineral water at 115° flows into a two-foot by three-foot source pool and then through a ditch to a three-foot by four-foot pool big enough for one or two people, where the water has cooled to 108°. The only way to further cool this tub is to block up or divert the water flow. The apparent local custom is clothing optional.

There are no services on the premises, but there is room for three or four cars to park overnight. It is seven miles to all other services.

Directions: From the town of Santiago, go east 5 miles to the town of Agua Caliente. Continue east 1.5 miles to Rancho El Chorro. Pass the nature preserve (El Santuario) .5 miles, then go .3 miles further to the end of the road and the springs.

GOING NATURAL IN PALM SPRINGS

❑   The following listings cover a growing industry in Palm Springs—going uncovered in lush, upscale surroundings. These clothing optional resorts have varying amenities, but all of them will arrange for airport pickup, are open all year, and accept credit cards. The pools use tap water and are gas heated and chlorine treated. Phone for rates, reservations, and directions.

Courtesy of Desert Stars

DESERT STARS RESORT
1491 Via Soledad   760 325-2686
Palm Springs, CA 92264

This small, intimate retreat was the nation's first clothing optional B&B, now catering to a male clientele. It's unique residential, wind-free cove location is within walking distance to famous Tahquitz Canyon, with waterfalls and natural swimming pools.

The lush grounds of this quiet enclave are lovingly maintained in pristine condition. All of the rooms have a Country French decor and are complete with every amenity including private patios for most. The soaking tub is set on its own patio surrounded by grapefruit and lemon trees and features a choice of two heat settings. The central courtyard pool is solar heated to between 85-92°.

MORNINGSIDE INN
888 N. Indian Canyon   760 325-2668
                              800 916-2668

Palm Springs, CA 92262

Exclusive, secluded, clothing-optional bed and breakfast for couples in the heart of Palm Springs.

Suites and cabana rooms are available. Suites contain fully equipped kitchens, and some have patios. The pool and spa, a covered workout area and a massage table are available for your use along with a barbeque area. A misting system operates to keep customers comfortable all year around.

Snacks, afternoon sweet tray and beverages and lunch on the weekends are available for your enjoyment. See web page at www.morningsideinn.com.

Courtesy of Morningside inn

Courtesy of Raffles

Courtesy of Terra Cotta

RAFFLES PALM SPRINGS HOTEL
760 320-3949

Palm Springs, CA 92262

An exotic clothing-optional oasis named for the Singapore Raffles and located in the ??? ern part of Palm Springs.

A large hydrojet ??? at 102°, and a swimming pool ??? . Clothing is optional throughout ???

Facilitie ??? es include rooms with kitchenettes, a B??? ly landscaped central patio garden, cooled by an automatic misting system in the summer, outdoor barbeque area, and continental breakfast.

CLOSED

THE TERRA COTTA INN
2388 E. Racquet Club Road

760 322-6059

Palm Springs, CA 92262

A premier clothing-optional resort for couples surrounding secluded, romantic gardens. Situated on a private, colorful acre with magnificent mountain vistas.

A large, pristine pool is heated year round, and the fifteen-person hydropool spa is maintained at 102°. Enjoy the beautiful mountain views from both the pool and the spa, open twenty-four hours a day. The pool patio is micro-mist cooled for relaxing sunbathing in all temperatures.

The seventeen luxurious rooms are lavishly appointed. The charming grounds feature a private shady fountain retreat and several sun patios. A special suite is available with a private patio, sunken tub, and terrarium bathroom garden. A clubhouse, barbeque facilities, and bicycles are available for your use. Amenities include a sumptuous poolside breakfast, hot hors d'oeuvres in the afternoon, and pampering services such as massage and spa treatments. Phone for a free brochure, 800 786-6938.

DESERT SHADOWS INN RESORT AND VILLAS

1533 Chaparral   760 325-6410
Palm Springs, CA 92262

A secluded retreat for the discerning naturist with a magnificent view of the San Jacinto Mountains. Only minutes away from downtown Palm Springs.

Three grand pools are heated to 86°. The main pool has a waterfall created by jets of water flowing from three stone lions. The "quiet" pool has classical music playing softly in the background from behind flowering bougainvillea and citrus trees. The villa pool has three distinct entrances and steps for sitting comfortably in the crystal clear water. Two magnificent outdoor spas are heated to 102°. The original spa rests under a canopy complete with skylights for star gazing and is surrounded by our unique misting system. The second spa is 250 square feet in a free-form clover pattern making pockets for relaxing or socializing.

Choose from the private courtyard rooms, the main chaparral rooms or the two-story deluxe villas complete with private whirlpool baths. A full service restaurant on the property means you never have to leave the acres of lushly landscaped grounds. Steam room, massage, facials, hair salon, manicures and pedicures, and herbal body wraps are offered. A handicap accessible room is available.

Gracious hospitality and luxurious ambiance make this a premiere resort location.

GOING NATURAL—PLACES TO STAY

To help those of you who like to stay in places that cater to the naturist lifestyle, included is a list of clubs offering varying types of accommodations. Always call first to check on available amenities.

ARIZONA

Arizona Hidden Valley Retreat   520 568-4027
55551 W. La Barranca, Maricopa, AZ 85239

El Dorado Hot Spring   602 393-0750
PO Box 10, Tonopah, AZ 85354
(See listing in Arizona for full description)

Jardin del Sol   520 682-2537
PO Box 39, Marana, AZ 85653-0039

Shangri La II   602 465-5959
46834 N. Shangri La Rd., New River, AZ 85027

CALIFORNIA

Buff Creek Nudist Resort   919 880-0803
1924 Glen Helen Rd., Devore, CA 92407

Chris Andrews

Lupin Naturist Club   408 353-2250
PO Box 1274., Los Gatos, CA 95030

McConville   909 678-2333
40051 Long Canyon Rd., Lake Elsinor, CA 92530

Olive Dell Ranch   909 825-6619
26520 Keissel Rd., Colton, CA 92324-9526

Sequoians Family Nudist Park   510 582-0194
10200 Cull Canyon Rd., Castro Valley, CA 94546

Elysium Fields   310 455-1000

Justine Hill

814 Robinson Rd., Topanga, CA 90290

Glen Eden Sun Club   800 843-6833
25999 Glen Eden Rd., Corona, CA 91719

Laguna Del Sol   916 687-6550
8683 Rawhide Lane, Wilton, CA 95693

Courtesy of Silver Valley

Silver Valley Sun Club   760 257-4239
48382 Silver Valley Rd., Newberry Springs, CA 92365

Swallows   619 445-3754
1631 Harbison Canyon Rd., El Cajon, CA 92019

COLORADO

Mountain Air Ranch   303 697-4083
PO Box 855
Indian Hills, CO 80455

NEVADA

Las Vegas Sun Club   702 723-5463
PO Box 12322, East Las Vegas, NV 89112

NEW MEXICO
  No landed clubs

TEXAS

Courtesy of Bluebonnet

Bluebonnet   940 627-2313
CR 1180, Box 146
Alvord, TX 76225

Live Oak Nudist Resort   409 878-2216
R#1 Box 916
Washington, TX 77880

Natural Horisun   409 657-3061
1715 F.M. 442
Boling, TX 77420

Riverside Ranch   830 393-2387
PO Box 14413
San Antonio, TX 78214

Sahnoans   512 273-2257
PO Box 142233
Austin, TX 78714

Phil Wilcox

Sandpipers Holiday Park   210 383-7589
Rt 7, Box 309, Edinburg, TX 78539

Sunny Pines   903 873-3311
PO Box 133, Wills Point, TX 75169

Vista Grande Ranch   817 598-1312
1149 FM 1885 Road, Weatherford, TX 76088

UTAH
  No landed clubs

BAJA (Mexico)

Eden Ranch (near Loreto, Baja Sur)
01152 (113) 30700

INDEX

This index is designed to help you locate a listing when you start with the location name. The description of the location will be found on the page number given for that name.

Within the index the abbreviations listed below are used to identify the specific state or geographical area of the location. The number shown after each state listed below is the page number where the KEY MAP of that state will be found.

AZ = Arizona / 90
BJ = Baja (Mexico) / 190
CCA = Central California / 122
CO = Colorado / 46
NV = Nevada / 20
NM = New Mexico / 72
NCA = Northern California / 104
SCA = Southern California / 166
TX = Texas / 68
UT = Utah / 36

NUBP = Not Usable By the Public
Some springs that have recently become NUBP are still included in the directory with an explanation as to what happened.

213

Name			
Street			
City		State	Zip
		Order Quan.	Amount
Hot Springs and Hot Pools of the Northwest $18.95			
Hot Springs and Hot Pools of the Southwest $18.95			
Postage: $3 first book, $2 each additional book			

Canadians: Please send in US dollars

BOOK   Make check to: AQUA THERMAL ACCESS (831) 426-2956

MAIL ORDER   Mail to: 55 Azalea Lane, Santa Cruz, CA 95060   TOTAL

Name			
Street			
City		State	Zip
		Order Quan.	Amount
Hot Springs and Hot Pools of the Northwest $18.95			
Hot Springs and Hot Pools of the Southwest $18.95			
Postage: $3 first book, $2 each additional book			

Canadians: Please send in US dollars

BOOK   Make check to: AQUA THERMAL ACCESS (831) 426-2956

MAIL ORDER   Mail to: 55 Azalea Lane, Santa Cruz, CA 95060   TOTAL

Aqua Thermal Access is expanding its forays into total decadence and enjoyment. We have established an imprint called Seasonal Feasts which will publish cookbooks. Our first offering, *From Duff to Dinner*, includes fungal recipes that are just a bit unusual and with some interesting ingredients. I can't think of anything better than to go out and hunt wild mushrooms, soak in the afternoon, and prepare a wonderful dinner with the fresh mushrooms. And, maybe soak again. Please join us.

Name			
Street			
City		State	Zip
		Order Quan.	Amount
From Duff to Dinner	$12.95		
Postage: $3 first book, $2 each additional book			
Canadians: Please send in US dollars			
BOOK MAIL ORDER	Make check to: SEASONAL FEASTS (831) 426-2956 Mail to: 55 Azalea Lane, Santa Cruz, CA 95060	TOTAL	

Name			
Street			
City		State	Zip
		Order Quan.	Amount
From Duff to Dinner	$12.95		
Postage: $3 first book, $2 each additional book			
Canadians: Please send in US dollars			
BOOK MAIL ORDER	Make check to: SEASONAL FEASTS (831) 426-2956 Mail to: 55 Azalea Lane, Santa Cruz, CA 95060	TOTAL	

If you discover that the description of a location needs to be revised, or you find a location not in the book, jot down the pertinent information below and send it to:

ATA Directory Editor
55 Azalea Lane
Santa Cruz, CA 95060
831 426-2956
e-mail: hsprings@ix.netcom.com